Amazon Elastic File System User Guide

A catalogue record for this book is available from the Hong Kong Public Libraries.

Published in Hong Kong by Samurai Media Limited.

Email: info@samuraimedia.org

ISBN 9789888408238

Contents

What Is Amazon Elastic File System?

Amazon Elastic File System (Amazon EFS) provides simple, scalable file storage for use with Amazon EC2. With Amazon EFS, storage capacity is elastic, growing and shrinking automatically as you add and remove files, so your applications have the storage they need, when they need it.

Amazon EFS has a simple web services interface that allows you to create and configure file systems quickly and easily. The service manages all the file storage infrastructure for you, avoiding the complexity of deploying, patching, and maintaining complex file system deployments.

Amazon EFS supports the Network File System versions 4.0 and 4.1 (NFSv4) protocol, so the applications and tools that you use today work seamlessly with Amazon EFS. Multiple Amazon EC2 instances can access an Amazon EFS file system at the same time, providing a common data source for workloads and applications running on more than one instance or server.

With Amazon EFS, you pay only for the storage used by your file system. You don't need to provision storage in advance and there is no minimum fee or setup cost. For more information, see Amazon EFS Pricing.

The service is designed to be highly scalable, highly available, and highly durable. Amazon EFS file systems store data and metadata across multiple Availability Zones in a region and can grow to petabyte scale, drive high levels of throughput, and allow massively parallel access from Amazon EC2 instances to your data.

Amazon EFS provides file system access semantics, such as strong data consistency and file locking. For more information, see Data Consistency in Amazon EFS.

Amazon EFS also allows you to control access to your file systems through Portable Operating System Interface (POSIX) permissions. For more information, see Security.

Amazon EFS supports two forms of encryption for file systems, encryption in transit and encryption at rest. You can enable encryption at rest when creating an Amazon EFS file system. If you do, all your data and metadata is encrypted. You can enable encryption in transit when you mount the file system. For more information, see Encrypting Data and Metadata in EFS.

Amazon EFS is designed to provide the throughput, IOPS, and low latency needed for a broad range of workloads. With Amazon EFS, throughput and IOPS scale as a file system grows, and file operations are delivered with consistent, low latencies. For more information, see Amazon EFS Performance.

Note
Using Amazon EFS with Microsoft Windows Amazon EC2 instances is not supported.

Are you a first-time user of Amazon EFS?

If you are a first-time user of Amazon EFS, we recommend you read the following sections in order:

1. For an Amazon EFS product and pricing overview, see Amazon EFS.

2. For an Amazon EFS technical overview, see Amazon EFS: How It Works.

3. Try the introductory exercises:

   - Getting Started
   - Walkthroughs

If you would like to learn more about Amazon EFS, the following topics discuss the service in greater detail:

- Creating Resources for Amazon EFS
- Managing Amazon EFS File Systems
- Amazon EFS API

Amazon EFS: How It Works

Following, you can find a description about how Amazon EFS works, its implementation details, and security considerations.

Topics

- Overview
- How Amazon EFS Works with Amazon EC2
- How Amazon EFS Works with AWS Direct Connect
- Implementation Summary
- Authentication and Access Control
- Data Consistency in Amazon EFS

Overview

Amazon EFS provides file storage in the AWS Cloud. With Amazon EFS, you can create a file system, mount the file system on an Amazon EC2 instance, and then read and write data to and from your file system. You can mount an Amazon EFS file system in your VPC, through the Network File System versions 4.0 and 4.1 (NFSv4) protocol.

For a list of Amazon EC2 Linux Amazon Machine Images (AMIs) that support this protocol, see NFS Support. We recommend using a current generation Linux NFSv4.1 client, such as those found in Amazon Linux and Ubuntu AMIs. For some AMIs, you'll need to install an NFS client to mount your file system on your Amazon EC2 instance. For instructions, see Installing the NFS Client.

You can access your Amazon EFS file system concurrently from Amazon EC2 instances in your Amazon VPC, so applications that scale beyond a single connection can access a file system. Amazon EC2 instances running in multiple Availability Zones within the same region can access the file system, so that many users can access and share a common data source.

Note the following restrictions:

- You can mount an Amazon EFS file system on instances in only one VPC at a time.
- Both the file system and VPC must be in the same AWS Region.

For a list of AWS regions where you can create an Amazon EFS file system, see the Amazon Web Services General Reference.

To access your Amazon EFS file system in a VPC, you create one or more *mount targets* in the VPC. A mount target provides an IP address for an NFSv4 endpoint at which you can mount an Amazon EFS file system. You mount your file system using its DNS name, which will resolve to the IP address of the EFS mount target in the same Availability Zone as your EC2 instance. You can create one mount target in each Availability Zone in a region. If there are multiple subnets in an Availability Zone in your VPC, you create a mount target in one of the subnets, and all EC2 instances in that Availability Zone share that mount target.

Mount targets themselves are designed to be highly available. When designing your application for high availability and the ability to failover to other Availability Zones, keep in mind that the IP addresses and DNS for your mount targets in each Availability Zone are static.

After mounting the file system via the mount target, you use it like any other POSIX-compliant file system. For information about NFS-level permissions and related considerations, see Network File System (NFS)–Level Users, Groups, and Permissions.

You can mount your Amazon EFS file systems on your on-premises datacenter servers when connected to your Amazon VPC with AWS Direct Connect. You can mount your EFS file systems on on-premises servers to migrate data sets to EFS, enable cloud bursting scenarios, or backup your on-premises data to EFS.

Amazon EFS file systems can be mounted on Amazon EC2 instances, or on-premises through an AWS Direct Connect connection.

How Amazon EFS Works with Amazon EC2

The following illustration shows an example VPC accessing an Amazon EFS file system. Here, EC2 instances in the VPC have file systems mounted.

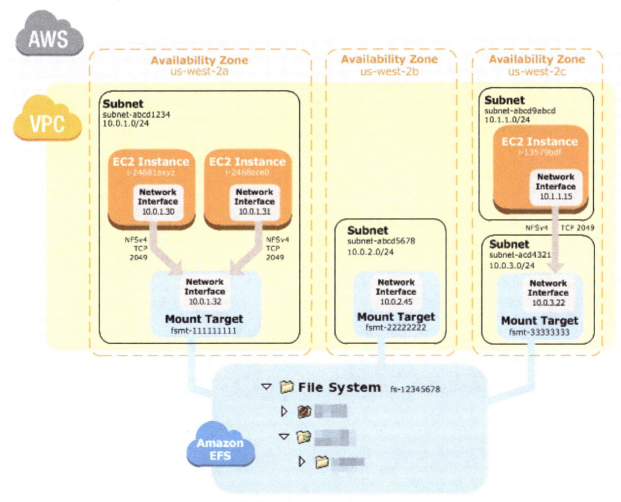

In this illustration, the VPC has three Availability Zones, and each has one mount target created in it. We recommend that you access the file system from a mount target within the same Availability Zone. Note that one of the Availability Zones has two subnets. However, a mount target is created in only one of the subnets. Creating this setup works as follows:

1. Create your Amazon EC2 resources and launch your Amazon EC2 instance. For more information on Amazon EC2, see Amazon EC2 - Virtual Server Hosting.

2. Create your Amazon EFS file system.

3. Connect to your Amazon EC2 instance, and mount the Amazon EFS file system.

For detailed steps, see Getting Started with Amazon Elastic File System.

How Amazon EFS Works with AWS Direct Connect

By using an Amazon EFS file system mounted on an on-premises server, you can migrate on-premises data into the AWS Cloud hosted in an Amazon EFS file system. You can also take advantage of bursting, meaning that you can move data from your on-premises servers into Amazon EFS, analyze it on a fleet of Amazon EC2 instances in your Amazon VPC, and then store the results permanently in your file system or move the results back to your on-premises server.

Keep the following considerations in mind when using Amazon EFS with AWS Direct Connect:

- Your on-premises server must have a Linux based operating system. We recommend Linux kernel version 4.0 or later.
- For the sake of simplicity, we recommend mounting an Amazon EFS file system on an on-premises server using a mount target IP address instead of a DNS name.
- AWS VPN is not supported for accessing an Amazon EFS file system from an on-premises server.

There is no additional cost for on-premises access to your Amazon EFS file systems. Note that you'll be charged for the AWS Direct Connect connection to your Amazon VPC. For more information, see AWS Direct Connect Pricing.

The following illustration shows an example of how to access an Amazon EFS file system from on-premises (the on-premises servers have the file systems mounted).

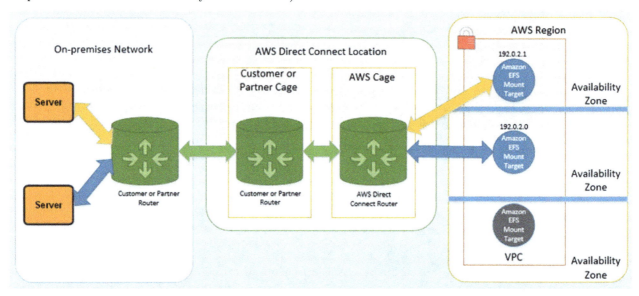

You can use any one of the mount targets in your VPC as long as the subnet of the mount target is reachable by using the AWS Direct Connect connection between your on-premises server and your Amazon VPC. To access Amazon EFS from a on-premises server, you need to add a rule to your mount target security group to allow inbound traffic to the NFS port (2049) from your on-premises server.

To create a setup like this, you do the following:

1. Establish an AWS Direct Connect connection between your on-premises data center and your Amazon VPC. For more information on AWS Direct Connect, see AWS Direct Connect.

2. Create your Amazon EFS file system.

3. Mount the Amazon EFS file system on your on-premises server.

For detailed steps, see Walkthrough 5: Create and Mount a File System On-Premises with AWS Direct Connect.

Implementation Summary

In Amazon EFS, a file system is the primary resource. Each file system has properties such as ID, creation token, creation time, file system size in bytes, number of mount targets created for the file system, and the file system state. For more information, see CreateFileSystem.

Amazon EFS also supports other resources to configure the primary resource. These include mount targets and tags:

- **Mount target** – To access your file system, you must create mount targets in your VPC. Each mount target has the following properties: the mount target ID, the subnet ID in which it is created, the file system ID for which it is created, an IP address at which the file system may be mounted, and the mount target state. You can use the IP address or the DNS name in your `mount` command. Each file system has a DNS name of the following form.

```
1 file-system-id.efs.aws-region.amazonaws.com
```

You can specify this DNS name in your `mount` command to mount the Amazon EFS file system. Suppose you create an `efs-mount-point` subdirectory off of your home directory on your EC2 instance or on-premises server. Then, you can use the mount command to mount the file system. For example, on an Amazon Linux AMI, you can use following `mount` command.

```
1 $ sudo mount -t nfs -o nfsvers=4.1,rsize=1048576,wsize=1048576,hard,timeo=600,retrans=2,
    noresvport file-system-DNS-name:/ ~/efs-mount-point
```

For more information, see Creating Mount Targets. First, you need to install the NFS client on your EC2 instance. The Getting Started exercise provides step-by-step instructions.

- **Tags** – To help organize your file systems, you can assign your own metadata to each of the file systems you create. Each tag is a key-value pair.

You can think of mount targets and tags as *subresources* that don't exist without being associated with a file system.

Amazon EFS provides API operations for you to create and manage these resources. In addition to the create and delete operations for each resource, Amazon EFS also supports a describe operation that enables you to retrieve resource information. You have the following options for creating and managing these resources:

- Use the Amazon EFS console – For an example, see Getting Started.
- Use the Amazon EFS command line interface (CLI) – For an example, see Walkthrough 1: Create Amazon EFS File System and Mount It on an EC2 Instance Using the AWS CLI.
- You can also manage these resources programmatically as follows:
  - Use the AWS SDKs – The AWS SDKs simplify your programming tasks by wrapping the underlying Amazon EFS API. The SDK clients also authenticate your requests by using access keys that you provide. For more information, see Sample Code and Libraries.
  - Call the Amazon EFS API directly from your application – If you cannot use the SDKs for some reason, you can make the Amazon EFS API calls directly from your application. However, you need to write the necessary code to authenticate your requests if you use this option. For more information about the Amazon EFS API, see Amazon EFS API.

Authentication and Access Control

You must have valid credentials to make Amazon EFS API requests, such as create a file system. In addition, you must also have permissions to create or access resources. By default, when you use the root account credentials of your AWS account you can create and access resources owned by that account. However, we do not recommend using root account credentials. In addition, any AWS Identity and Access Management (IAM) users and roles you create in your account must be granted permissions to create or access resources. For more information about permissions, see Authentication and Access Control for Amazon EFS.

Data Consistency in Amazon EFS

Amazon EFS provides the open-after-close consistency semantics that applications expect from NFS.

In Amazon EFS, write operations will be durably stored across Availability Zones when:

- An application performs a synchronous write operation (for example, using the `open` Linux command with the `O_DIRECT` flag, or the `fsync` Linux command).
- An application closes a file.

Amazon EFS provides stronger consistency guarantees than open-after-close semantics depending on the access pattern. Applications that perform synchronous data access and perform non-appending writes will have read-after-write consistency for data access.

Setting Up

Before you use Amazon EFS for the first time, complete the following tasks:

1. Sign up for AWS
2. Create an IAM User

Sign up for AWS

When you sign up for Amazon Web Services (AWS), your AWS account is automatically signed up for all services in AWS, including Amazon EFS. You are charged only for the services that you use.

With Amazon EFS, you pay only for the storage you use. For more information about Amazon EFS usage rates, see the Amazon Elastic File System Pricing. If you are a new AWS customer, you can get started with Amazon EFS for free. For more information, see AWS Free Usage Tier.

If you have an AWS account already, skip to the next task. If you don't have an AWS account, use the following procedure to create one.

To create an AWS account

1. Open https://aws.amazon.com/, and then choose **Create an AWS Account**. **Note**
   This might be unavailable in your browser if you previously signed into the AWS Management Console. In that case, choose **Sign in to a different account**, and then choose **Create a new AWS account**.

2. Follow the online instructions.

   Part of the sign-up procedure involves receiving a phone call and entering a PIN using the phone keypad.

Note your AWS account number, because you'll need it for the next task.

Create an IAM User

Services in AWS, such as Amazon EFS, require that you provide credentials when you access them, so that the service can determine whether you have permissions to access its resources. AWS recommends that you do not use the root credentials of your AWS account to make requests. Instead, create an IAM user, and grant that user full access. We refer to these users as administrator users. You can use the administrator user credentials, instead of root credentials of your account, to interact with AWS and perform tasks, such as create a bucket, create users, and grant them permissions. For more information, see Root Account Credentials vs. IAM User Credentials in the *AWS General Reference* and IAM Best Practices in the *IAM User Guide*.

If you signed up for AWS but have not created an IAM user for yourself, you can create one using the IAM console.

To create an IAM user for yourself and add the user to an Administrators group

1. Use your AWS account email address and password to sign in as the *AWS account root user* to the IAM console at https://console.aws.amazon.com/iam/. **Note**
   We strongly recommend that you adhere to the best practice of using the **Administrator** IAM user below and securely lock away the root user credentials. Sign in as the root user only to perform a few account and service management tasks.

2. In the navigation pane of the console, choose **Users**, and then choose **Add user**.

3. For **User name**, type **Administrator**.

4. Select the check box next to **AWS Management Console access**, select **Custom password**, and then type the new user's password in the text box. You can optionally select **Require password reset** to force the user to create a new password the next time the user signs in.

5. Choose **Next: Permissions**.

6. On the **Set permissions for user** page, choose **Add user to group**.

7. Choose **Create group**.

8. In the **Create group** dialog box, type **Administrators**.

9. For **Filter**, choose **Job function**.

10. In the policy list, select the check box for **AdministratorAccess**. Then choose **Create group**.

11. Back in the list of groups, select the check box for your new group. Choose **Refresh** if necessary to see the group in the list.

12. Choose **Next: Review** to see the list of group memberships to be added to the new user. When you are ready to proceed, choose **Create user**.

You can use this same process to create more groups and users, and to give your users access to your AWS account resources. To learn about using policies to restrict users' permissions to specific AWS resources, go to Access Management and Example Policies.

To sign in as this new IAM user, sign out of the AWS Management Console, and then use the following URL, where *your_aws_account_id* is your AWS account number without the hyphens (for example, if your AWS account number is 1234-5678-9012, your AWS account ID is 123456789012):

```
1 https://your_aws_account_id.signin.aws.amazon.com/console/
```

Enter the IAM user name and password that you just created. When you're signed in, the navigation bar displays *your_user_name***@***your_aws_account_id*.

If you don't want the URL for your sign-in page to contain your AWS account ID, you can create an account alias. From the IAM dashboard, click **Create Account Alias** and enter an alias, such as your company name. To sign in after you create an account alias, use the following URL:

```
1 https://your_account_alias.signin.aws.amazon.com/console/
```

To verify the sign-in link for IAM users for your account, open the IAM console and check under **AWS Account Alias** on the dashboard.

Getting Started with Amazon Elastic File System

Topics

- Assumptions
- Related Topics
- Step 1: Create Your EC2 Resources and Launch Your EC2 Instance
- Step 2: Create Your Amazon EFS File System
- Step 3: Connect to Your Amazon EC2 Instance and Mount the Amazon EFS File System
- Step 4: Sync Files from Existing File Systems to Amazon EFS Using EFS File Sync
- Step 5: Clean Up Resources and Protect Your AWS Account

This Getting Started exercise shows you how to quickly create an Amazon Elastic File System (Amazon EFS) file system, mount it on an Amazon Elastic Compute Cloud (Amazon EC2) instance in your VPC, and test the end-to-end setup.

There are four steps you need to perform to create and use your first Amazon EFS file system:

- Create your Amazon EC2 resources and launch your instance.
- Create your Amazon EFS file system.
- Connect to your Amazon EC2 instance and mount the Amazon EFS file system.
- Clean up your resources and protect your AWS account.

Assumptions

For this exercise, we assume the following:

- You're already familiar with using the Amazon EC2 console to launch instances.
- Your Amazon VPC, Amazon EC2, and Amazon EFS resources are all in the same region. This guide uses the US West (Oregon) Region (us-west-2).
- You have a default VPC in the region that you're using for this Getting Started exercise. If you don't have a default VPC, or if you want to mount your file system from a new VPC with new or existing security groups, you can still use this Getting Started exercise. To do so, configure Security Groups for Amazon EC2 Instances and Mount Targets.
- You have not changed the default inbound access rule for the default security group.

You can use the root credentials of your AWS account to sign in to the console and try the Getting Started exercise. However, AWS Identity and Access Management (IAM) recommends that you do not use the root credentials of your AWS account. Instead, create an administrator user in your account and use those credentials to manage resources in your account. For more information, see Setting Up.

Related Topics

This guide also provides a walkthrough to perform a similar Getting Started exercise using AWS Command Line Interface (AWS CLI) commands to make the Amazon EFS API calls. For more information, see Walkthrough 1: Create Amazon EFS File System and Mount It on an EC2 Instance Using the AWS CLI.

Step 1: Create Your EC2 Resources and Launch Your EC2 Instance

Before you can launch and connect to an Amazon EC2 instance, you need to create a key pair, unless you already have one. You can create a key pair using the Amazon EC2 console and then you can launch your EC2 instance.

Note
Using Amazon EFS with Microsoft Windows Amazon EC2 instances is not supported.

To create a key pair

- Follow the steps in Setting Up with Amazon EC2 in the *Amazon EC2 User Guide for Linux Instances* to create a key pair. If you already have a key pair, you do not need to create a new one and you can use your existing key pair for this exercise.

To launch the EC2 instance

1. Open the Amazon EC2 console at https://console.aws.amazon.com/ec2/.

2. Choose **Launch Instance**.

3. In **Step 1: Choose an Amazon Machine Image (AMI)**, find an Amazon Linux AMI at the top of the list and choose **Select**.

4. In **Step 2: Choose an Instance Type**, choose **Next: Configure Instance Details**.

5. In **Step 3: Configure Instance Details**, choose **Network**, and then choose the entry for your default VPC. It should look something like `vpc-xxxxxxx (172.31.0.0/16)(default)`.

   1. Choose **Subnet**, and then choose a subnet in any Availability Zone.

   2. Choose **Next: Add Storage**.

6. Choose **Next: Tag Instance**.

7. Name your instance and choose **Next: Configure Security Group**.

8. In **Step 6: Configure Security Group**, review the contents of this page, ensure that **Assign a security group** is set to **Create a new security group**, and verify that the inbound rule being created has the following default values.

   - **Type:** SSH
   - **Protocol:** TCP
   - **Port Range:** 22
   - **Source:** Anywhere 0.0.0.0/0

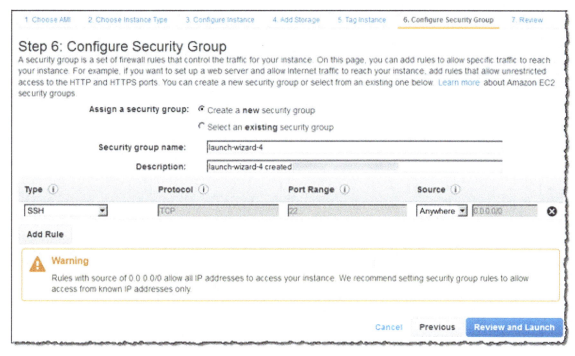

Note

You can configure the EFS file system to mount on your EC2 instance automatically. For more information, see Configuring an EFS File System to Mount Automatically at EC2 Instance Launch.

9. Choose **Review and Launch**.

10. Choose **Launch**.

11. Select the check box for the key pair that you created, and then choose **Launch Instances**.

12. Choose **View Instances**.

13. Choose the name of the instance you just created from the list, and then choose **Actions**.

    1. From the menu that opens, choose **Networking** and then choose **Change Security Groups**.

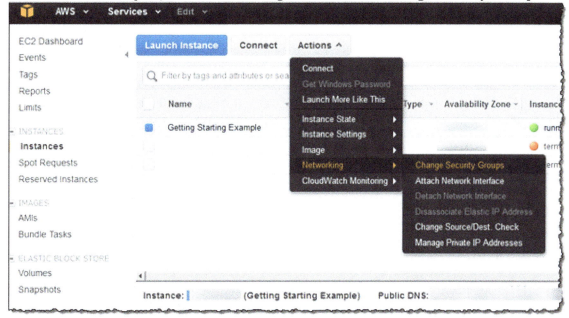

2. Select the check box next to the security group with the description **default VPC security group**.

3. Choose **Assign Security Groups**.

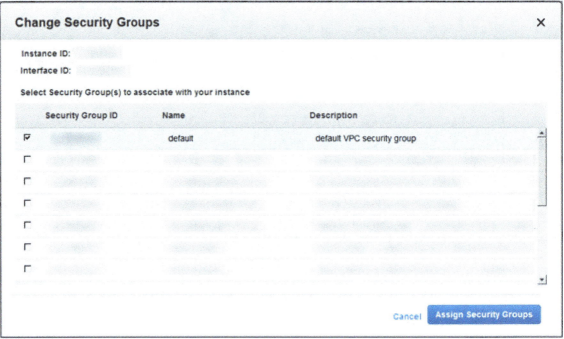

Note

In this step, you assign your VPC's default security group to the Amazon EC2 instance. Doing this ensures that the instance is a member of the security group that the Amazon EFS file system mount target authorizes for connection in Step 2: Create Your Amazon EFS File System.

By using your VPC's default security group, with its default inbound and outbound rules, you are potentially opening up this instance and this file system to potential threats from within your VPC. Make sure that you follow Step 5: Clean Up Resources and Protect Your AWS Account at the end of this Getting Started exercise to remove resources exposed to your VPC's default security group for this example. For more information, see Security Groups for Amazon EC2 Instances and Mount Targets.

14. Choose your instance from the list.

15. On the **Description** tab, make sure that you have two entries listed next to **security groups**—one for the default VPC security group and one for the security group that you created when you launched the instance.

16. Make a note of the values listed next to **VPC ID** and **Public DNS**. You need those values later in this exercise.

Step 2: Create Your Amazon EFS File System

In this step, you create your Amazon EFS file system.

To create your Amazon EFS file system

1. Open the Amazon EFS Management Console at https://console.aws.amazon.com/efs/.

2. Choose **Create File System**.

3. Choose your default VPC from the **VPC** list. It has the same **VPC ID** that you noted at the end of Step 1: Create Your EC2 Resources and Launch Your EC2 Instance.

4. Select the check boxes for all of the Availability Zones. Make sure that they all have the default subnets, automatic IP addresses, and the default security groups chosen. These are your mount targets. For more information, see Creating Mount Targets.

5. Choose **Next Step**.

6. Name your file system, keep **general purpose** selected as your default performance mode, and choose **Next Step**.

7. Choose **Create File System**.

8. Choose your file system from the list and make a note of the **File system ID** value. You'll need this value for the next step.

Step 3: Connect to Your Amazon EC2 Instance and Mount the Amazon EFS File System

You can connect to your Amazon EC2 instance from a computer running Windows or Linux. To connect to your Amazon EC2 instance and mount the Amazon EFS file system, you need the **File system ID** value for the mount target for your Amazon EFS file system. You made a note of this value at the end of Step 2: Create Your Amazon EFS File System.

To connect to your Amazon EC2 instance and mount the Amazon EFS file system

1. Connect to your Amazon EC2 instance. For more information, see Connecting to Your Linux Instance from Windows Using PuTTY or Connecting to Your Linux Instance Using SSH in the *Amazon EC2 User Guide for Linux Instances.*

2. After you've connected, install the amazon-efs-utils package, which has the Amazon EFS mount helper.

   Run the following command to install amazon-efs-utils.

   ```
   1 sudo yum install -y amazon-efs-utils
   ```

Note
For more information on the amazon-efs-utils package, including installation instructions for other Linux distributions, see Using the amazon-efs-utils Tools.

1. Make a directory for the mount point with the following command.

   ```
   1 $ sudo mkdir efs
   ```

2. Mount the Amazon EFS file system to the directory that you created. Use the following command and replace `file-system-id` with your **File System ID** value.

   ```
   1 sudo mount -t efs fs-12345678:/ /mnt/efs
   ```

Note
We recommend that you wait 90 seconds after creating a mount target before you mount your file system.

1. Change directories to the new directory that you created with the following command.

   ```
   1 $ cd efs
   ```

2. Make a subdirectory and change the ownership of that subdirectory to your EC2 instance user. Then navigate to that new directory with the following commands.

   ```
   1 $ sudo mkdir getting-started
   2 $ sudo chown ec2-user getting-started
   3 $ cd getting-started
   ```

3. Create a text file with the following command.

   ```
   1 $ touch test-file.txt
   ```

4. List the directory contents with the following command.

   ```
   1 $ ls -al
   ```

As a result, the following file is created.

```
1 -rw-rw-r-- 1 ec2-user ec2-user 0 Aug 15 15:32 test-file.txt
```

Step 4: Sync Files from Existing File Systems to Amazon EFS Using EFS File Sync

Now that you have created a functioning Amazon EFS file system, you can use EFS File Sync to sync files from an existing file system to Amazon EFS. EFS File Sync can sync your file data, and also file system metadata such as ownership, time stamps, and access permissions.

In this step, we assume that you have the following:

- A source NFS file system that you can sync from. This source system needs to be accessible over NFS version 3 or version 4. The source file system can be on-premises or on Amazon EC2.
- A destination Amazon EFS file system to sync to. If you don't have an Amazon EFS file system, create one. For more information, see Getting Started with Amazon Elastic File System.
- DNS access as detailed following:
  - For sync agents hosted on Amazon EC2, your sync agent requires access to a DNS server configured in your Amazon VPC. This server can be the default Amazon DNS server. For more information, see Using DNS with Your VPC in the *Amazon VPC User Guide*.
  - For sync agents hosted on-premises, your sync agent requires access to a functioning DNS server that can communicate with AWS.

To sync files from an existing file system to Amazon EFS

1. Open the Amazon EFS Management Console at https://console.aws.amazon.com/efs/.

2. Download and deploy a sync agent. For on-premises deployment, the sync agent is provided as a virtual machine (VM) image for VMware ESXi. For an AWS Cloud deployment, you can create an Amazon EC2 instance from the community Amazon Machine Image (AMI).

3. Create a sync task and configure your source and destination file systems.

4. Start your sync task to begin syncing files from the source file system to the Amazon EFS file system.

5. Monitor your sync task on the Amazon EFS console or from Amazon CloudWatch. For more information, see Monitoring EFS File Sync with Amazon CloudWatch.

For more details on the EFS File Sync process, see the following:

- For information about how to sync files from an on-premises file system to Amazon EFS, see Walkthrough 7: Sync Files from an On-Premises File System to Amazon EFS by Using EFS File Sync.
- For information about how to sync files from Amazon EC2 to Amazon EFS, see Walkthrough 8: Sync a File System from Amazon EC2 to Amazon EFS Using EFS File Sync.

Step 5: Clean Up Resources and Protect Your AWS Account

This guide includes walkthroughs that you can use to further explore Amazon EFS. Before you perform this clean-up step, you can use the resources you've created and connected to in this Getting Started exercise in those walkthroughs. For more information, see Walkthroughs. After you have finished the walkthroughs or if you don't want to explore the walkthroughs, you should follow these steps to clean up your resources and protect your AWS account.

To clean up resources and protect your AWS account

1. Connect to your Amazon EC2 instance.

2. Unmount the Amazon EFS file system with the following command.

```
1 $ sudo umount efs
```

3. Open the Amazon EFS console at https://console.aws.amazon.com/efs/.

4. Choose the Amazon EFS file system that you want to delete from the list of file systems.

5. For **Actions**, choose **Delete file system**.

6. In the **Permanently delete file system** dialog box, type the file system ID for the Amazon EFS file system that you want to delete, and then choose **Delete File System**.

7. Open the Amazon EC2 console at https://console.aws.amazon.com/ec2/.

8. Choose the Amazon EC2 instance that you want to terminate from the list of instances.

9. For **Actions**, choose **Instance State** and then choose **Terminate**.

10. In **Terminate Instances**, choose **Yes, Terminate** to terminate the instance that you created for this Getting Started exercise.

11. In the navigation pane, choose **Security Groups**.

12. Select the name of the security group that you created for this Getting Started exercise in Step 1: Create Your EC2 Resources and Launch Your EC2 Instance as a part of the Amazon EC2 instance launch wizard.
    Warning
    Don't delete the default security group for your VPC.

13. For **Actions**, choose **Delete Security Group**.

14. In **Delete Security Group**, choose **Yes, Delete** to delete the security group you created for this Getting Started exercise.

Creating Resources for Amazon EFS

Amazon EFS provides elastic, shared file storage that is POSIX-compliant. The file system you create supports concurrent read and write access from multiple Amazon EC2 instances and is accessible from all of the Availability Zones in the AWS Region where it is created.

You can mount an Amazon EFS file system on EC2 instances in your Amazon Virtual Private Cloud (Amazon VPC) using the Network File System versions 4.0 and 4.1 protocol (NFSv4). For more information, see Amazon EFS: How It Works.

Topics

- Creating an Amazon Elastic File System
- Creating Mount Targets
- Creating Security Groups

As an example, suppose you have one or more EC2 instances launched in your VPC. Now you want to create and use a file system on these instances. Following are the typical steps you need to perform to use Amazon EFS file systems in the VPC:

- **Create an Amazon EFS file system** – When creating a file system, we recommend that you consider using the **Name** tag because the **Name** tag value appears in the console and makes it easier to identify. You can also add other optional tags to the file system.
- **Create mount targets for the file system** – To access the file system in your VPC and mount the file system to your Amazon EC2 instance, you must create mount targets in the VPC subnets.
- **Create security groups** – Both an Amazon EC2 instance and a mount target need to have associated security groups. These security groups act as a virtual firewall that controls the traffic between them. You can use the security group you associated with the mount target to control inbound traffic to your file system by adding an inbound rule to the mount target security group that allows access from a specific EC2 instance. Then, you can mount the file system only on that EC2 instance.

If you are new to Amazon EFS, we recommend that you try the following exercises that provide a first-hand, end-to-end experience of using an Amazon EFS file system:

- Getting Started – The Getting Started exercise provides a console-based end-to-end setup in which you create a file system, mount it on an EC2 instance, and test the setup. The console takes care of many things for you and helps you set up the end-to-end experience quickly.
- Walkthrough 1: Create Amazon EFS File System and Mount It on an EC2 Instance Using the AWS CLI – The walkthrough is similar to the Getting Started exercise, but it uses the AWS Command Line Interface (AWS CLI) to perform most of the tasks. Because the AWS CLI commands closely map to the Amazon EFS API, the walkthrough can help you familiarize yourself with the Amazon EFS API operations.

For more information about creating and accessing a file system, see the following topics.

Topics

- Creating an Amazon Elastic File System
- Creating Mount Targets
- Creating Security Groups

Creating an Amazon Elastic File System

Following, you can find an explanation about how to create an Amazon EFS file system and optional tags for the file system. This section explains how to create these resources using both the console and the AWS Command Line Interface (AWS CLI).

Note

If you are new to Amazon EFS, we recommend you go through the Getting Started exercise, which provides console-based end-to-end instructions to create and access a file system in your VPC. For more information, see Getting Started.

Topics

- Requirements
- Permissions Required
- Creating a File System

Requirements

To create a file system, the only requirement is that you create a token to ensure idempotent operation. If you use the console, it generates the token for you. For more information, see CreateFileSystem. After you create a file system, Amazon EFS returns the file system description as JSON. Following is an example.

```
1  {
2      "SizeInBytes": {
3          "Value": 6144
4      },
5      "CreationToken": "console-d7f56c5f-e433-41ca-8307-9d9c0example",
6      "CreationTime": 1422823614.0,
7      "FileSystemId": "fs-c7a0456e",
8      "PerformanceMode" : "generalPurpose",
9      "NumberOfMountTargets": 0,
10     "LifeCycleState": "available",
11     "OwnerId": "231243201240"
12 }
```

If you use the console, the console displays this information in the user interface.

After creating a file system, you can create optional tags for the file system. Initially, the file system has no name. You can create a **Name** tag to assign a file system name. Amazon EFS provides the CreateTags operation for creating tags. Each tag is simply a key-value pair.

Permissions Required

For all operations, such as creating a file system and creating tags, a user must have AWS Identity and Access Management permissions for the corresponding API action and resource.

You can perform any Amazon EFS operations using the root credentials of your AWS account, but using root credentials is not recommended. If you create IAM users in your account, you can grant them permissions for Amazon EFS actions with user policies. You can also use roles to grant cross-account permissions. For more information about managing permissions for the API actions, see Authentication and Access Control for Amazon EFS.

Creating a File System

You can create a file system using the Amazon EFS console or using the AWS Command Line Interface. You can also create file systems programmatically using AWS SDKs.

Creating a File System Using the Amazon EFS Console

The Amazon EFS console provides an integrated experience. In the console, you can specify VPC subnets to create mount targets and optional file system tags when you create a file system.

To create the file system mount targets in your VPC, you must specify VPC subnets. The console prepopulates the list of VPCs in your account that are in the selected AWS Region. First, you select your VPC, and then the console lists the Availability Zones in the VPC. For each Availability Zone, you can select a subnet from the list. After you select a subnet, you can either specify an available IP address in the subnet or let Amazon EFS choose an address.

When creating a file system, you also choose a performance mode. There are two performance modes to choose from—General Purpose and Max I/O. For the majority of use cases, we recommend that you use the general purpose performance launch mode for your file system. For more information about the different performance modes, see Performance Modes.

You can enable encryption at rest when creating a file system. If you enable encryption at rest for your file system, all data and metadata stored on it is encrypted. You can enable encryption in transit later, when you mount the file system. For more information about Amazon EFS encryption, see Security.

When you choose **Create File System**, the console sends a series of API requests to create the file system. The console then sends API requests to create tags and mount targets for the file system. The following example console shows the **MyFS** file system. It has the **Name** tag and three mount targets that are being created. The mount target lifecycle state must be **Available** before you can use it to mount the file system on an EC2 instance.

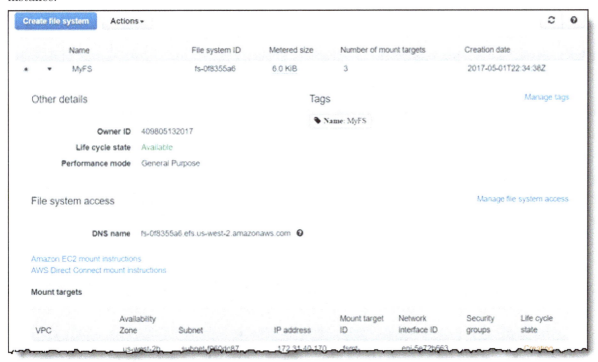

For instructions on how to create an Amazon EFS file system using the console, see Step 1: Create Your EC2 Resources and Launch Your EC2 Instance.

Creating a File System Using the AWS CLI

When using the AWS CLI, you create these resources in order. First, you create a file system. Then, you can create mount targets and optional tags for the file system using corresponding AWS CLI commands.

The following examples use the `adminuser` as the `profile` parameter value. You need to use an appropriate user profile to provide your credentials. For information about the AWS CLI, see Getting Set Up with the AWS Command Line Interface in the *AWS Command Line Interface User Guide.*

- To create a file system, use the Amazon EFS `create-file-system` CLI command (corresponding operation is CreateFileSystem), as shown following.

```
1 $ aws efs create-file-system \
2 --creation-token creation-token \
3 --region aws-region \
4 --profile adminuser
```

For example, the following `create-file-system` command creates a file system in the **us-west-2** region. The command specifies **MyFirstFS** as the creation token. For a list of AWS regions where you can create an Amazon EFS file system, see the Amazon Web Services General Reference.

```
1 $  aws efs create-file-system \
2 --creation-token MyFirstFS \
3 --region us-west-2 \
4 --profile adminuser
```

After successfully creating the file system, Amazon EFS returns the file system description as JSON, as shown in the following example.

```
1  {
2      "SizeInBytes": {
3          "Value": 6144
4      },
5      "CreationToken": "MyFirstFS",
6      "CreationTime": 1422823614.0,
7      "FileSystemId": "fs-c7a0456e",
8      "PerformanceMode" : "generalPurpose",
9      "NumberOfMountTargets": 0,
10      "LifeCycleState": "available",
11      "OwnerId": "231243201240"
12  }
```

Amazon EFS also provides the `describe-file-systems` CLI command (corresponding operation is DescribeFileSystems) that you can use to retrieve a list of file systems in your account, as shown following:

```
1 $  aws efs describe-file-systems \
2 --region aws-region \
3 --profile adminuser
```

Amazon EFS returns a list of the file systems in your AWS account created in the specified region.

- To create tags, use the Amazon EFS `create-tags` CLI command (the corresponding API operation is CreateTags). The following example command adds the `Name` tag to the file system.

```
1 aws efs create-tags \
2 --file-system-id File-System-ID \
3 --tags Key=Name,Value=SomeExampleNameValue \
4 --region aws-region \
5 --profile adminuser
```

You can retrieve a list of tags created for a file system using the `describe-tags` CLI command (corresponding operation is DescribeTags), as shown following.

```
1 aws efs describe-tags \
2 --file-system-id File-System-ID \
3 --region aws-region \
4 --profile adminuser
```

Amazon EFS returns these descriptions as JSON. The following is an example of tags returned by the `DescribeTags` operation. It shows a file system as having only the `Name` tag.

```
1 {
2     "Tags": [
3         {
4             "Value": "MyFS",
5             "Key": "Name"
6         }
7     ]
8 }
```

Creating Mount Targets

After you create a file system, you can create mount targets and then you can mount the file system on EC2 instances in your VPC, as shown in the following illustration.

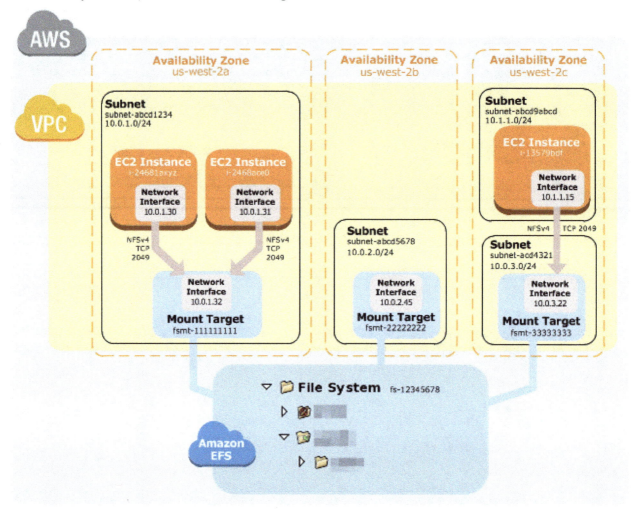

For more information about creating a file system, see Creating an Amazon Elastic File System.

The mount target security group acts as a virtual firewall that controls the traffic. For example, it determines which Amazon EC2 instances can access the file system. This section explains the following:

- Mount target security groups and how to enable traffic.

- How to mount the file system on your Amazon EC2 instance.

- NFS-level permissions considerations.

  Initially, only the root user on the Amazon EC2 instance has read-write-execute permissions on the file system. This topic discusses NFS-level permissions and provides examples that show you how to grant permissions in common scenarios. For more information, see Network File System (NFS)–Level Users, Groups, and Permissions.

You can create mount targets for a file system using the console, using AWS Command Line Interface, or programmatically using the AWS SDKs. When using the console, you can create mount targets when you first create a file system or after the file system is created.

Creating a Mount Target Using the Amazon EFS console

Perform the steps in the following procedure to create a mount target using the console. As you follow the console steps, you can also create one or more mount targets. You can create one mount target for each Availability Zone in your VPC.

To create an Amazon EFS file system (console)

1. Sign in to the AWS Management Console and open the Amazon EFS console at https://console.aws.amazon.com/efs/.

2. Choose **Create File System**.

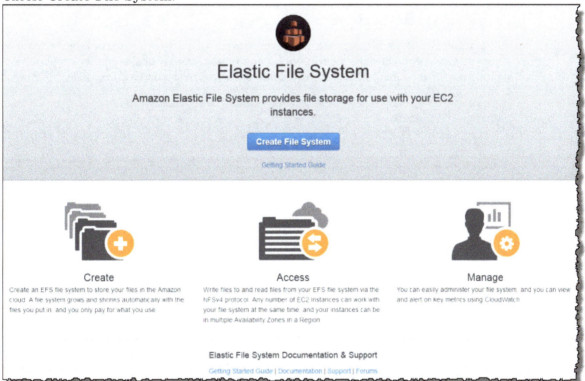

Note
The console shows the preceding page only if you don't already have any Amazon EFS file systems. If you have created file systems, the console shows a list of your file systems. On the list page, choose **Create File System**.

3. On the **Step 1: Configure File System Access** page, select the VPC and the Availability Zone in the VPC where you want the console to create one or more mount targets for the file system that you are creating. This VPC should be the same Amazon VPC in which you created your Amazon EC2 instance in the preceding section.

    1. Select a Amazon VPC from the **VPC** list. **Warning**
    If the Amazon VPC you want is not listed, verify the region in the global navigation in the Amazon EFS console.

    2. In the **Create Mount Targets** section, select all of the Availability Zones listed.

    We recommend that you create mount targets in all Availability Zones. You can then mount your file system on Amazon EC2 instances created in any of the Amazon VPC subnets. **Note**
    You can access a file system on an Amazon EC2 instance in one Availability Zone by using a mount target created in another Availability Zone, but there are costs associated with cross–Availability Zone access.

For each Availability Zone, do the following:

- Choose a **Subnet** from the list where you want to create the mount target.

    You can create one mount target in each Availability Zone. If you have multiple subnets in an Availability Zone where you launched your Amazon EC2 instance, you don't have to create mount target in the same subnet, it can be any subnet in the Availability Zone.

- Leave **IP Address** select to **Automatic**. Amazon EFS will select one of the available IP addresses for the mount target.

- Specify the **Security Group** you created specifically for the mount target, or the default security group for the default VPC. Both security groups will have the necessary inbound rule that allows inbound access from the EC2 instance security group.

    Click in the **Security Group** box and the console will show you the available security groups. Here you can select a specific security group and remove the **Default** security group, or leave the default in place, depending on how you configured your Amazon EC2 instance.

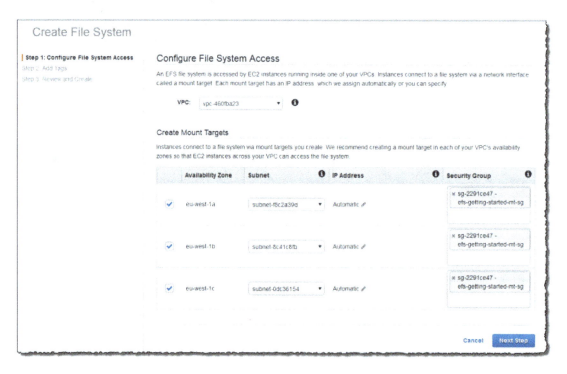

4. On the **Step 2: Configure optional settings** page, specify a value for the **Name** tag (**MyExampleFileSystem**) and choose your performance mode.

    The console prepopulates the **Name** tag because Amazon EFS uses its value as the file system display name.

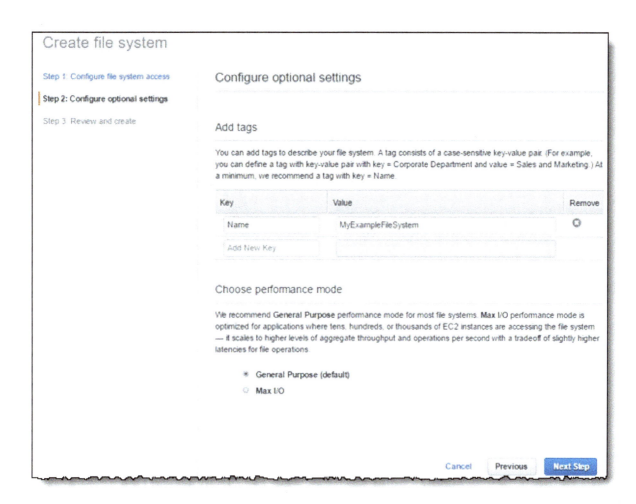

5. On the **Step 3: Review and Create** page, choose **Create File System**.

Create file system

Step 1: Configure file system access

Step 2: Configure optional settings

Step 3: Review and create

Review and create

Review the configuration below before proceeding to create your file system.

File system access

VPC	Availability Zone	Subnet	IP address	Security groups
	us-west-2a		Automatic	
vpc- (default)	us-west-2b		Automatic	
	us-west-2c		Automatic	

Optional settings

Tags	● Name: MyExampleFileSystem
Performance mode	General Purpose (default)

Cancel   Previous   **Create File System**

6. The console shows the newly created file system on the **File Systems** page. Verify that all mount targets show the **Life Cycle State** as **Available**. It might take a few moments before the mount targets become available (you can expand/collapse the file system in the EFS console to force it to refresh).

7. Under **File system access**, you'll see the file system's **DNS name**. Make a note of this DNS name. In the next section, you use the DNS name to mount the file system on the Amazon EC2 instance through the mount target. The Amazon EC2 instance on which you mount the file system can resolve the file system's DNS name to the mount target's IP address.

Now you are ready to mount the Amazon EFS file system on an Amazon EC2 instance.

Creating a Mount Target using the AWS CLI

To create a mount target using AWS CLI, use the `create-mount-target` CLI command (corresponding operation is CreateMountTarget), as shown following.

```
1 $ aws efs create-mount-target \
2 --file-system-id file-system-id \
3 --subnet-id  subnet-id \
4 --security-group ID-of-the-security-group-created-for-mount-target \
5 --region aws-region \
6 --profile adminuser
```

After successfully creating the mount target, Amazon EFS returns the mount target description as JSON as shown in the following example.

```
1 {
```

```
2      "MountTargetId": "fsmt-f9a14450",
3      "NetworkInterfaceId": "eni-3851ec4e",
4      "FileSystemId": "fs-b6a0451f",
5      "LifeCycleState": "available",
6      "SubnetId": "subnet-b3983dc4",
7      "OwnerId": "23124example",
8      "IpAddress": "10.0.1.24"
9 }
```

You can also retrieve a list of mount targets created for a file system using the `describe-mount-targets` CLI command (corresponding operation is DescribeMountTargets), as shown following.

```
1 $ aws efs describe-mount-targets \
2 --file-system-id file-system-id \
3 --region aws-region \
4 --profile adminuser
```

For an example, see Walkthrough 1: Create Amazon EFS File System and Mount It on an EC2 Instance Using the AWS CLI.

Creating Security Groups

Note

The following section is specific to Amazon EC2 and discusses how to create security groups so you can use Secure Shell (SSH) to connect to any instances that have mounted Amazon EFS file systems. If you're not using SSH to connect to your Amazon EC2 instances, you can skip this section.

Both an Amazon EC2 instance and a mount target have associated security groups. These security groups act as a virtual firewall that controls the traffic between them. If you don't provide a security group when creating a mount target, Amazon EFS associates the default security group of the VPC with it.

Regardless, to enable traffic between an EC2 instance and a mount target (and thus the file system), you must configure the following rules in these security groups:

- The security groups you associate with a mount target must allow inbound access for the TCP protocol on the NFS port from all EC2 instances on which you want to mount the file system.
- Each EC2 instance that mounts the file system must have a security group that allows outbound access to the mount target on the NFS port.

For more information about security groups, see Amazon EC2 Security Groups in the *Amazon EC2 User Guide for Linux Instances*.

Creating Security Groups Using the AWS Management Console

You can use the AWS Management Console to create security groups in your VPC. To connect your Amazon EFS file system to your Amazon EC2 instance, you'll need to create two security groups: one for your Amazon EC2 instance and another for your Amazon EFS mount target.

1. Create two security groups in your VPC. For instructions, see Creating a Security Group in the *Amazon VPC User Guide*.

2. In the VPC console, verify the default rules for these security groups. Both security groups should have only an outbound rule that allows traffic to leave.

3. You need to authorize additional access to the security groups as follows:

4. Add a rule to the EC2 security group to allow inbound access, as shown following. Optionally, you can restrict the **Source** address.

   For instructions, see Adding and Removing Rules in the *Amazon VPC User Guide*.

5. Add a rule to the mount target security group to allow inbound access from the EC2 security group, as shown following (where the EC2 security group is identified as the source):

Note

You don't need to add an outbound rule because the default outbound rule allows all traffic to leave (otherwise, you will need to add an outbound rule to open TCP connection on the NFS port, identifying the mount target security group as the destination).

6. Verify that both security groups now authorize inbound and outbound access as described in this section.

Creating Security Groups Using the AWS CLI

For an example that shows how to create security groups using the AWS CLI, see Step 1: Create Amazon EC2 Resources.

Using File Systems

Amazon Elastic File System presents a standard file system interface that support full file system access semantics. Using NFSv4.1, you can mount your Amazon EFS file system on any Amazon Elastic Compute Cloud (Amazon EC2) Linux-based instance. Once mounted, you can work with the files and directories just like you would with a local file system. For more information on mounting, see Mounting File Systems.

You can also use EFS File Sync to copy file from any file system to Amazon EFS. For more information on mounting, see Amazon EFS File Sync.

After you create a file system and mount it on your EC2 instance, there are a few things you need to know in order to use it effectively:

- **Users, groups, and related NFS-Level permissions management** – When you first create the file system, there is only one root directory at /. By default, only the root user (UID 0) has read-write-execute permissions. In order for other users to modify the file system, the root user must explicitly grant them access. For more information, see Network File System (NFS)–Level Users, Groups, and Permissions.

Related Topics

Amazon EFS: How It Works

Getting Started

Walkthroughs

Network File System (NFS)–Level Users, Groups, and Permissions

Topics

- Example Amazon EFS File System Use Cases and Permissions
- User and group ID permissions on files and directories within a file system
- No Root Squashing
- Permissions Caching
- Changing File System Object Ownership

After creating a file system, by default, only the root user (UID 0) has read-write-execute permissions. In order for other users to modify the file system, the root user must explicitly grant them access.

Amazon EFS file system objects have a Unix-style mode associated with them. This value defines the permissions for performing actions on that object, and users familiar with Unix-style systems can easily understand how Amazon EFS behaves with respect to these permissions.

Additionally, on Unix-style systems, users and groups are mapped to numeric identifiers, which Amazon EFS uses to represent file ownership. File system objects (that is, files, directories, etc.) on Amazon EFS are owned by a single owner and a single group. Amazon EFS uses these numeric IDs to check permissions when a user attempts to access a file system object.

This section provides examples of permissions and discusses Amazon EFS–specific NFS permissions considerations.

Example Amazon EFS File System Use Cases and Permissions

After you create an Amazon EFS file system and mount targets for the file system in your VPC, you can mount the remote file system locally on your Amazon EC2 instance. The `mount` command can mount any directory in the file system. However, when you first create the file system, there is only one root directory at `/`.

The following `mount` command mounts the root directory of an Amazon EFS file system, identified by the file system DNS name, on the `/efs-mount-point` local directory.

```
1  sudo mount -t nfs -o nfsvers=4.1,rsize=1048576,wsize=1048576,hard,timeo=600,retrans=2,noresvport
       file-system-id.efs.aws-region.amazonaws.com:/ efs-mount-point
```

Note that the root user and root group own the mounted directory.

```
[ec2-user@ip-172-31-43-70 efs]$ ls -al
total 8
drwxr-xr-x 2 root     root      6144 Aug 29  2016 .
drwx------ 5 ec2-user ec2-user  4096 May  1 21:44 ..
[ec2-user@ip-172-31-43-70 efs]$
```

The initial permissions mode allows:

- `read-write-execute` permissions to the owner *root*
- `read-execute` permissions to the group *root*
- `read-execute` permissions to others

Note that only the root user can modify this directory. The root user can also grant other users permissions to write to this directory. For example:

- Create writable per-user subdirectories. For step-by-step instructions, see Walkthrough 3: Create Writable Per-User Subdirectories and Configure Automatic Remounting on Reboot.
- Allow users to write to the Amazon EFS file system root. A user with root privileges can grant other users access to the file system.

43

- To change the Amazon EFS file system ownership to a non-*root* user and group, use the following:

```
1 $ sudo chown user:group /EFSroot
```

- To change permissions of the file system to something more permissive, use the following:

```
1 $ sudo chmod 777 /EFSroot
```

This command grants read-write-execute privileges to all users on all EC2 instances that have the file system mounted.

User and group ID permissions on files and directories within a file system

Files and directories in an Amazon EFS file system support standard Unix-style read/write/execute permissions based on the user ID and group ID asserted by the mounting NFSv4.1 client. When a user attempts to access files and directories, Amazon EFS checks their user ID and group IDs to verify the user has permission to access the objects. Amazon EFS also uses these IDs as the owner and group owner for new files and directories the user creates. Amazon EFS does not examine user or group names—it only uses the numeric identifiers.

Note
When you create a user on an EC2 instance, you can assign any numeric UID and GID to the user. The numeric user IDs are set in the /etc/passwd file on Linux systems. The numeric group IDs are in the /etc/group file. These files define the mappings between names and IDs. Outside of the EC2 instance, Amazon EFS does not perform any authentication of these IDs, including the root ID of 0.

If a user accesses an Amazon EFS file system from two different EC2 instances, depending on whether the UID for the user is the same or different on those instances, you see different behavior as follows:

- If the user IDs are the same on both EC2 instances, Amazon EFS considers them to be the same user, regardless of the EC2 instance they use. The user experience when accessing the file system is the same from both EC2 instances.
- If the user IDs are not the same on both EC2 instances, Amazon EFS considers them to be different users, and the user experience will not be the same when accessing the Amazon EFS file system from the two different EC2 instances.
- If two different users on different EC2 instances share an ID, Amazon EFS considers them the same user.

You might consider managing user ID mappings across EC2 instances consistently. Users can check their numeric ID using the id command, as shown following:

```
1 $ id
2
3 uid=502(joe) gid=502(joe) groups=502(joe)
```

Turn Off the ID Mapper

The NFS utilities in the operating system include a daemon called an ID Mapper that manages mapping between user names and IDs. In Amazon Linux, the daemon is called rpc.idmapd and on Ubuntu is called idmapd. It translates user and group IDs into names, and vice versa. However, Amazon EFS deals only with numeric IDs. We recommend you turn this process off on your EC2 instances (on Amazon Linux the mapper is usually disabled, in which case don't enable the ID mapper), as shown following:

```
1 $  service rpcidmapd status
2 $  sudo service rpcidmapd stop
```

No Root Squashing

When root squashing is enabled, the root user is converted to a user with limited permissions on the NFS server.

Amazon EFS behaves like a Linux NFS server with `no_root_squash`. If a user or group ID is 0, Amazon EFS treats that user as the `root` user, and bypasses permissions checks (allowing access and modification to all file system objects).

Permissions Caching

Amazon EFS caches file permissions for a small time period. As a result, there may be a brief window where a user who had access to a file system object but the access was revoked recently can still access that object.

Changing File System Object Ownership

Amazon EFS enforces the POSIX `chown_restricted` attribute. This means only the root user can change the owner of a file system object. While the root or the owner user can change the owner group of a file system object, unless the user is root, the group can only be changed to one that the owner user is a member of.

Amazon EFS File Sync

Amazon EFS File Sync copies files from an existing on-premises or cloud file system into an Amazon EFS file system. EFS File Sync securely and efficiently copies files over the internet or an AWS Direct Connect connection. It copies file data and file system metadata such as ownership, timestamps, and access permissions. For information about how to use AWS Direct Connect, see Walkthrough 5: Create and Mount a File System On-Premises with AWS Direct Connect.

Note
You don't need to set up AWS Direct Connect to use EFS File Sync.

Topics

- Requirements for EFS File Sync
- EFS File Sync Architecture
- How EFS File Sync Transfers Files

Requirements for EFS File Sync

Unless otherwise noted, the following are required for creating Amazon EFS File Sync.

Hardware Requirements

When deploying Amazon EFS File Sync on-premises, you must make sure that the underlying hardware on which you are deploying the file sync VM can dedicate the following minimum resources:

- Four virtual processors assigned to the VM.
- 32 GB of RAM assigned to the VM
- 80 GB of disk space for installation of VM image and system data

When deploying Amazon EFS File Sync on Amazon EC2, the instance size must be at least **xlarge** for your Amazon EFS File Sync to function. We recommend using one of the **Memory optimized r4.xlarge** instance types.

Supported Hypervisors and Host Requirements

You can choose to run EFS File Sync either on-premises as a virtual machine (VM), or in AWS as an Amazon Elastic Compute Cloud (Amazon EC2) instance.

EFS File Sync supports the following hypervisor versions and hosts:

- VMware ESXi Hypervisor (version 4.1, 5.0, 5.1, 5.5, 6.0 or 6.5) – A free version of VMware is available on the VMware website. You also need a VMware vSphere client to connect to the host.
- EC2 instance – EFS File Sync provides an Amazon Machine Image (AMI) that contains the EFS File Sync VM image. We recommend using the **Memory optimized r4.xlarge** instance types.

Supported NFS Protocols

EFS File Sync supports NFS v3.x, NFS v4.0 and NFS v4.1.

Allowing EFS File Sync Access Through Firewalls and Routers

EFS File Sync requires access to the following endpoints to communicate with AWS. If you use a firewall or router to filter or limit network traffic, you must configure your firewall and router to allow these service endpoints for outbound communication to AWS.

The following endpoints are required by EFS File Sync.

```
1  cp-sync.$region.amazonaws.com
2  activation-sync.$region.amazonaws.com
3  ec2-*.amazonaws.com
4  repo.$region.amazonaws.com
5  repo.default.amazonaws.com
6  packages.$region.amazonaws.com
7  0.amazon.pool.ntp.org
8  1.amazon.pool.ntp.org
9  2.amazon.pool.ntp.org
10 3.amazon.pool.ntp.org
11 54.201.223.107
```

For information about supported AWS Regions, see Amazon Elastic File System in the AWS General Reference.

The Amazon CloudFront endpoint is required before activation for the sync agent to get the list of available AWS Regions.

```
1  https://d4kdq0yaxexbo.cloudfront.net/
```

Network and Port Requirements

EFS File Sync requires the following ports for its operation.

From	To	Protocol	Port	How Used
EFS File Sync VM	AWS	TCP	443 (HTTPS)	For communication from EFS File Sync VM to the AWS service endpoint. For information about service endpoints, see Allowing EFS File Sync Access Through Firewalls and Routers.

From	To	Protocol	Port	How Used
Your web browser	EFS File Sync VM	TCP	80 (HTTP)	By local systems to obtain the sync agent activation key. Port 80 is used only during activation of the EFS File Sync agent. EFS File Sync VM doesn't require port 80 to be publicly accessible. The required level of access to port 80 depends on your network configuration. If you activate your sync agent from the Amazon EFS Management Console, the host from which you connect to the console must have access to port 80.
EFS File Sync VM	Domain Name Service (DNS) server	TCP/UDP	53 (DNS)	For communication between EFS File Sync VM and the DNS server.
EFS File Sync VM	AWS	TCP	22 (Support channel)	Allows AWS Support to access your EFS File Sync to help you with troubleshooting EFS File Sync issues. You don't need this port open for normal operation, but it is required for troubleshooting.
EFS File Sync VM	NTP server	UDP	123 (NTP)	By local systems to synchronize VM time to the host time.

From	To	Protocol	Port	How Used
EFS File Sync VM	NFS Server	TCP/UDP	2049 (NFS)	By EFS File Sync VM to mount a source NFS file system. Supports NFS v3.x, NFS v4.0 and NFS v4.1.

Following is an illustration of the required ports and lists the ports required by EFS File Sync.

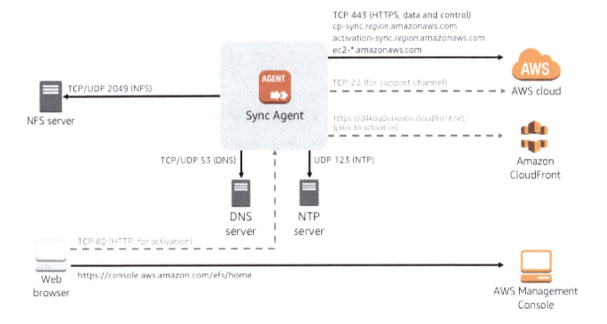

EFS File Sync Architecture

EFS File Sync provides the following benefits:

- Efficient high-performance parallel data transfer that tolerates unreliable and high-latency networks.
- Encryption of data transferred from your IT environment to AWS.
- Data transfer rate up to five times faster than standard Linux copy tools.
- Full and incremental syncs for repetitive transfers.

The following diagram shows a high-level view of the EFS File Sync architecture.

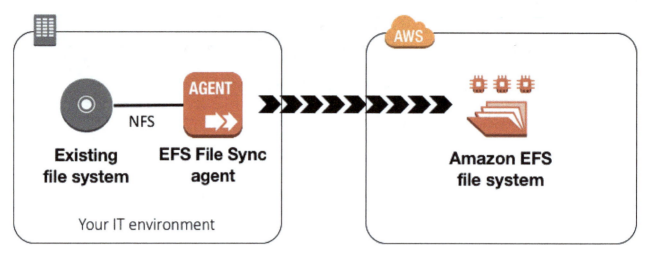

To sync files from an existing file system to Amazon EFS

1. Open the Amazon EFS Management Console at https://console.aws.amazon.com/efs/.

2. Download and deploy a sync agent. For on-premises deployment, the sync agent is provided as a virtual machine (VM) image for VMware ESXi. For an AWS Cloud deployment, you can create an Amazon EC2 instance from the community Amazon Machine Image (AMI).

3. Create a sync task and configure your source and destination file systems.

4. Start your sync task to begin syncing files from the source file system to the Amazon EFS file system.

5. Monitor your sync task on the Amazon EFS console or from Amazon CloudWatch. For more information, see Monitoring EFS File Sync with Amazon CloudWatch.

For more details on the EFS File Sync process, see the following:

- For information about how to sync files from an on-premises file system to Amazon EFS, see Walkthrough 7: Sync Files from an On-Premises File System to Amazon EFS by Using EFS File Sync.
- For information about how to sync files from Amazon EC2 to Amazon EFS, see Walkthrough 8: Sync a File System from Amazon EC2 to Amazon EFS Using EFS File Sync.

How EFS File Sync Transfers Files

When a sync task starts, it goes through three different statuses: **Preparing**, **Syncing** and **Verifying**. In the **Preparing** status, EFS File Sync examines the source and destination file systems to determine which files to sync. It does so by recursively scanning the contents of the source and destination file systems for differences. The files it examines include files that have been modified, deleted, added and files that have their metadata modified.

After the scanning is done, and the differences are calculated, EFS File Sync transitions to the **Syncing** status. At this point, EFS File Sync starts transferring files from the source file system to the destination Amazon EFS file system. Only files that have been added, modified, or deleted are transferred. This incremental transfer doesn't depend on the sync task you use but rather depends on the contents of your source and destination file system. In the Configure sync settings dialog box, you can choose which metadata in source file system you want to preserve. You can also configure your sync tasks settings to keep or delete files in the destination even if they aren't found in the source file system.

After the syncing is done, EFS File Sync verifies consistency between the source and destination file systems. This is the **Verifying** status. By default, EFS File Sync uses a full consistency verification of your source and destination when transferring files. During the **verifying** phase of a sync task, EFS File Sync rescans the content of the source and destination for any differences. If no differences are found, the task succeeds. Otherwise, the task is marked with a verification failure. For information about EFS File Sync status, see Understanding Sync Task Status.

Best Practices for Data Transfer from an On-Premises Storage Array

You might want to transfer data from an on-premises enterprise storage array to Amazon EFS. In this case, files in the source file system might be modified by another application while the files are being transferred from Network File System (NFS) to Amazon EFS.

To ensure that EFS File Sync successfully performs a transfer with full consistency verification, we recommend that the source location point to a read-only snapshot. This setup ensures that files at the source location can't be modified while the files are being transferred, and makes sure that verification works.

For information about how to take a snapshot in an enterprise storage array, see one of the following:

- EMC VNX: How to create a VNX snapshot and attach it to a server
- EMC VMAX: EMC TimeFinder Product Description Guide
- NetApp: Snapshot management
- HPE 3PAR: Snapshots and copy data management
- HDS: Hitachi Copy-on-Write Snapshot User Guide

Related Topics

Step 2: Create a Sync Task

Understanding Sync Task Status

Using the amazon-efs-utils Tools

Following, you can find a description of amazon-efs-utils, an open-source collection of Amazon EFS tools.

Topics

- Overview
- Installing the amazon-efs-utils Package on Amazon Linux
- Installing the amazon-efs-utils Package on Other Linux Distributions
- Upgrading Stunnel
- EFS Mount Helper

Overview

The amazon-efs-utils package is an open-source collection of Amazon EFS tools. There's no additional cost to use amazon-efs-utils, and you can download these tools from GitHub here: https://github.com/aws/efs-utils. The amazon-efs-utils package is available in the Amazon Linux package repositories, and you can build and install the package on other Linux distributions.

The amazon-efs-utils package comes with a mount helper and tooling that makes it easier to perform encryption of data in transit for Amazon EFS. A *mount helper* is a program that you use when you mount a specific type of file system. We recommend that you use the mount helper included in amazon-efs-utils to mount your Amazon EFS file systems.

The following dependencies exist for amazon-efs-utils and are installed when you install the amazon-efs-utils package:

- NFS client (the nfs-utils package)
- Network relay (stunnel package, version 4.56 or later)
- Python (version 2.7 or later)
- OpenSSL 1.0.2 or newer

Note
By default, when using the Amazon EFS mount helper with Transport Layer Security (TLS), the mount helper enforces the use of the Online Certificate Status Protocol (OCSP) and certificate hostname checking. The Amazon EFS mount helper uses the stunnel program for its TLS functionality. Some versions of Linux don't include a version of stunnel that supports these TLS features by default. When using one of those Linux versions, mounting an Amazon EFS file system using TLS fails.
When you've installed the amazon-efs-utils package, to upgrade your system's version of stunnel, see Upgrading Stunnel.
For issues with encryption, see Troubleshooting Encryption.

The following Linux distributions support amazon-efs-utils:

- Amazon Linux 2
- Amazon Linux
- Red Hat Enterprise Linux (and derivatives such as CentOS) version 7 and newer
- Ubuntu 16.04 LTS and newer

In the following sections, you can find out how to install amazon-efs-utils on your Linux instances.

Installing the amazon-efs-utils Package on Amazon Linux

The amazon-efs-utils package is available for installation in Amazon Linux and the Amazon Machine Images (AMIs) for Amazon Linux 2.

Note
If you're using AWS Direct Connect, you can find installation instructions in Walkthrough 5: Create and Mount a File System On-Premises with AWS Direct Connect.

To install the amazon-efs-utils package

1. Make sure that you've created an Amazon Linux or Amazon Linux 2 EC2 instance. For information on how to do this, see Step 1: Launch an Instance in the* Amazon EC2 User Guide for Linux Instances.*

2. Access the terminal for your instance through Secure Shell (SSH), and log in with the appropriate user name. For more information on how to do this, see Connecting to Your Linux Instance Using SSH in the *Amazon EC2 User Guide for Linux Instances.*

3. Run the following command to install amazon-efs-utils.

```
1 sudo yum install -y amazon-efs-utils
```

Installing the amazon-efs-utils Package on Other Linux Distributions

If you don't want to get the amazon-efs-utils package from Amazon Linux or Amazon Linux 2 AMIs, the amazon-efs-utils package is also available on GitHub.

To clone amazon-efs-utils from GitHub

1. Make sure that you've created an Amazon EC2 instance of the supported AMI type. For more information on how to do this, see Step 1: Launch an Instance in the *Amazon EC2 User Guide for Linux Instances.*

2. Access the terminal for your instance through Secure Shell (SSH), and log in with the appropriate user name. For more information on how to do this, see Connecting to Your Linux Instance Using SSH in the *Amazon EC2 User Guide for Linux Instances.*

3. If you haven't done so already, install gi with the following command.

```
1 sudo yum -y install git
```

4. From the terminal, clone the amazon-efs-utils tool from GitHub to a directory of your choice, with the following command.

```
1 git clone https://github.com/aws/efs-utils
```

Because you need the bash command **make**, you can install it with the following command if your operating system doesn't already have it.

```
1    sudo yum -y install make
```

After you clone the package, you can build and install amazon-efs-utils using one of the following methods, depending on the package type supported by your Linux distribution:

- **RPM** – This package type is supported by Amazon Linux, Red Hat Linux, CentOS, and similar.
- **DEB** – This package type is supported by Ubuntu, Debian, and similar.

To build and install amazon-efs-utils as an RPM package

1. Open a terminal on your client and navigate to the directory that has the cloned amazon-efs-utils package from GitHub (for example "/home/centos/efs-utils").

2. If you haven't done so already, install the rpm-builder package with the following command.

```
1 sudo yum -y install rpm-build
```

3. Build the package with the following command.

```
1 sudo make rpm
```

4. Install the amazon-efs-utils package with the following command.

```
1  sudo yum -y install ./build/amazon-efs-utils*rpm
```

To build and install amazon-efs-utils as a DEB package

1. Open a terminal on your client and navigate to the directory that has the cloned amazon-efs-utils package from GitHub.

2. Install the binutils package, a dependency for building DEB packages.

```
1  sudo apt-get -y install binutils
```

3. Build the package with the following command.

```
1  ./build-deb.sh
```

4. Install the package with the following command.

```
1  sudo apt-get -y install ./build/amazon-efs-utils*deb
```

Upgrading Stunnel

Using encryption of data in transit with the Amazon EFS mount helper requires OpenSSL version 1.0.2 or newer, and a version of stunnel that supports both OSCP and certificate hostname checking. The Amazon EFS mount helper uses the stunnel program for its TLS functionality. Note that some versions of Linux don't include a version of stunnel that supports these TLS features by default. When using one of those Linux versions, mounting an Amazon EFS file system using TLS fails.

After installing the Amazon EFS mount helper, you can upgrade your system's version of stunnel with the following instructions.

To upgrade stunnel

1. Open a terminal on your Linux client, and run the following commands in order.

2. `sudo yum install -y gcc openssl-devel tcp_wrappers-devel`

3. `sudo curl -o stunnel-5.46.tar.gz https://www.stunnel.org/downloads/stunnel-5.45.tar.gz`

4. `sudo tar xvfz stunnel-5.46.tar.gz`

5. `cd stunnel-5.46/`

6. `sudo ./configure`

7. `sudo make`

8. The current amazon-efs-utils package is installed in `bin/stunnel`. So that the new version can be installed, remove that directory with the following command.

```
1  sudo rm /bin/stunnel
```

9. `sudo make install`

10.

Note
The default CentOS shell is csh, which has different syntax than the bash shell. The following code first invokes bash, then runs.

```
1  bash
```

```
1 if [[ -f /bin/stunnel ]]; then
2 sudo mv /bin/stunnel /root
3 fi
```

1. `sudo ln -s /usr/local/bin/stunnel /bin/stunnel`

After you've installed a version of stunnel with the required features, you can mount your file system using TLS with the recommended settings.

If you are unable to install the required dependencies, you can optionally disable OCSP and certificate hostname checking inside the Amazon EFS mount helper configuration. We do not recommend that you disable these features in production environments. To disable OCSP and certificate host name checking, do the following:

1. Using your text editor of choice, open the `/etc/amazon/efs/efs-utils.conf` file.

2. Set the `stunnel_check_cert_hostname` value to false.

3. Set the `stunnel_check_cert_validity` value to false.

4. Save the changes to the file and close it.

For more information on using encryption of data in transit, see Mounting File Systems.

EFS Mount Helper

The Amazon EFS mount helper simplifies mounting your file systems. It includes the Amazon EFS recommended mount options by default. Additionally, the mount helper has built-in logging for troubleshooting purposes. If you encounter an issue with your Amazon EFS file system, you can share these logs with AWS Support.

How It Works

The mount helper defines a new network file system type, called `efs`, which is fully compatible with the standard `mount` command in Linux. The mount helper also supports mounting an Amazon EFS file system at instance boot time automatically by using entries in the `/etc/fstab` configuration file.

Warning
Use the `_netdev` option, used to identify network file systems, when mounting your file system automatically. If `_netdev` is missing, your EC2 instance might stop responding. This result is because network file systems need to be initialized after the compute instance starts its networking. For more information, see Automatic Mounting Fails and the Instance Is Unresponsive.

When encryption of data in transit is declared as a mount option for your Amazon EFS file system, the mount helper initializes a client stunnel process, and a supervisor process called `amazon-efs-mount-watchdog`. Stunnel is a multipurpose network relay that is open-source. The client stunnel process listens on a local port for inbound traffic, and the mount helper redirects NFS client traffic to this local port. The mount helper uses TLS version 1.2 to communicate with your file system.

Using TLS requires certificates, and these certificates are signed by a trusted Amazon Certificate Authority. For more information on how encryption works, see Encrypting Data and Metadata in EFS.

Using the EFS Mount Helper

The mount helper helps you mount your EFS file systems on your Linux EC2 instances. For more information, see Mounting File Systems.

Getting Support Logs

The mount helper has built-in logging for your Amazon EFS file system. You can share these logs with AWS Support for troubleshooting purposes.

You can find the logs stored in `/var/log/amazon/efs` for systems with the mount helper installed. These logs are for the mount helper, the stunnel process itself, and for the `amazon-efs-mount-watchdog` process that monitors the stunnel process.

Note
The watchdog process ensures that each mount's stunnel process is running, and stops the stunnel when the Amazon EFS file system is unmounted. If for some reason a stunnel process is terminated unexpectedly, the watchdog process restarts it.

You can change the configuration of your logs in `/etc/amazon/efs/amazon-efs-utils.conf`. However, doing so requires unmounting and then remounting the file system with the mount helper for the changes to take effect. Log capacity for the mount helper and watchdog logs is limited to 20 MiB. Logs for the stunnel process are disabled by default.

Important
You can enable logging for the stunnel process logs. However, enabling the stunnel logs can use up a nontrivial amount of space on your file system.

Using amazon-efs-utils with AWS Direct Connect

You can mount your Amazon EFS file systems on your on-premises data center servers when connected to your Amazon VPC with AWS Direct Connect. Using amazon-efs-utils also makes mounting simpler with the mount helper and allows you to enable encryption of data in transit. To see how to use amazon-efs-utils with AWS Direct Connect to mount Amazon EFS file systems onto on-premises Linux clients, see Walkthrough 5: Create and Mount a File System On-Premises with AWS Direct Connect.

Related Topics

For more information on the Amazon EFS mount helper, see these related topics:

- Encrypting Data and Metadata in EFS
- Mounting File Systems

Managing Amazon EFS File Systems

File system management tasks refer to creating and deleting file systems, managing tags, and managing network accessibility of an existing file system. Managing network accessibility is about creating and managing mount targets.

You can perform these file system management tasks using the Amazon EFS console, AWS Command Line Interface (AWS CLI), or programmatically, as discussed in the following sections.

Topics

- Managing File System Network Accessibility
- Managing File System Tags
- Metering – How Amazon EFS Reports File System and Object Sizes
- Managing Amazon EFS File Sync
- Deleting an Amazon EFS File System
- Managing Access to Encrypted File Systems

If you are new to Amazon EFS, we recommend that you try the following exercises that provide you with first-hand end-to-end experience using an Amazon EFS file system:

- Getting Started – This exercise provides a console-based, end-to-end setup in which you create a file system, mount it on an EC2 instance, and test the setup. The console takes care of many things for you and thus helps you quickly set up the end-to-end experience.
- Walkthrough 1: Create Amazon EFS File System and Mount It on an EC2 Instance Using the AWS CLI – This walkthrough is similar to the Getting Started exercise, but it uses the AWS CLI to perform most of the tasks. Because the CLI commands closely map to the Amazon EFS API, the walkthrough can help you familiarize yourself with the Amazon EFS API.

Managing Access to Encrypted File Systems

Using Amazon EFS, you can create encrypted file systems. Amazon EFS supports two forms of encryption for file systems, encryption in transit and encryption at rest. Any key management you need to perform is only related to encryption at rest. Amazon EFS automatically manages the keys for encryption in transit.

If you create a file system that uses encryption at rest, data and metadata are encrypted at rest. Amazon EFS uses AWS Key Management Service (AWS KMS) for key management. When you create a file system using encryption at rest, you specify a customer master key (CMK). The CMK can be `aws/elasticfilesystem` (the AWS-managed CMK for Amazon EFS), or it can be a CMK that you manage.

File data—the contents of your files—is encrypted at rest using the CMK that you specified when you created your file system. Metadata—file names, directory names, and directory contents—is encrypted by a key that Amazon EFS manages.

The AWS-managed CMK for your file system is used as the master key for the metadata in your file system, for example file names, directory names, and directory contents. You own the CMK used to encrypt file data (the contents of your files) at rest.

You manage who has access to your CMKs and the contents of your encrypted file systems. This access is controlled by both AWS Identity and Access Management (IAM) policies and AWS KMS. IAM policies control a user's access to Amazon EFS API actions. AWS KMS key policies control a user's access to the CMK you specified when the file system was created. For more information, see the following:

- IAM Users in the *IAM User Guide*
- Using Key Policies in AWS KMS in the *AWS Key Management Service Developer Guide*
- Using Grants in the *AWS Key Management Service Developer Guide.*

As a key administrator, you can import external keys and you can modify keys by enabling, disabling, or deleting them. The state of the CMK that you specified (when you created the file system with encryption at rest) affects access to its contents. The CMK must be in the `enabled` state for users to have access to the contents of an encrypted-at-rest file system.

Performing Administrative Actions on Amazon EFS Customer Master Keys

Following, you can find how to enable, disable, or delete the CMKs associated with your Amazon EFS file system. You can also learn about the behavior to expect from your file system when you perform these actions.

Disabling, Deleting, or Revoking Access to the CMK for a File System

You can disable or delete your custom CMKs, or you can revoke Amazon EFS access to your CMKs. Disabling and revoking access for Amazon EFS to your keys are reversible actions. Exercise significant caution when deleting CMKs. Deleting a CMK is an irreversible action.

If you disable or delete the CMK used for your mounted file system, the following is true:

- That CMK can't be used as the master key for new encrypted-at-rest file systems.
- Existing encrypted-at-rest file systems that use that CMK stop working after a period of time.

If you revoke Amazon EFS access to a grant for any existing mounted file system, the behavior is the same as if you disabled or deleted the associated CMK. In other words, the encrypted-at-rest file system continues to function, but stops working after a period of time.

To prevent access to a mounted encrypted-at-rest file system that has a CMK that you disabled, deleted, or revoked Amazon EFS access to, unmount the file system and delete your Amazon EFS mount targets.

You can't immediately delete an AWS KMS key, but you can instead schedule a key to be deleted. The earliest a CMK can be deleted is seven days after the key has been scheduled for deletion. When a key is scheduled for deletion, it behaves as if it is disabled. You can also cancel a key's scheduled deletion. For more information on deleting a master key in AWS KMS, see Deleting Customer Master Keys in the *AWS Key Management Service Developer Guide*.

The following procedure outlines how to disable a CMK.

To disable a CMK

1. Open the **Encryption Keys** section of the IAM console at https://console.aws.amazon.com/iam/home# encryptionKeys.

2. For **Region**, choose the appropriate AWS Region. Don't use the AWS Region selector in the navigation bar (top right corner).

3. Select the check box next to the alias of each CMK that you want to disable. **Note**
You can't disable AWS-managed CMKs, which are denoted by the orange AWS icon.

4. To disable a CMK, choose **Key actions, Disable**.

The following procedure outlines how to enable a CMK.

To enable a CMK

1. Open the **Encryption Keys** section of the IAM console at https://console.aws.amazon.com/iam/home# encryptionKeys.

2. For **Region**, choose the appropriate AWS Region. Don't use the AWS Region selector in the navigation bar (top right corner).

3. Select the check box next to the alias of each CMK that you want to enable. **Note**
You can't enable AWS-managed CMKs, which are denoted by the orange AWS icon.

4. To enable a CMK, choose **Key actions, Enable**.

Related Topics

- For more information on encrypted data and metadata at rest in Amazon EFS, see Encrypting Data and Metadata in EFS.
- For example key policies, see Amazon EFS Key Policies for AWS KMS.
- For a list of AWS CloudTrail log entries associated with an encrypted file system, see Amazon EFS Log File Entries for Encrypted-at-Rest File Systems.
- For more information on determining what accounts and services have access to your CMKs, see Determining Access to an AWS KMS Customer Master Key in the *AWS Key Management Service Developer Guide*.

Managing File System Network Accessibility

You mount your file system on an EC2 instance in your VPC using a mount target that you create for the file system. Managing file system network accessibility refers to managing the mount targets.

The following illustration shows how EC2 instances in a VPC access an Amazon EFS file system using a mount target.

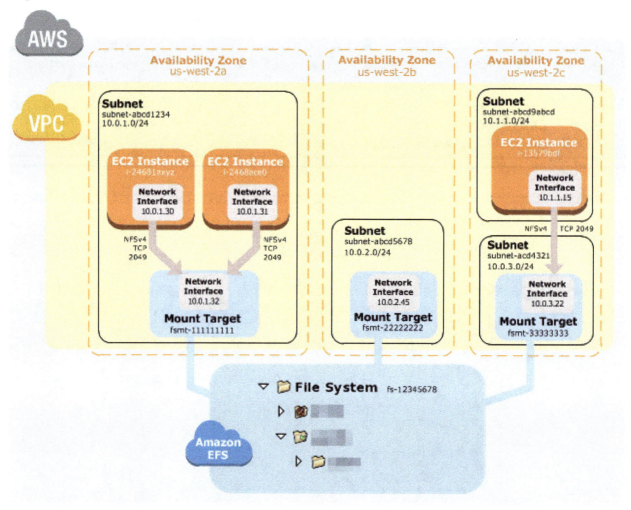

The illustration shows three EC2 instances launched in different VPC subnets accessing an Amazon EFS file system. The illustration also shows one mount target in each of the Availability Zones (regardless of the number of subnets in each Availability Zone).

You can create only one mount target per Availability Zone. If an Availability Zone has multiple subnets, as shown in one of the zones in the illustration, you create a mount target in only one of the subnets. As long as you have one mount target in an Availability Zone, the EC2 instances launched in any of its subnets can share the same mount target.

Managing mount targets refers to these activities:

- **Creating and deleting mount targets in a VPC** – At a minimum, you should create a mount target in each Availability Zone from which you want to access the file system. **Note**
  We recommend that you create mount targets in all the Availability Zones so you can easily mount the file system on EC2 instances that you might launch in any of the Availability Zones.

  If you delete a mount target, the operation forcibly breaks any mounts of the file system via the mount target being deleted, which might disrupt instances or applications using those mounts. To avoid application disruption, stop applications and unmount the file system before deleting the mount target.

You can use a file system only in one VPC at a time. That is, you can create mount targets for the file system in one VPC at a time. If you want to access the file system from another VPC, you must delete the mount targets from the current VPC and then create new mount targets in another VPC.

- **Updating the mount target configuration** – When you create a mount target, you associate security groups with the mount target. A security group acts as a virtual firewall that controls the traffic to and from the mount target. You can add inbound rules to control access to the mount target, and thus the file system. After creating a mount target, you might want to modify the security groups assigned to them.

Each mount target also has an IP address. When you create a mount target, you can choose an IP address from the subnet where you are placing the mount target. If you omit a value, Amazon EFS selects an unused IP address from that subnet.

There is no Amazon EFS operation to change the IP address after creating a mount target, so you cannot change the IP address programmatically or by using the AWS CLI. But the console enables you to change the IP address. Behind the scenes, the console deletes the mount target and creates the mount target again. **Warning**
If you change the IP address of a mount target, you break any existing file system mounts and you need to remount the file system.

None of the configuration changes to file system network accessibility affects the file system itself. Your file system and data remain.

The following sections provide information about managing network accessibility of your file system.

Topics

- Creating or Deleting Mount Targets in a VPC
- Creating Mount Targets in Another VPC
- Updating the Mount Target Configuration

Creating or Deleting Mount Targets in a VPC

To access an Amazon EFS file system in a VPC, you need mount targets. For an Amazon EFS file system, the following is true:

- You can create one mount target in each Availability Zone.
- If the VPC has multiple subnets in an Availability Zone, you can create a mount target in only one of those subnets. All EC2 instances in the Availability Zone can share the single mount target.

Note
We recommend that you create a mount target in each of the Availability Zones. There are cost considerations for mounting a file system on an EC2 instance in an Availability Zone through a mount target created in another Availability Zone. For more information, see Amazon EFS. In addition, by always using a mount target local to the instance's Availability Zone, you eliminate a partial failure scenario. If the mount target's zone goes down, you can't access your file system through that mount target.

For more information about the operation, see CreateMountTarget.

You can delete mount targets. A mount target deletion forcibly breaks any mounts of the file system via that mount target, which might disrupt instances or applications using those mounts. For more information, see DeleteMountTarget.

Using the Console

Use the following procedure to create new mount targets, delete, or update existing mount targets using the AWS Management Console.

1. In the Amazon EFS console, select the file system, choose **Actions**, and then choose **Manage File System Access**.

   The console displays the **Manage File System Access** page with a list of file system mount targets you have created in the selected VPC. The console shows a list of Availability Zones and mount target information, if there is a mount target in that Availability Zone.

   The console shows that the file system has one mount target in the **eu-west-2c** Availability Zone, as shown following:

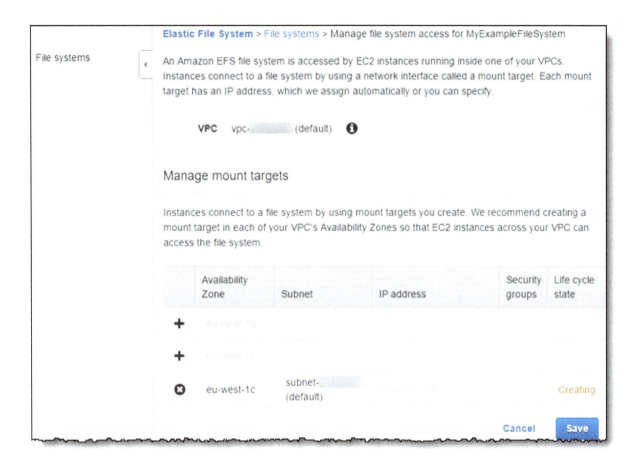

2. To create new mount targets

   1. Click on the left side in the specific **Availability Zone** row.

   2. If the Availability Zone has multiple subnets, select a subnet from the **Subnet** list.

   3. Amazon EFS automatically selects an available IP address, or you can provide another IP address explicitly.

   4. Choose a **Security Group** from the list.

      For more information about security groups, see Amazon EC2 Security Groups in the *Amazon EC2 User Guide for Linux Instances*.

3. To delete a mount target, choose the **X** next to the Availability Zone from which you want to remove a mount target.

Using the AWS CLI

To create a mount target, use the `create-mount-target` AWS CLI command (corresponding operation is CreateMountTarget), as shown following:

```
1 $ aws efs create-mount-target \
2 --file-system-id file-system-ID (for which to create the mount target) \
3 --subnet-id  vpc-subnet-ID (in which to create mount target) \
4 --security-group security-group IDs (to associate with the mount target) \
5 --region aws-region (for example, us-west-2) \
6 --profile adminuser
```

The AWS Region (the `region` parameter) must be the VPC region.

You can get a list of mount targets created for a file system using the `describe-mount-target` AWS CLI command (corresponding operation is DescribeMountTargets), as shown following:

```
1 $ aws efs describe-mount-targets \
2 --file-system-id file-system-ID \
3 --region aws-region-where-file-system-exists \
4 --profile adminuser
```

Here's a sample response:

```
1 {
2     "MountTargets": [
3         {
4             "MountTargetId": "fsmt-52a643fb",
5             "NetworkInterfaceId": "eni-f11e8395",
6             "FileSystemId": "fs-6fa144c6",
7             "LifeCycleState": "available",
8             "SubnetId": "subnet-15d45170",
9             "OwnerId": "23124example",
10            "IpAddress": "10.0.2.99"
11        },
12        {
13            "MountTargetId": "fsmt-55a643fc",
14            "NetworkInterfaceId": "eni-14a6ae4d",
15            "FileSystemId": "fs-6fa144c6",
16            "LifeCycleState": "available",
17            "SubnetId": "subnet-0b05fc52",
18            "OwnerId": "23124example",
19            "IpAddress": "10.0.19.174"
20        }
21    ]
22 }
```

To delete an existing mount target, use the `delete-mount-target` AWS CLI command (corresponding operation is DeleteMountTarget), as shown following:

```
1 $ aws efs delete-mount-target \
2 --mount-target-id mount-target-ID-to-delete \
3 --region aws-region-where-mount-target-exists \
4 --profile adminuser
```

Creating Mount Targets in Another VPC

You can use an Amazon EFS file system in one VPC at a time. That is, you create mount targets in a VPC for your file system, and use those mount targets to provide access to the file system from EC2 instances in that VPC. To access the file system from EC2 instances in another VPC, you must first delete the mount targets from the current VPC and then create new mount targets in another VPC.

Working with VPC Peering in Amazon EFS

A *VPC peering connection *is a networking connection between two VPCs that enables you to route traffic between them using private Internet Protocol version 4 (IPv4) or Internet Protocol version 6 (IPv6) addresses. For more information on VPC peering, see What is VPC Peering? in the *Amazon VPC Peering Guide*.

For Amazon EFS, you can work with VPC peering within a single AWS Region when using C5 or M5 instances. However, other VPC private connectivity mechanisms such as a VPN connection, interregion VPC peering, and intraregion VPC peering using other instance types are not supported.

Using the Console

1. In the Amazon EFS console, select the file system, choose **Actions**, and then choose **Manage File System Access**.

   The console displays the **Manage File System Access** page with a list of mount targets you created for the file system in a VPC. The following illustration shows a file system that has three mount targets, one in each Availability Zones.

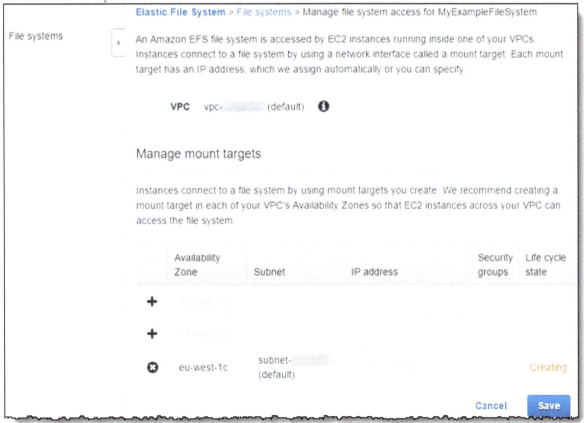

2. To change the VPC, select another VPC from the **VPC** list.

   The console clears all of the mount target information and lists only the Availability Zone.

3. Create mount targets in one or more Availability Zones as follows:

   1. If the Availability Zone has multiple subnets, select a subnet from the **Subnet** list.

   2. Amazon EFS automatically selects an available IP address, or you can provide another IP address explicitly.

   3. Choose the security groups that you want to associate.

      For information about security groups, see Amazon EC2 Security Groups in the *Amazon EC2 User Guide for Linux Instances*.

4. Choose **Save**.

   The console first deletes the mount targets from the previous VPC and then creates new mount targets in the new VPC that you selected.

Using the CLI

To use a file system in another VPC, you must first delete any mount targets you previously created in a VPC and then create new mount targets in another VPC. For example AWS CLI commands, see Creating or Deleting Mount Targets in a VPC.

Updating the Mount Target Configuration

After you create a mount target for your file system, you may want to update security groups that are in effect. You cannot change the IP address of an existing mount target. To change IP address you must delete the mount target and create a new one with the new address. Deleting a mount target breaks any existing file system mounts.

Modifying the Security Group

Security groups define inbound/outbound access. When you change security groups associated with a mount target, make sure that you authorize necessary inbound/outbound access so that your EC2 instance can communicate with the file system.

For more information about security groups, see Amazon EC2 Security Groups in the *Amazon EC2 User Guide for Linux Instances*.

Using the Console

1. In the Amazon EFS console, select the file system, choose **Actions**, and then choose **Manage File System Access**.

   The console displays the **Manage File System Access** page with a list of Availability Zones and mount target information, if there is a mount target in the Availability Zone.

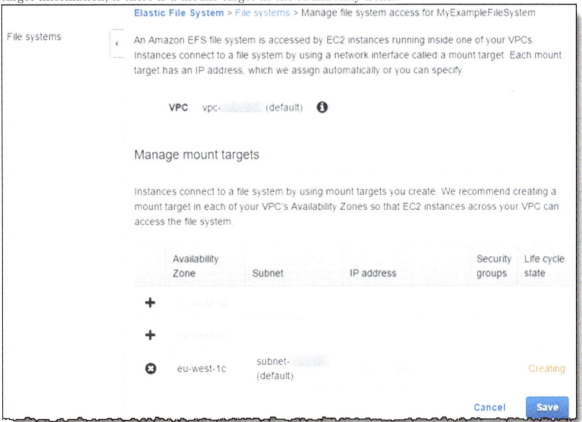

2. In the **Security Group** column, you can add or remove security groups. Choose **X** to remove an existing security group. Choose the **Security Group** box to select from other available security groups.

If you remove all security groups, Amazon EFS assigns the VPC's default security group.

Using the CLI

To modify security groups that are in effect for a mount target, use the `modify-mount-target-security-group` AWS CLI command (corresponding operation is ModifyMountTargetSecurityGroups) to replace any existing security groups, as shown following:

```
1 $ aws efs modify-mount-target-security-groups \
2 --mount-target-id mount-target-ID-whose-configuration-to-update \
3 --security-groups  security-group-ids-separated-by-space \
4 --region aws-region-where-mount-target-exists \
5 --profile adminuser
```

Managing File System Tags

You can create new tags, update values of existing tags, or delete tags associated with a file system.

Using the Console

The console lists existing tags associated with a file system. You can add new tags, change values of existing tags, or delete existing tags.

1. Open the Amazon Elastic File System console at https://console.aws.amazon.com/efs/.

2. Choose the file system.

3. Choose **Action** and then choose **Manage Tags**.

4. On the **Manage Tags** page, add or delete tags. For each new tag, provide a **Key** and its **Value**.

5. Choose **Save**.

Using the AWS CLI

You can use the `create-tags` CLI command to add new tags, `delete-tags` to delete existing tags, or use the `describe-tags` command to retrieve tags associated with a file system. Each CLI command corresponds to the CreateTags, DeleteTags, and DescribeTags Amazon EFS operations.

For an example walkthrough of the AWS CLI commands that you can use to add and list tags, see Step 2.1: Create Amazon EFS File System.

The following `delete-tags` command removes the tag keys `test1` and `test2` from the tag list of the specified file system.

```
1 $ aws efs \
2 delete-tags \
3 --file-system-id fs-c5a1446c \
4 --tag-keys "test1" "test2" \
5 --region us-west-2 \
6 --profile adminuser
```

Metering – How Amazon EFS Reports File System and Object Sizes

This section explains how Amazon EFS reports file system sizes and sizes of objects within a file system.

Metering Amazon EFS File System Objects

Customer-visible objects in an Amazon EFS system can be regular files, directories, symbolic links, and special files (FIFOs and sockets). Each of these objects is metered for 2 kibibytes (KiB) of metadata (for its inode) and one or more increments of 4 KiB of data. The following list explains the metered data size for different types of file system objects.

- **Regular files** – The metered data size of a regular file is the logical size of the file rounded to the next 4-KiB increment, except that it may be less for sparse files.

  A sparse file is a file to which data is not written to all positions of the file before its logical size is reached. For a sparse file, if the actual storage used is less than the logical size rounded to the next 4-KiB increment, Amazon EFS reports actual storage used as the metered data size.

- **Directories** – The metered data size of a directory is the actual storage used for the directory entries and the data structure that holds them, rounded to the next 4 KiB increment. The metered data size doesn't include the actual storage used by the file data.

- **Symbolic links and special files** – The metered data size for these objects is always 4 KiB.

When Amazon EFS reports the space used for an object, through the NFSv4.1 `space_used` attribute, it includes the object's current metered data size, but not its metadata size. There are two utilities available for measuring the disk usage of a file, the `du` and `stat` utilities. Here's an example of how to use the `du` utility, on an empty file, with the `-k` option to return the output in kilobytes:

```
1 $ du -k file
2 4        file
```

Here's an example of how to use the `stat` utility on an empty file to return the file's disk usage:

```
1 $ /usr/bin/stat --format="%b*%B" file | bc
2 4096
```

To measure the size of a directory, use the `stat` utility, find the `Blocks` value, and then multiply that value by the block size. Here's an example of how to use the `stat` utility on an empty directory:

```
1 $ /usr/bin/stat --format="%b*%B" . | bc
2 4096
```

Metering an Amazon EFS File System

The metered size of an entire Amazon EFS file system is the sum of the sizes (including metadata) of all of its current objects. The size of each object is calculated from a representative sampling that represents the size of the object during the metered hour, for example the hour from 8:00 am to 9:00 am.

For example, an empty file contributes 6 KiB (2 KiB metadata + 4 KiB data) to the metered size of its file system. Upon creation, a file system has a single empty root directory and therefore has a metered size of 6 KiB.

The metered sizes of a particular file system define the usage for which the owner account is billed for that file system for that hour.

Note
The computed metered size doesn't represent a consistent snapshot of the file system at any particular time

during that hour. Instead, it represents the sizes of the objects that existed in the file system at varying times within each hour, or possibly the hour before it. These sizes are summed to determine the file system's metered size for the hour. The metered size of a file system is thus eventually consistent with the metered sizes of the objects stored when there are no writes to the file system.

This metered size for an Amazon EFS file system can be seen in the following ways:

- **DescribeFileSystems API** – Used in SDKs, HTTP, and the AWS CLI.
- **File Systems table** – For each file system listed in the AWS Management Console.
- **DF command** – In Linux, the `df` command can be run at the terminal prompt of an EC2 instance. Use the `df` command and not the `du` command. Don't use the `du` command on the root of the file system for storage metering purposes. The results don't provide full data.

Note
The metered size is also used to determine your I/O throughput baseline and burst rates. For more information, see Throughput Scaling in Amazon EFS.

Managing Amazon EFS File Sync

In this section, you can find information about how to manage your Amazon EFS File Sync.

Topics

- Deleting a Sync Agent
- Deleting a Sync Task
- Understanding Sync Agent Status
- Understanding Sync Task Status
- Performing Tasks on the EFS File Sync VM Local Console
- Performing Tasks on Amazon EC2 EFS File Sync Local Console

Deleting a Sync Agent

If you no longer need a sync agent, you can delete it from the Amazon EFS Management Console.

To delete a sync agent

1. Choose **File syncs**, choose **Agents**, and then choose the sync agent that you want to delete.

2. For **Actions**, choose **Delete**.

3. In the **Confirm deletion of sync agent** dialog box, choose **Check box confirm deletion**, and then choose **OK**.

Deleting a Sync Task

If you no longer need a sync task, you can delete it from the Amazon EFS Management Console.

To delete a sync task

1. Choose **File syncs**, choose **Tasks**, and then choose the sync task that you want to delete.

2. For **Actions**, choose **Delete**.

3. In the **Confirm deletion of sync task** dialog box, choose **Check box confirm deletion**, and then choose **OK**.

Understanding Sync Agent Status

The following table describes each sync agent status, and if and when you should take action based on the status. When a sync agent is in use, it has **Running** status all or most of the time.

Sync Agent Status	Meaning
Running	The sync agent is configured properly and is available to use. The Running status is the normal running status for a sync agent.
Offline	The sync agent's VM or EC instance is turned off or the agent is in an unhealthy state. When the issue that caused the unhealthy state is resolved, the agent returns to Running status.

Understanding Sync Task Status

The following table described each sync task status, and if and when you should take action based on the status.

Sync Task Status	Meaning
Available	The sync task is configured properly and is available to be started.
Completed	The task creating process has completed.
Creating	EFS File Sync is creating the sync task.
Starting	The task creating process has started.
Preparing	The sync task is examining the source and destination file systems to determine which files to sync.
Syncing	EFS File Sync is syncing file from the source file system to the destination Amazon EFS file system.
Verifying	EFS File Sync is verifying consistency between the source and destination file systems.

Performing Tasks on the EFS File Sync VM Local Console

For an EFS File Sync deployed on-premises, you can perform the following maintenance tasks using the VM host's local console.

Topics

- Logging in to the Local Console Using Default Credentials
- Configuring Your EFS File Sync Network
- Viewing Your EFS File Sync System Resource Status
- Synchronizing Your EFS File Sync VM Time
- Running EFS File Sync Commands on the Local Console

Logging in to the Local Console Using Default Credentials

When the VM is ready for you to log in, the login screen is displayed.

To log in to the EFS File Sync's local console

- If this is your first time logging in to the local console, log in to the VM with the user name: *admin* and password: *password*. Otherwise, use your credentials to log in.

After you log in, you see the** Amazon EFS File Sync** **Configuration** main menu, as shown in the following screenshot.

```
AWS Appliance Activation - Configuration

#######################################################
##  Currently connected network adapters:
##
##  eth0:
#######################################################

1: Network Configuration
2: View System Resource Check (0 Errors)
3: System Time Management
4: Command Prompt

Press "x" to exit session

Enter command: _
```

Note

We recommend changing the default password. You do this by running the `passwd` command from the EFS File Sync Command Prompt (item 5 on the main menu). For information about how to run the command, see Running EFS File Sync Commands on the Local Console.

To	See
Configure your network	Configuring Your EFS File Sync Network.
View system resource check	Viewing Your EFS File Sync System Resource Status.
Manage VM time	Synchronizing Your EFS File Sync VM Time.
Run Local console commands	Running EFS File Sync Commands on the Local Console.

To shut down EFS File Sync, type **0**.

To exit the configuration session, type **x** to exit the menu.

Configuring Your EFS File Sync Network

The default network configuration for the EFS File Sync is Dynamic Host Configuration Protocol (DHCP). With DHCP, your EFS File Sync is automatically assigned an IP address. In some cases, you might need to manually assign your EFS File Sync's IP as a static IP address, as described following.

To configure your EFS File Sync to use static IP addresses

1. Log in to your EFS File Sync's local console.

2. On the Amazon EFS File Sync **Configuration** main menu, type option **1** to begin configuring a static IP address.

```
AWS Appliance Activation - Configuration

##################################################
##   Currently connected network adapters:
##
##   eth0: ▓▓▓▓▓▓▓▓▓▓▓
##################################################

1: Network Configuration
2: View System Resource Check (0 Errors)
3: System Time Management
4: Command Prompt

Press "x" to exit session

Enter command: _
```

3. Choose one of the following options on the **Amazon EFS File Sync Configuration** menu:

```
AWS Appliance Activation - Network Configuration

1: Describe Adapter
2: Configure DHCP
3: Configure Static IP
4: Reset all to DHCP
5: Set Default Adapter
6: View DNS Configuration
7: View Routes

Press "x" to exit

Enter command: _
```

[See the AWS documentation website for more details]

Viewing Your EFS File Sync System Resource Status

When your gateway starts, it checks its virtual CPU cores, root volume size, and RAM and determines whether these system resources are sufficient for your EFS File Sync to function properly. You can view the results of this check on the EFS File Sync's local console.

To view the status of a system resource check

1. Log in to your EFS File Sync's local console.

2. In the **EFS File Sync Configuration** main menu, type **2** to view the results of a system resource check.

```
AWS Appliance Activation - Configuration

#################################################
##   Currently connected network adapters:
##
##   eth0: ▓▓▓ ▓▓▓ ▓▓▓ ▓▓
#################################################

1: Network Configuration
2: View System Resource Check (0 Errors)
3: System Time Management
4: Command Prompt

Press "x" to exit session

Enter command: _
```

The console displays an [**OK**], [**WARNING**], or [**FAIL**] message for each resource as described in the table following.
[See the AWS documentation website for more details]

The console also displays the number of errors and warnings next to the resource check menu option.

The following screenshot shows a [**FAIL**] message and the accompanying error message.

Synchronizing Your EFS File Sync VM Time

After your EFS File Sync is deployed and running, in some scenarios the EFS File Sync VM's time can drift. For example, if there is a prolonged network outage and your hypervisor host and EFS File Sync do not get time updates, then the EFS File Sync VM's time will be different from the true time. When there is a time drift, a discrepancy occurs between the stated times when operations such as snapshots occur and the actual times that the operations occur.

For an EFS File Sync deployed on VMware ESXi, setting the hypervisor host time and synchronizing the VM time to the host is sufficient to avoid time drift.

Running EFS File Sync Commands on the Local Console

The EFS File Sync console helps provide a secure environment for configuring and diagnosing issues with your EFS File Sync. Using the console commands, you can perform maintenance tasks such as saving routing tables or connecting to AWS Support.

To run a configuration or diagnostic command

1. Log in to your EFS File Sync's local console.

2. On the **EFS File Sync Configuration** main menu, type option 4 for **Command Prompt**.

```
    AWS Appliance Activation - Configuration

    ##############################################################
    ##   Currently connected network adapters:
    ##
    ##   eth0:
    ##############################################################

    1: Network Configuration
    2: View System Resource Check (0 Errors)
    3: System Time Management
    4: Command Prompt

    Press "x" to exit session

    Enter command: _
```

3. On the EFS File Sync console, type **h**, and then press the **Return** key.

   The console displays the **Available Commands** menu with the available commands and after the menu a **Command Prompt**, as shown in the following screenshot.

```
AVAILABLE COMMANDS
ip                      Show / manipulate routing, devices, and tunnels
save-routing-table      Save newly added routing table entry
ifconfig                View or configure network interfaces
iptables                Administration tool for IPv4 packet filtering and NAT
save-iptables           Persist IP tables
passwd                  Update authentication tokens
open-support-channel    Connect to AWS Support
h                       Display available command list
exit                    Return to Configuration menu

Command: _
```

Note
The man command is disabled in the EFS File Sync local console.

Performing Tasks on Amazon EC2 EFS File Sync Local Console

Some maintenance tasks require that you log in to the local console when running an EFS File Sync deployed on an Amazon EC2 instance. In this section, you can find information about how to log in to the local console and perform maintenance tasks.

Topics

- Logging In to Amazon EC2 EFS File Sync Local Console
- Viewing EFS File Sync System Resource Status
- Running EFS File Sync Commands on the Local Console

Logging In to Amazon EC2 EFS File Sync Local Console

You can connect to your Amazon EC2 instance by using a Secure Shell (SSH) client. For detailed information, see Connect to Your Instance in the *Amazon EC2 User Guide.* To connect this way, you will need the SSH key pair you specified when you launched the instance. For information about Amazon EC2 key pairs, see Amazon EC2 Key Pairs in the *Amazon EC2 User Guide.*

To log in to the EFS File Sync local console

1. Log in to your local console. If you are connecting to your EC2 instance from a Windows computer, log in as user name: *admin* and password: *password.* Otherwise, use your credentials to log in

2. After you log in, you see the **Amazon EFS File Sync Configuration** main menu, as shown in the following screenshot.

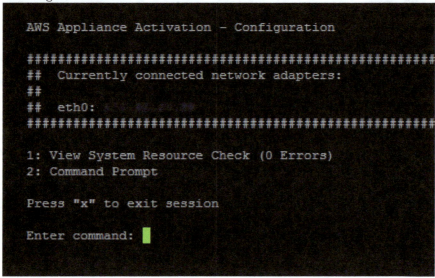

[See the AWS documentation website for more details]

To shut down the EFS File Sync, type **0**.

To exit the configuration session, type **x** to exit the menu.

Viewing EFS File Sync System Resource Status

When your EFS File Sync starts, it checks its virtual CPU cores, root volume size, and RAM and determines whether these system resources are sufficient for your EFS File Sync to function properly. You can view the results of this check on the EFS File Sync's local console.

To view the status of a system resource check

1. Log in to your EFS File Sync's local console. For instructions, see Logging In to Amazon EC2 EFS File Sync Local Console.

2. In the **Amazon EFS File Sync Configuration** main menu, type **1** to view the results of a system resource check.

```
AWS Appliance Activation - Configuration

#####################################################
##   Currently connected network adapters:
##
##   eth0:
#####################################################

1: View System Resource Check (0 Errors)
2: Command Prompt

Press "x" to exit session

Enter command: █
```

The console displays an [**OK**], [**WARNING**], or [**FAIL**] message for each resource as described in the table following.
[See the AWS documentation website for more details]

The console also displays the number of errors and warnings next to the resource check menu option.

The following screenshot shows a [**FAIL**] message and the accompanying error message.

Running EFS File Sync Commands on the Local Console

The EFS File Sync local console helps provide a secure environment for configuring and diagnosing issues with your EFS File Sync. Using the local console commands, you can perform maintenance tasks such as saving routing tables or connecting to AWS Support.

To run a configuration or diagnostic command

1. Log in to your EFS File Sync's local console. For instructions, see Logging In to Amazon EC2 EFS File Sync Local Console.

2. In the **Amazon EFS File Sync Configuration** main menu, type **2** for **EFS File Sync Console**.

```
AWS Appliance Activation - Configuration

#####################################################
##   Currently connected network adapters:
##
##   eth0:
#####################################################

1: View System Resource Check (0 Errors)
2: Command Prompt

Press "x" to exit session

Enter command: █
```

3. In the EFS File Sync console, type **h**, and then press the **Return** key.

The console displays the **Available Commands** menu with the available commands. After the menu, a **EFS File Sync Console** prompt appears, as shown in the following screenshot.

```
AVAILABLE COMMANDS
ip                        Show / manipulate routing, devices, and tunnels
save-routing-table        Save newly added routing table entry
ifconfig                  View or configure network interfaces
iptables                  Administration tool for IPv4 packet filtering and NAT
save-iptables             Persist IP tables
open-support-channel      Connect to AWS Support
h                         Display available command list
exit                      Return to Configuration menu

Command: █
```

Note

The man command is disabled in the EFS File Sync local console.

Deleting an Amazon EFS File System

File system deletion is a destructive action that you can't undo. You lose the file system and any data you have in it. Any data that you delete from a file system is gone, and you can't restore the data.

Important
You should always unmount a file system before you delete it.

Using the Console

1. Open the Amazon Elastic File System console at https://console.aws.amazon.com/efs/.

2. Select the file system that you want to delete.

3. Choose **Action** and then choose **Delete File System**.

4. In **Permanently Delete File System** confirmation box, type the file system ID and then choose **Delete File System**.

   The console simplifies the file deletion for you. First it deletes the associated mount targets, and then it deletes the file system.

Using the CLI

Before you can use the AWS CLI command to delete a file system, you must delete all of the mount targets created for the file system.

For example AWS CLI commands, see Step 4: Clean Up.

Related Topics

Managing Amazon EFS File Systems

Mounting File Systems

In the following section, you can learn how to mount your Amazon EFS file system on a Linux instance using the Amazon EFS mount helper. In addition, you can find how to use the file `fstab` to automatically remount your file system after any system restarts.

Before the Amazon EFS mount helper was available, we recommended mounting your Amazon EFS file systems using the standard Linux NFS client. For more information on those changes, see Mounting File Systems Without the EFS Mount Helper.

Note
Before you can mount a file system, you must create, configure, and launch your related AWS resources. For detailed instructions, see Getting Started with Amazon Elastic File System.

Topics

- Troubleshooting AMI and Kernel Versions
- Installing the amazon-efs-utils Package
- Mounting with the EFS Mount Helper
- Mounting Your Amazon EFS File System Automatically
- Additional Mounting Considerations

Troubleshooting AMI and Kernel Versions

To troubleshoot issues related to certain Amazon Machine Image (AMI) or kernel versions when using Amazon EFS from an Amazon EC2 instance, see Troubleshooting AMI and Kernel Issues.

Installing the amazon-efs-utils Package

To mount your Amazon EFS file system on your Amazon EC2 instance, we recommend that you use the mount helper in the amazon-efs-utils package. The amazon-efs-utils package is an open-source collection of Amazon EFS tools. For more information, see Installing the amazon-efs-utils Package on Amazon Linux.

Mounting with the EFS Mount Helper

You can mount an Amazon EFS file system on a number of clients using the Amazon EFS mount helper. The following sections, you can find the mount helper process for the different types of clients.

Topics

- Mounting on Amazon EC2 with the EFS Mount Helper
- Mounting on Your On-Premises Linux Client with the EFS Mount Helper over AWS Direct Connect

Mounting on Amazon EC2 with the EFS Mount Helper

You can mount an Amazon EFS file system on an Amazon EC2 instance using the Amazon EFS mount helper. For more information on the mount helper, see EFS Mount Helper. To use the mount helper, you need the following:

- **An Amazon EFS file system ID** – After you create an Amazon EFS file system, you can get that file system's ID from the console or programmatically through the Amazon EFS API. This ID is in this format: `fs-12345678`.

- **An Amazon EFS mount target** – You create mount targets in your VPC. If you create your file system in the console, you create your mount targets at the same time. For more information, see Creating a Mount Target Using the Amazon EFS console.
- **An Amazon EC2 instance running a supported distribution of Linux** – The supported Linux distributions for mounting your file system with the mount helper are Amazon Linux 2, Amazon Linux 2017.09 and newer, Red Hat Enterprise Linux (and derivatives such as CentOS) version 7 and newer, and Ubuntu 16.04 LTS and newer.
- **The Amazon EFS mount helper installed** – The mount helper is a tool in amazon-efs-utils. For information on how to install amazon-efs-utils, see Installing the amazon-efs-utils Package on Amazon Linux.

To mount your Amazon EFS file system with the mount helper

1. Access the terminal for your instance through Secure Shell (SSH), and log in with the appropriate user name. For more information on how to do this, see Connecting to Your Linux Instance Using SSH in the *Amazon EC2 User Guide for Linux Instances.*

2. Run the following command to mount your file system.

```
1 sudo mount -t efs fs-12345678:/ /mnt/efs
```

Alternatively, if you want to use encryption of data in transit, you can mount your file system with the following command.

```
1 sudo mount -t efs -o tls fs-12345678:/ /mnt/efs
```

You also have the option of mounting automatically by adding an entry to your `/etc/fstab` file. When you mount automatically using `/etc/fstab`, you must add the `_netdev` mount option. For more information, see Updating an Existing EC2 Instance to Mount Automatically.

Note
Mounting with the mount helper automatically uses the following mount options that are optimized for Amazon EFS:
`nfsvers=4.1 rsize=1048576 wsize=1048576 hard timeo=600 retrans=2`

To use the `mount` command, the following must be true:

- The connecting EC2 instance must be in a VPC and must be configured to use the DNS server provided by Amazon. For information about the Amazon DNS server, see DHCP Options Sets in the *Amazon VPC User Guide.*
- The VPC of the connecting EC2 instance must have DNS hostnames enabled. For more information, see Viewing DNS Hostnames for Your EC2 Instance in the *Amazon VPC User Guide.*

Note
We recommend that you wait 90 seconds after creating a mount target before you mount your file system. This wait lets the DNS records propagate fully in the AWS Region where the file system is.

Mounting on Your On-Premises Linux Client with the EFS Mount Helper over AWS Direct Connect

You can mount your Amazon EFS file systems on your on-premises data center servers when connected to your Amazon VPC with AWS Direct Connect. Mounting your Amazon EFS file systems with amazon-efs-utils also makes mounting simpler with the mount helper and allows you to enable encryption of data in transit.

To see how to use amazon-efs-utils with AWS Direct Connect to mount Amazon EFS file systems onto on-premises Linux clients, see Walkthrough 5: Create and Mount a File System On-Premises with AWS Direct Connect.

Mounting Your Amazon EFS File System Automatically

You can use `fstab` to automatically mount your Amazon EFS file system using the mount helper whenever the Amazon EC2 instance it is mounted on reboots. For more information on the mount helper, see EFS Mount Helper. You can set up automatic mounting in two ways. You can update the `/etc/fstab` file in your EC2 instance after you connect to the instance for the first time, or you can configure automatic mounting of your EFS file system when you create your EC2 instance.

Updating an Existing EC2 Instance to Mount Automatically

To automatically remount your Amazon EFS file system directory when the Amazon EC2 instance reboots, you can use the file `fstab`. The file `fstab` contains information about file systems, and the command `mount -a`, which runs during instance startup, mounts the file systems listed in the `fstab` file.

Note
Before you can update the /etc/fstab file of your EC2 instance, make sure that you've already created your Amazon EFS file system. For more information, see Step 2: Create Your Amazon EFS File System in the Amazon EFS Getting Started exercise.

To update the /etc/fstab file in your EC2 instance

1. Connect to your EC2 instance, and open the `/etc/fstab` file in an editor.

2. Add the following line to the `/etc/fstab` file.

```
1 fs-12345678:/ /mnt/efs efs defaults,_netdev 0 0
```

   If you're mounting without amazon-efs-utils, see Mounting Automatically. **Warning**
   Use the `_netdev` option, used to identify network file systems, when mounting your file system automatically. If `_netdev` is missing, your EC2 instance might stop responding. This result is because network file systems need to be initialized after the compute instance starts its networking. For more information, see Automatic Mounting Fails and the Instance Is Unresponsive.

3. Save the changes to the file.

Your EC2 instance is now configured to mount the EFS file system whenever it restarts.

Note
If your Amazon EC2 instance needs to start regardless of the status of your mounted Amazon EFS file system, you'll want to add the `nofail` option to your file system's entry in your `etc/fstab` file.

The line of code you added to the /etc/fstab file does the following.

Field	Description
`fs-12345678:/`	The ID for your Amazon EFS file system. You can get this ID from the console or programmatically from the CLI or an AWS SDK.
`/mnt/efs`	The mount point for the EFS file system on your EC2 instance.
`efs`	The type of file system. When you're using the mount helper, this type is always `efs`.
`mount options`	Mount options for the file system. This is a comma-separated list of the following options: [See the AWS documentation website for more details]

Field	Description
0	A nonzero value indicates that the file system should be backed up by dump. For EFS, this value should be 0.
0	The order in which fsck checks file systems at boot. For EFS file systems, this value should be 0 to indicate that fsck should not run at startup.

Configuring an EFS File System to Mount Automatically at EC2 Instance Launch

You can configure an Amazon EC2 instance to mount your Amazon EFS file system automatically when it is first launched with a script that works with cloud-init. You add the script during the **Launch Instance** wizard of the EC2 management console. For an example of how to launch an EC2 instance from the console, see Getting Started.

The script installs the NFS client and writes an entry in the /etc/fstab file that will identify the mount target DNS name as well as the subdirectory in your EC2 instance on which to mount the EFS file system. The script ensures the file gets mounted when the EC2 instance is launched and after each system reboot.

For more information about the customized version of cloud-init used by Amazon Linux, see http://docs.aws. amazon.com/AWSEC2/latest/UserGuide/AmazonLinuxAMIBasics.html#CloudInit in the *Amazon EC2 User Guide for Linux Instances*.

To configure your EC2 instance to mount an EFS file system automatically at launch

1. Open the Amazon EC2 console in your web browser, and begin the **Launch Instance** wizard.

2. When you reach **Step 3: Configure Instance Details**, configure your instance details, expand the **Advanced** section, and then do the following:

   1. Paste the following script into **User data**. You must update the script by providing the appropriate values for *fs-12345678* and */mnt/efs*:

```
1 #cloud-config
2 repo_update: true
3 repo_upgrade: all
4
5 packages:
6 - amazon-efs-utils
7
8 runcmd:
9 - file_system_id_01=fs-12345678
10 - efs_directory=/mnt/efs
11
12 - mkdir -p ${efs_directory}
13 - echo "${file_system_id_01}:/ ${efs_directory} efs tls,_netdev" >> /etc/fstab
14 - mount -a -t efs defaults
```

Warning
Use the _netdev option, used to identify network file systems, when mounting your file system automatically. If _netdev is missing, your EC2 instance might stop responding. This result is because network file systems need to be initialized after the compute instance starts its networking. For more information, see Automatic Mounting Fails and the Instance Is Unresponsive.

1   If you are specifying a custom path to your mount point, as in the example, you may want to use
       `mkdir -p`, because the `-p` option creates intermediate parent directories as needed\.
       The `- chown` line of the preceding example changes the ownership of the directory at the
       mount point from the root user to the default Linux system user account for Amazon Linux, `
       ec2-user`\. You can specify any user with this command, or leave it out of the script to
       keep ownership of that directory with the root user\.
2
3   For more information about user data scripts, see [Adding User Data](http://docs.aws.amazon.com
       /AWSEC2/latest/UserGuide/ec2-instance-metadata.html#instancedata-add-user-data) in the *
       Amazon EC2 User Guide for Linux Instances*\.

    1. Complete the **Launch Instance** wizard. **Note**
       To verify that your EC2 instance is working correctly, you can integrate these steps into the Getting
       Started exercise. For more information, see Getting Started.

    Your EC2 instance is now configured to mount the EFS file system at launch.

Additional Mounting Considerations

When mounting your Amazon EFS file system on an Amazon EC2 instance, note the following additional considerations:

- We recommend the following default Linux mount option values:

```
1 rsize=1048576
2 wsize=1048576
3 hard
4 timeo=600
5 retrans=2
6 noresvport
```

- If you must change the IO size parameters (`rsize` and `wsize`), we recommend that you use the largest size possible (up to `1048576`) to avoid diminished performance.

- If you must change the timeout parameter (`timeo`), we recommend that you use a value of at least 150, which is equivalent to 15 seconds. The timeo parameter is in deciseconds, so 15 seconds is equal to 150 deciseconds.

- We recommend that you use the hard mount option. However, if you use a soft mount, you need to set the `timeo` parameter to at least 150 deciseconds.

- With the `noresvport` option, the NFS client uses a new Transmission Control Protocol (TCP) source port when a network connection is reestablished. Doing this helps ensure uninterrupted availability after a network recovery event.

- Avoid setting any other mount options that are different from the defaults. For example, changing read or write buffer sizes, or disabling attribute caching can result in reduced performance.

- Amazon EFS ignores source ports. If you change Amazon EFS source ports, it doesn't have any effect.

- Amazon EFS does not support any of the Kerberos security variants. For example, the following will cause a mount to fail:

```
1 $ mount -t nfs4 -o krb5p <DNS_NAME>:/ /efs/
```

- We recommend that you mount your file system using its DNS name, which will resolve to the IP address of the Amazon EFS mount target in the same Availability Zone as your Amazon EC2 instance. If you use a mount target in a different Availability Zone as your Amazon EC2 instance, you will incur the standard Amazon EC2 data transfer charges for data sent across Availability Zones, and you may see increased latencies for file system operations.

- For more mount options, and detailed explanations of the defaults, refer to the `man fstab` and `man nfs` pages.

Unmounting File Systems

Before you delete a file system, we recommend that you unmount it from every Amazon EC2 instance that it's connected to. You can unmount a file system on your Amazon EC2 instance by running the `umount` command on the instance itself. You can't unmount an Amazon EFS file system through the AWS CLI, the AWS Management Console, or through any of the AWS SDKs. To unmount an Amazon EFS file system connected to an Amazon EC2 instance running Linux, use the `umount` command as follows:

```
1 umount /mnt/efs
```

We recommend that you do not specify any other `umount` options. Avoid setting any other `umount` options that are different from the defaults.

You can verify that your Amazon EFS file system has been unmounted by running the `df` command to display the disk usage statistics for the file systems currently mounted on your Linux-based Amazon EC2 instance. If the Amazon EFS file system that you want to unmount isn't listed in the `df` command output, this means that the file system is unmounted.

Example Example: Identify the Mount Status of an Amazon EFS File System and Unmount It

```
1 $ df -T
2 Filesystem Type 1K-blocks Used Available Use% Mounted on
3 /dev/sda1 ext4 8123812 1138920 6884644 15% /
4 availability-zone.file-system-id.efs.aws-region.amazonaws.com :/ nfs4 9007199254740992 0
      9007199254740992 0% /mnt/efs
```

```
1 $ umount /mnt/efs
```

```
1 $ df -T
```

```
1 Filesystem Type 1K-blocks Used Available Use% Mounted on
2 /dev/sda1 ext4 8123812 1138920 6884644 15% /
```

Monitoring Amazon EFS

Monitoring is an important part of maintaining the reliability, availability, and performance of Amazon EFS and your AWS solutions. You should collect monitoring data from all of the parts of your AWS solution so that you can more easily debug a multi-point failure if one occurs. Before you start monitoring Amazon EFS, however, you should create a monitoring plan that includes answers to the following questions:

- What are your monitoring goals?
- What resources will you monitor?
- How often will you monitor these resources?
- What monitoring tools will you use?
- Who will perform the monitoring tasks?
- Who should be notified when something goes wrong?

The next step is to establish a baseline for normal Amazon EFS performance in your environment, by measuring performance at various times and under different load conditions. As you monitor Amazon EFS, you should consider storing historical monitoring data. This stored data will give you a baseline to compare against with current performance data, identify normal performance patterns and performance anomalies, and devise methods to address issues.

For example, with Amazon EFS, you can monitor network throughput, I/O for read, write, and/or metadata operations, client connections, and burst credit balances for your file systems. When performance falls outside your established baseline, you might need change the size of your file system or the number of connected clients to optimize the file system for your workload.

To establish a baseline you should, at a minimum, monitor the following items:

- Your file system's network throughput.
- The number of client connections to a file system.
- The number of bytes for each file system operation, including data read, data write, and metadata operations.

Monitoring Tools

AWS provides various tools that you can use to monitor Amazon EFS. You can configure some of these tools to do the monitoring for you, while some of the tools require manual intervention. We recommend that you automate monitoring tasks as much as possible.

Automated Monitoring Tools

You can use the following automated monitoring tools to watch Amazon EFS and report when something is wrong:

- **Amazon CloudWatch Alarms** – Watch a single metric over a time period that you specify, and perform one or more actions based on the value of the metric relative to a given threshold over a number of time periods. The action is a notification sent to an Amazon Simple Notification Service (Amazon SNS) topic or Amazon EC2 Auto Scaling policy. CloudWatch alarms do not invoke actions simply because they are in a particular state; the state must have changed and been maintained for a specified number of periods. For more information, see Monitoring with Amazon CloudWatch.
- **Amazon CloudWatch Logs** – Monitor, store, and access your log files from AWS CloudTrail or other sources. For more information, see Monitoring Log Files in the *Amazon CloudWatch User Guide*.
- **Amazon CloudWatch Events** – Match events and route them to one or more target functions or streams to make changes, capture state information, and take corrective action. For more information, see What is Amazon CloudWatch Events in the *Amazon CloudWatch User Guide*.
- **AWS CloudTrail Log Monitoring** – Share log files between accounts, monitor CloudTrail log files in real time by sending them to CloudWatch Logs, write log processing applications in Java, and validate that your log files have not changed after delivery by CloudTrail. For more information, see Working with CloudTrail Log Files in the *AWS CloudTrail User Guide*.

Manual Monitoring Tools

Another important part of monitoring Amazon EFS involves manually monitoring those items that the Amazon CloudWatch alarms don't cover. The Amazon EFS, CloudWatch, and other AWS console dashboards provide an at-a-glance view of the state of your AWS environment. We recommend that you also check the log files on file system.

- From the Amazon EFS console, you can find the following items for your file systems:
  - The current metered size
  - The number of mount targets
  - The life cycle state
- CloudWatch home page shows:
  - Current alarms and status
  - Graphs of alarms and resources
  - Service health status

In addition, you can use CloudWatch to do the following:
  - Create customized dashboards to monitor the services you use
  - Graph metric data to troubleshoot issues and discover trends
  - Search and browse all your AWS resource metrics
  - Create and edit alarms to be notified of problems

Monitoring with Amazon CloudWatch

You can monitor file systems using Amazon CloudWatch, which collects and processes raw data from Amazon EFS into readable, near real-time metrics. These statistics are recorded for a period of 15 months, so that you can access historical information and gain a better perspective on how your web application or service is performing. By default, Amazon EFS metric data is automatically sent to CloudWatch at 1-minute periods. For more information about CloudWatch, see What Are Amazon CloudWatch, Amazon CloudWatch Events, and Amazon CloudWatch Logs? in the *Amazon CloudWatch User Guide*.

Amazon CloudWatch Metrics for Amazon EFS

The `AWS/EFS` namespace includes the following metrics.

Metric	Description
BurstCreditBalance	The number of burst credits that a file system has. Burst credits allow a file system to burst to throughput levels above a file system's baseline level for periods of time. For more information, see Throughput scaling in Amazon EFS. The `Minimum` statistic is the smallest burst credit balance for any minute during the period. The `Maximum` statistic is the largest burst credit balance for any minute during the period. The `Average` statistic is the average burst credit balance during the period. Units: Bytes Valid statistics: `Minimum`, `Maximum`, `Average`
ClientConnections	The number of client connections to a file system. When using a standard client, there is one connection per mounted Amazon EC2 instance. To calculate the average `ClientConnections` for periods greater than one minute, divide the `Sum` statistic by the number of minutes in the period. Units: Count of client connections Valid statistics: `Sum`
DataReadIOBytes	The number of bytes for each file system read operation. The `Sum` statistic is the total number of bytes associated with read operations. The `Minimum` statistic is the size of the smallest read operation during the period. The `Maximum` statistic is the size of the largest read operation during the period. The `Average` statistic is the average size of read operations during the period. The `SampleCount` statistic provides a count of read operations. Units: [See the AWS documentation website for more details] Valid statistics: `Minimum`, `Maximum`, `Average`, `Sum`, `SampleCount`

Metric	Description
DataWriteIOBytes	The number of bytes for each file write operation. The `Sum` statistic is the total number of bytes associated with write operations. The `Minimum` statistic is the size of the smallest write operation during the period. The `Maximum` statistic is the size of the largest write operation during the period. The `Average` statistic is the average size of write operations during the period. The `SampleCount` statistic provides a count of write operations. Units: [See the AWS documentation website for more details] Valid statistics: `Minimum, Maximum, Average, Sum, SampleCount`
MetadataIOBytes	The number of bytes for each metadata operation. The `Sum` statistic is the total number of bytes associated with metadata operations. The `Minimum` statistic is the size of the smallest metadata operation during the period. The `Maximum` statistic is the size of the largest metadata operation during the period. The `Average` statistic is the size of the average metadata operation during the period. The `SampleCount` statistic provides a count of metadata operations. Units: [See the AWS documentation website for more details] Valid statistics: `Minimum, Maximum, Average, Sum, SampleCount`
PercentIOLimit	Shows how close a file system is to reaching the I/O limit of the General Purpose performance mode. If this metric is at 100% more often than not, consider moving your application to a file system using the Max I/O performance mode. This metric is only submitted for file systems using the General Purpose performance mode. Units: [See the AWS documentation website for more details]
PermittedThroughput	The maximum amount of throughput a file system is allowed, given the file system size and `BurstCreditBalance`. For more information, see Amazon EFS Performance. The `Minimum` statistic is the smallest throughput permitted for any minute during the period. The `Maximum` statistic is the highest throughput permitted for any minute during the period. The `Average` statistic is the average throughput permitted during the period. Units: Bytes per second Valid statistics: `Minimum, Maximum, Average`

Metric	Description
TotalIOBytes	The number of bytes for each file system operation, including data read, data write, and metadata operations. The Sum statistic is the total number of bytes associated with all file system operations. The Minimum statistic is the size of the smallest operation during the period. The Maximum statistic is the size of the largest operation during the period. The Average statistic is the average size of an operation during the period. The SampleCount statistic provides a count of all operations. To calculate the average operations per second for a period, divide the SampleCount statistic by the number of seconds in the period. To calculate the average throughput (Bytes per second) for a period, divide the Sum statistic by the number of seconds in the period. Units: [See the AWS documentation website for more details] Valid statistics: Minimum, Maximum, Average, Sum, SampleCount

Bytes Reported in CloudWatch

As with Amazon S3 and Amazon EBS, Amazon EFS CloudWatch metrics are reported as raw *Bytes*. Bytes are not rounded to either a decimal or binary multiple of the unit. Keep this in mind when calculating your burst rate using the data you get from the metrics. For more information on bursting, see Throughput Scaling in Amazon EFS.

Amazon EFS Dimensions

Amazon EFS metrics use the EFS namespace and provides metrics for a single dimension, FileSystemId. A file system's ID can be found in the Amazon EFS management console, and it takes the form of fs-XXXXXXXX.

How Do I Use Amazon EFS Metrics?

The metrics reported by Amazon EFS provide information that you can analyze in different ways. The list below shows some common uses for the metrics. These are suggestions to get you started, not a comprehensive list.

How do I?	Relevant Metrics
How can I determine my throughput?	You can monitor the daily `Sum` statistic of the `TotalIOBytes` metric to see your throughput.
How can I track the number of Amazon EC2 instances that are connected to a file system?	You can monitor the `Sum` statistic of the `ClientConnections` metric. To calculate the average `ClientConnections` for periods greater than one minute, divide the sum by the number of minutes in the period.
How can I see my burst credit balance?	You can see your balance by monitoring the `BurstCreditBalance` metric for your file system. For more information on bursting and burst credits, see Throughput Scaling in Amazon EFS.

Monitoring EFS File Sync with Amazon CloudWatch

You can monitor EFS File Sync using Amazon CloudWatch, which collects and processes raw data from Amazon EFS into readable, near real-time metrics. These statistics are recorded for a period of 15 months, so that you can access historical information and gain a better perspective on how EFS File Sync. By default, EFS File Sync metric data is automatically sent to CloudWatch at 5-minute periods. For more information about CloudWatch, see What Are Amazon CloudWatch, Amazon CloudWatch Events, and Amazon CloudWatch Logs? in the *Amazon CloudWatch User Guide*.

The AWS/FileSync namespace includes the following metrics.

Metric	Description
FilesTransferred	The number of files transferred from a source file system to the Amazon EFS file system. A file is considered to be transferred if any aspect of the required syncing increments this metric. In this case, this metric is incremented. However, if only metadata is changed then no actual data is transferred. units: Count
PhysicalBytesTransferred	The total number of bytes transferred over the network when the sync agent reads from the source file system to the Amazon EFS file system. Unit: Bytes
LogicalBytesTransferred	The total size of the files or directories transferred to the Amazon EFS file system. Metadata is not included in this metric. Units: Bytes

Amazon EFS File Sync Dimensions

EFS File Sync metrics use the AWS/FileSync namespace and provide metrics for the following dimensions:

- HostId—the unique ID of your host server.
- HostName—the name or domain of your host server.
- SyncSetId—the ID of the sync set. It takes the form set-12345678912345678

Accessing CloudWatch Metrics

You can see Amazon EFS metrics for CloudWatch in many ways. You can view them through the CloudWatch console, or you can access them using the CloudWatch CLI or the CloudWatch API. The following procedures show you how to access the metrics using these various tools.

To view metrics using the CloudWatch console

1. Open the CloudWatch console at https://console.aws.amazon.com/cloudwatch/.

2. In the navigation pane, choose **Metrics**.

3. Select the **EFS** namespace.

4. (Optional) To view a metric, type its name in the search field.

5. (Optional) To filter by dimension, select **FileSystemId**.

To access metrics from the AWS CLI

- Use the http://docs.aws.amazon.com/cli/latest/reference/cloudwatch/list-metrics.html command with the `--namespace "AWS/EFS"` namespace. For more information, see the AWS CLI Command Reference.

To access metrics from the CloudWatch API

- Call `[GetMetricStatistics](http://docs.aws.amazon.com/AmazonCloudWatch/latest/APIReference/API_GetMetricStatistics.html)`. For more information, see Amazon CloudWatch API Reference.

Creating CloudWatch Alarms to Monitor Amazon EFS

You can create a CloudWatch alarm that sends an Amazon SNS message when the alarm changes state. An alarm watches a single metric over a time period you specify, and performs one or more actions based on the value of the metric relative to a given threshold over a number of time periods. The action is a notification sent to an Amazon SNS topic or Auto Scaling policy.

Alarms invoke actions for sustained state changes only. CloudWatch alarms don't invoke actions simply because they are in a particular state; the state must have changed and been maintained for a specified number of periods.

One important use of CloudWatch alarms for Amazon EFS is to enforce encryption at rest for your file system. You can enable encryption at rest for an Amazon EFS file system when it's created. To enforce data encryption-at-rest policies for Amazon EFS file systems, you can use Amazon CloudWatch and AWS CloudTrail to detect the creation of a file system and verify that encryption at rest is enabled. For more information, see Walkthrough 6: Enforcing Encryption on an Amazon EFS File System at Rest.

Note
Currently, you can't enforce encryption in transit.

The following procedures outline how to create alarms for Amazon EFS.

To set alarms using the CloudWatch console

1. Sign in to the AWS Management Console and open the CloudWatch console at https://console.aws.amazon.com/cloudwatch/.

2. Choose **Create Alarm**. This launches the **Create Alarm Wizard**.

3. Choose **EFS Metrics** and scroll through the Amazon EFS metrics to locate the metric you want to place an alarm on. To display just the Amazon EFS metrics in this dialog box, search on the file system id of your file system. Select the metric to create an alarm on and choose **Next**.

4. Fill in the **Name**, **Description**, **Whenever** values for the metric.

5. If you want CloudWatch to send you an email when the alarm state is reached, in the **Whenever this alarm:** field, choose **State is ALARM**. In the **Send notification to:** field, choose an existing SNS topic. If you select **Create topic**, you can set the name and email addresses for a new email subscription list. This list is saved and appears in the field for future alarms. **Note**
If you use **Create topic** to create a new Amazon SNS topic, the email addresses must be verified before they receive notifications. Emails are only sent when the alarm enters an alarm state. If this alarm state change happens before the email addresses are verified, they do not receive a notification.

6. At this point, the **Alarm Preview** area gives you a chance to preview the alarm you're about to create. Choose **Create Alarm**.

To set an alarm using the AWS CLI

- Call [put\-metric\-alarm](http://docs.aws.amazon.com/cli/latest/reference/put-metric-alarm.html). For more information, see *AWS CLI Command Reference*.

To set an alarm using the CloudWatch API

- Call [PutMetricAlarm](http://docs.aws.amazon.com/AmazonCloudWatch/latest/APIReference/API_PutMetricAlarm.html). For more information, see *Amazon CloudWatch API Reference*

Using Metric Math with Amazon EFS

Using metric math, you can query multiple CloudWatch metrics and use math expressions to create new time series based on these metrics. You can visualize the resulting time series in the CloudWatch console and add them to dashboards. For example, you can use Amazon EFS metrics to take the sample count of `DataRead` operations divided by 60. The result is the average number of reads per second on your file system for a given 1-minute period. For more information on metric math, see Use Metric Math in the* Amazon CloudWatch User Guide.*

Following, find some useful metric math expressions for Amazon EFS.

Topics

- Metric Math: Throughput in MiB/Second
- Metric Math: Percent Throughput
- Metric Math: Throughput IOPS
- Metric Math: Percentage of IOPS
- Metric Math: Average I/O Size in KiB
- Using Metric Math Through an AWS CloudFormation Template for Amazon EFS

Metric Math: Throughput in MiB/Second

To calculate the average throughput (in MiB/second) for a time period, first choose a sum statistic (`DataReadIOBytes`, `DataWriteIOBytes`, `MetadataIOBytes`, or `TotalIOBytes`). Then convert the value to MiB, and divide that by the number of seconds in the period.

Suppose that your example logic is this: (sum of `TotalIOBytes` ÷ 1048576 (to convert to MiB)) ÷ seconds in the period

Then your CloudWatch metric information is the following.

ID	Usable Metrics	Statistic	Period
m1	[See the AWS documentation website for more details]	sum	1 minute

Your metric math ID and expression are the following.

ID	Expression
e1	(m1/1048576)/PERIOD(m1)

Metric Math: Percent Throughput

To calculate the percent throughput of the different I/O types (`DataReadIOBytes`, `DataWriteIOBytes`, or `MetadataIOBytes`) for a time period, first multiply the respective sum statistic by 100. Then divide the result by the sum statistic of `TotalIOBytes` for the same period.

Suppose that your example logic is this: (sum of `DataReadIOBytes` x 100 (to convert to percentage)) ÷ sum of `TotalIOBytes`

Then your CloudWatch metric information is the following.

ID	Usable Metric or Metrics	Statistic	Period
m1	[See the AWS documentation website for more details]	sum	1 minute
m2	[See the AWS documentation website for more details]	sum	1 minute

Your metric math ID and expression are the following.

ID	Expression
e1	(m2*100)/m1

Metric Math: Throughput IOPS

To calculate the average operations per second (IOPS) for a time period, divide the sample count statistic (`DataReadIOBytes`, `DataWriteIOBytes`, `MetadataIOBytes`, or `TotalIOBytes`) by the number of seconds in the period.

Suppose that your example logic is this: sample count of `DataWriteIOBytes` ÷ seconds in the period

Then your CloudWatch metric information is the following.

ID	Usable Metrics	Statistic	Period
m1	[See the AWS documentation website for more details]	sample count	1 minute

Your metric math ID and expression are the following.

ID	Expression
e1	m1/PERIOD(m1)

Metric Math: Percentage of IOPS

To calculate the percentage of IOPS per second of the different I/O types (`DataReadIOBytes`, `DataWriteIOBytes`, or `MetadataIOBytes`) for a time period, first multiply the respective sample count statistic by 100. Then divide that value by the sample count statistic of `TotalIOBytes` for the same period.

Suppose that your example logic is this: (sample count of `MetadataIOBytes` x 100 (to convert to percentage)) ÷ sample count of `TotalIOBytes`

Then your CloudWatch metric information is the following.

ID	Usable Metrics	Statistic	Period
m1	[See the AWS documentation website for more details]	sample count	1 minute

ID	Usable Metrics	Statistic	Period
m2	[See the AWS documentation website for more details]	sample count	1 minute

Your metric math ID and expression are the following.

ID	Expression
e1	(m2*100)/m1

Metric Math: Average I/O Size in KiB

To calculate the average I/O size (in KiB) for a period, divide the respective sum statistic for the `DataReadIOBytes`, `DataWriteIOBytes`, or `MetadataIOBytes` metric by the same sample count statistic of that metric.

Suppose that your example logic is this: (sum of `DataReadIOBytes` ÷ 1024 (to convert to KiB)) ÷ sample count of `DataReadIOBytes`

Then your CloudWatch metric information is the following.

ID	Usable Metrics	Statistic	Period
m1	[See the AWS documentation website for more details]	sum	1 minute
m2	[See the AWS documentation website for more details]	sample count	1 minute

Your metric math ID and expression are the following.

ID	Expression
e1	(m1/1024)/m2

Using Metric Math Through an AWS CloudFormation Template for Amazon EFS

You can also create metric math expressions through AWS CloudFormation templates. One such template is available for you to download and customize for use from the Amazon EFS tutorials on GitHub. For more information about using AWS CloudFormation templates, see Working with AWS CloudFormation Templates in the *AWS CloudFormation User Guide.*

Logging Amazon EFS API Calls with AWS CloudTrail

Amazon EFS is integrated with AWS CloudTrail, a service that captures AWS API calls and delivers the log files to an Amazon S3 bucket that you specify. CloudTrail captures API calls from the Amazon EFS console, the AWS CLI, or one of the AWS SDKs to the Amazon EFS API operations. Using the information collected by CloudTrail, you can determine the request that was made to Amazon EFS, the source IP address from which the request was made, who made the request, when it was made, and more.

Once you've created a trail, it starts logging events automatically for that region. It can take about 15 minutes for the logs to appear in the bucket. To learn more about CloudTrail, including how to configure and enable it, see the AWS CloudTrail User Guide.

Amazon EFS Information in CloudTrail

When CloudTrail logging is enabled in your AWS account, API calls made to Amazon EFS are tracked in CloudTrail log files, where they are written with other AWS service records. CloudTrail determines when to create and write to a new log file based on a time period and file size.

All Amazon EFS API calls are logged by CloudTrail. For example, calls to the `CreateFileSystem`, `CreateMountTarget` and `CreateTags` actions generate entries in the CloudTrail log files.

Each log file contains at least one API call. Some Amazon EFS API calls will trigger other API calls for other services. For example, the Amazon EFS `CreateMountTarget` API call will trigger a `CreateNetworkInterface` Amazon EC2 API call. For more information on which Amazon EFS API actions will trigger API calls in other services, see the **Required Permissions (API Actions)** column of the table in Amazon EFS API Permissions: Actions, Resources, and Conditions Reference.

Every log entry contains information about who generated the request. The user identity information in the log entry helps you determine the following:

- Whether the request was made with root or IAM user credentials
- Whether the request was made with temporary security credentials for a role or federated user
- Whether the request was made by another AWS service

For more information, see the CloudTrail userIdentity Element.

You can store your log files in your Amazon S3 bucket for as long as you want, but you can also define Amazon S3 lifecycle rules to archive or delete log files automatically. By default, your log files are encrypted with Amazon S3 server-side encryption (SSE).

If you want to be notified upon log file delivery, you can configure CloudTrail to publish Amazon SNS notifications when new log files are delivered. For more information, see Configuring Amazon SNS Notifications for CloudTrail.

You can also aggregate Amazon EFS log files from multiple AWS regions and multiple AWS accounts into a single Amazon S3 bucket.

For more information, see Receiving CloudTrail Log Files from Multiple Regions and Receiving CloudTrail Log Files from Multiple Accounts.

Understanding Amazon EFS Log File Entries

CloudTrail log files can contain one or more log entries. Each entry lists multiple JSON-formatted events. A log entry represents a single request from any source and includes information about the requested action, the date and time of the action, request parameters, and more. For information on what events are recorded, see the CloudTrail Record Contents in the AWS CloudTrail User Guide. Log entries are not an ordered stack trace of the public API calls, so they do not appear in any specific order.

The following example shows a CloudTrail log entry that demonstrates the `CreateTags` action when a tag for a file system is created from the console.

```
1  {
2      "eventVersion": "1.04",
3      "userIdentity": {
4          "type": "Root",
5          "principalId": "111122223333",
6          "arn": "arn:aws:iam::111122223333:root",
7          "accountId": "111122223333",
8          "accessKeyId": "AKIAIOSFODNN7EXAMPLE",
9          "sessionContext": {
10             "attributes": {
11                 "mfaAuthenticated": "false",
12                 "creationDate": "2017-03-01T18:02:37Z"
13             }
14         }
15     },
16     "eventTime": "2017-03-01T19:25:47Z",
17     "eventSource": "elasticfilesystem.amazonaws.com",
18     "eventName": "CreateTags",
19     "awsRegion": "us-west-2",
20     "sourceIPAddress": "192.0.2.0",
21     "userAgent": "console.amazonaws.com",
22     "requestParameters": {
23         "fileSystemId": "fs-00112233",
24         "tags": [{
25             "key": "TagName",
26             "value": "AnotherNewTag"
27         }
28         ]
29     },
30     "responseElements": null,
31     "requestID": "dEXAMPLE-feb4-11e6-85f0-736EXAMPLE75",
32     "eventID": "eEXAMPLE-2d32-4619-bd00-657EXAMPLEe4",
33     "eventType": "AwsApiCall",
34     "apiVersion": "2015-02-01",
35     "recipientAccountId": "111122223333"
36  }
```

The following example shows a CloudTrail log entry that demonstrates the `DeleteTags` action when a tag for a file system is deleted from the console.

```
1  {
2      "eventVersion": "1.04",
3      "userIdentity": {
4          "type": "Root",
5          "principalId": "111122223333",
6          "arn": "arn:aws:iam::111122223333:root",
7          "accountId": "111122223333",
8          "accessKeyId": "AKIAIOSFODNN7EXAMPLE",
9          "sessionContext": {
10             "attributes": {
11                 "mfaAuthenticated": "false",
12                 "creationDate": "2017-03-01T18:02:37Z"
13             }
```

```
14          }
15      },
16      "eventTime": "2017-03-01T19:25:47Z",
17      "eventSource": "elasticfilesystem.amazonaws.com",
18      "eventName": "DeleteTags",
19      "awsRegion": "us-west-2",
20      "sourceIPAddress": "192.0.2.0",
21      "userAgent": "console.amazonaws.com",
22      "requestParameters": {
23          "fileSystemId": "fs-00112233",
24          "tagKeys": []
25      },
26      "responseElements": null,
27      "requestID": "dEXAMPLE-feb4-11e6-85f0-736EXAMPLE75",
28      "eventID": "eEXAMPLE-2d32-4619-bd00-657EXAMPLEe4",
29      "eventType": "AwsApiCall",
30      "apiVersion": "2015-02-01",
31      "recipientAccountId": "111122223333"
32 }
```

Amazon EFS Log File Entries for Encrypted-at-Rest File Systems

Amazon EFS gives you the option of using encryption at rest, encryption in transit, or both, for your file systems. For more information, see Encrypting Data and Metadata in EFS.

If you're using an encrypted-at-rest file system, the calls that Amazon EFS makes on your behalf appear in your AWS CloudTrail logs as coming from an AWS-owned account. If you see one of the following account IDs in your CloudTrail logs, depending on the AWS Region that your file system is created in, this ID is one owned by the Amazon EFS service.

AWS Region	Account ID
US East (Ohio)	771736226457
US East (N. Virginia)	055650462987
US West (N. California)	208867197265
US West (Oregon)	736298361104
Asia Pacific (Seoul)	518632624599
EU (Frankfurt)	992038834663
EU (Ireland)	805538244694
Asia Pacific (Sydney)	288718191711

Amazon EFS Encryption Context for Encryption at Rest

Amazon EFS sends encryption context when making AWS KMS API requests to generate data keys and decrypt Amazon EFS data. The file system ID is the encryption context for all file systems that are encrypted at rest. In the requestParameters field of a CloudTrail log entry, the encryption context looks similar to the following.

```
1 "EncryptionContextEquals": {}
2 "aws:elasticfilesystem:filesystem:id" : "fs-4EXAMPLE"
```

Amazon EFS Performance

This topic provides an overview of Amazon EFS performance, discusses the two performance modes (General Purpose and Max I/O) available in Amazon EFS, reviews the Amazon EFS bursting model, and outlines some useful performance tips.

Performance Overview

Amazon EFS file systems are distributed across an unconstrained number of storage servers, enabling file systems to grow elastically to petabyte scale and allowing massively parallel access from Amazon EC2 instances to your data. The distributed design of Amazon EFS avoids the bottlenecks and constraints inherent to traditional file servers.

This distributed data storage design means that multithreaded applications and applications that concurrently access data from multiple Amazon EC2 instances can drive substantial levels of aggregate throughput and IOPS. Big data and analytics workloads, media processing workflows, content management, and web serving are examples of these applications.

In addition, Amazon EFS data is distributed across multiple Availability Zones (AZs), providing a high level of durability and availability. The following tables compare high-level performance and storage characteristics for Amazon's file and block cloud storage services.

Performance Comparison – Amazon EFS and Amazon EBS

	Amazon EFS	Amazon EBS Provisioned IOPS
Per-operation latency	Low, consistent latency.	Lowest, consistent latency.
Throughput scale	10+ GB per second.	Up to 2 GB per second.

Storage Characteristics Comparison – Amazon EFS and Amazon EBS

	Amazon EFS	Amazon EBS Provisioned IOPS
Availability and durability	Data is stored redundantly across multiple AZs.	Data is stored redundantly in a single AZ.
Access	Up to thousands of Amazon EC2 instances, from multiple AZs, can connect concurrently to a file system.	A single Amazon EC2 instance in a single AZ can connect to a file system.
Use cases	Big data and analytics, media processing workflows, content management, web serving, and home directories.	Boot volumes, transactional and NoSQL databases, data warehousing, and ETL.

The distributed nature of Amazon EFS enables high levels of availability, durability, and scalability. This distributed architecture results in a small latency overhead for each file operation. Due to this per-operation latency, overall throughput generally increases as the average I/O size increases, because the overhead is amortized over a larger amount of data. Amazon EFS supports highly parallelized workloads (for example, using concurrent operations from multiple threads and multiple Amazon EC2 instances), which enables high levels of aggregate throughput and operations per second.

Amazon EFS Use Cases

Amazon EFS is designed to meet the performance needs of the following use cases.

Big Data and Analytics

Amazon EFS provides the scale and performance required for big data applications that require high throughput to compute nodes coupled with read-after-write consistency and low-latency file operations.

Media Processing Workflows

Media workflows like video editing, studio production, broadcast processing, sound design, and rendering often depend on shared storage to manipulate large files. A strong data consistency model with high throughput and shared file access can cut the time it takes to perform these jobs and consolidate multiple local file repositories into a single location for all users.

Content Management and Web Serving

Amazon EFS provides a durable, high throughput file system for content management systems that store and serve information for a range of applications like websites, online publications, and archives.

Home Directories

Amazon EFS can provide storage for organizations that have many users that need to access and share common data sets. An administrator can use Amazon EFS to create a file system accessible to people across an organization and establish permissions for users and groups at the file or directory level.

File System Syncing to Amazon EFS

Amazon EFS File Sync provides efficient, high-performance parallel data sync that is tolerant to unreliable and high latency networks. Using this data sync, you can easily and efficiently sync files from an existing file system into Amazon EFS. For more information, see Amazon EFS File Sync.

Performance Modes

To support a wide variety of cloud storage workloads, Amazon EFS offers two performance modes. You select a file system's performance mode when you create it.

The two performance modes have no additional costs, so your Amazon EFS file system is billed and metered the same, regardless of your performance mode. For information about file system limits, see Limits for Amazon EFS File Systems.

Note
An Amazon EFS file system's performance mode can't be changed after the file system has been created.

General Purpose Performance Mode

We recommend the General Purpose performance mode for the majority of your Amazon EFS file systems. General Purpose is ideal for latency-sensitive use cases, like web serving environments, content management systems, home directories, and general file serving. If you don't choose a performance mode when you create your file system, Amazon EFS selects the General Purpose mode for you by default.

Max I/O Performance Mode

File systems in the Max I/O mode can scale to higher levels of aggregate throughput and operations per second with a tradeoff of slightly higher latencies for file operations. Highly parallelized applications and workloads, such as big data analysis, media processing, and genomics analysis, can benefit from this mode.

Using the Right Performance Mode

Our recommendation for determining which performance mode to use is as follows:

1. Create a new file system using the default General Purpose performance mode.

2. Run your application (or a use case similar to your application) for a period of time to test its performance.

3. Monitor the `PercentIOLimit` Amazon CloudWatch metric for Amazon EFS during the performance test. For more information about accessing this and other metrics, see Amazon CloudWatch Metrics.

If the `PercentIOLimit` percentage returned was at or near 100 percent for a significant amount of time during the test, your application should use the Max I/O performance mode. Otherwise, it should use the default General Purpose mode.

Throughput Scaling in Amazon EFS

Throughput on Amazon EFS scales as a file system grows. Because file-based workloads are typically spiky—driving high levels of throughput for short periods of time, and low levels of throughput the rest of the time—Amazon EFS is designed to burst to high throughput levels for periods of time.

All file systems, regardless of size, can burst to 100 MiB/s of throughput, and those over 1 TiB large can burst to 100 MiB/s per TiB of data stored in the file system. For example, a 10 TiB file system can burst to 1,000 MiB/s of throughput (`10 TiB x 100 MiB/s/TiB`). The portion of time a file system can burst is determined by its size, and the bursting model is designed so that typical file system workloads will be able to burst virtually any time they need to.

Amazon EFS uses a credit system to determine when file systems can burst. Each file system earns credits over time at a baseline rate that is determined by the size of the file system, and uses credits whenever it reads or writes data. The baseline rate is 50 MiB/s per TiB of storage (equivalently, 50 KiB/s per GiB of storage).

Accumulated burst credits give the file system permission to drive throughput above its baseline rate. A file system can drive throughput continuously at its baseline rate, and whenever it's inactive or driving throughput below its baseline rate, the file system accumulates burst credits.

For example, a 100 GiB file system can burst (at 100 MiB/s) for 5 percent of the time if it's inactive for the remaining 95 percent. Over a 24-hour period, the file system earns 432,000 MiBs worth of credit, which can be used to burst at 100 MiB/s for 72 minutes.

File systems larger than 1 TiB can always burst for up to 50 percent of the time if they are inactive for the remaining 50 percent.

The following table provides examples of bursting behavior.

File System Size	Aggregate Read/Write Throughput
A 100 GiB file system can...	[See the AWS documentation website for more details]
A 1 TiB file system can...	[See the AWS documentation website for more details]

File System Size	Aggregate Read/Write Throughput
A 10 TiB file system can...	[See the AWS documentation website for more details]
Generally, a larger file system can...	[See the AWS documentation website for more details]

Note

The minimum file system size used when calculating the baseline rate is 1 GiB, so all file systems have a baseline rate of at least 50 KiB/s. The file system size used when determining the baseline rate and burst rate is the same as the metered size available through the `DescribeFileSystems` operation. File systems can earn credits up to a maximum credit balance of 2.1 TiB for file systems smaller than 1 TiB, or 2.1 TiB per TiB stored for file systems larger than 1 TiB. This implies that file systems can accumulate enough credits to burst for up to 12 hours continuously. Newly created file systems begin with an initial credit balance of 2.1 TiB, which enables them to add data at the 100 MiB/s burst rate until they are large enough to run at 100 MiB/s continuously (that is, 2 TiB).

The following table provides more detailed examples of bursting behavior for file systems of different sizes.

File System Size (GiB)	Baseline Aggregate Throughput (MiB/s)	Burst Aggregate Throughput (MiB/s)	Maximum Burst Duration (Min/-Day)	% of Time File System Can Burst (Per Day)
10	0.5	100	7.2	0.5%
256	12.5	100	180	12.5%
512	25.0	100	360	25.0%
1024	50.0	100	720	50.0%
1536	75.0	150	720	50.0%
2048	100.0	200	720	50.0%
3072	150.0	300	720	50.0%
4096	200.0	400	720	50.0%

Note

As previously mentioned, new file systems have an initial burst credit balance of 2.1 TB. With this starting balance, you can burst at 100 MB/s for 6.12 hours (which is calculated by `2.1 x 1024 x (1024/100/3600)` to get 6.116 hours, rounded up to 6.12) without spending any credits that you're earning from your storage.

Managing Burst Credits

When a file system has a positive burst credit balance, it can burst. You can see the burst credit balance for a file system by viewing the `BurstCreditBalance` Amazon CloudWatch metric for Amazon EFS. For more information about accessing this and other metrics, see Monitoring Amazon EFS.

The bursting capability (both in terms of length of time and burst rate) of a file system is directly related to its size. Larger file systems can burst at larger rates for longer periods of time. Therefore, if your application needs to burst more (that is, if you find that your file system is running out of burst credits), you should increase the size of your file system.

Note

There's no provisioning with Amazon EFS, so to make your file system larger you need to add more data to it.

Use your historical throughput patterns to calculate the file system size you need to sustain your desired level of activity. The following steps outline how to do this:

1. Identify your throughput needs by looking at your historical usage. From the Amazon CloudWatch console, check the `sum` statistic of the `TotalIOBytes` metric with daily aggregation, for the past 14 days. Identify the day with the largest value for `TotalIOBytes`.

2. Divide this number by 24 hours, 60 minutes, 60 seconds, and 1024 bytes to get the average KiB/second your application required for that day.

3. Calculate the file system size (in GB) required to sustain this average throughput by dividing the average throughput number (in KB/s) by the baseline throughput number (50 KB/s/GiB) that EFS provides.

On-Premises Performance Considerations

The throughput bursting model for Amazon EFS file systems remains the same whether accessed from your on-premises servers or your Amazon EC2 instances. However, when accessing Amazon EFS file data from your on-premises servers, the maximum throughput is also constrained by the bandwidth of the AWS Direct Connect connection.

Because of the propagation delay tied to data traveling over long distances, the network latency of an AWS Direct Connect connection between your on-premises data center and your Amazon VPC can be tens of milliseconds. If your file operations are serialized, the latency of the AWS Direct Connect connection directly impacts your read and write throughput. In essence, the volume of data you can read or write during a period of time is bounded by the amount of time it takes for each read and write operation to complete. To maximize your throughput, parallelize your file operations so that multiple reads and writes are processed by Amazon EFS concurrently. Standard tools like GNU parallel enable you to parallelize the copying of file data.

Architecting for High Availability

To ensure continuous availability between your on-premises data center and your Amazon VPC, we recommend configuring two AWS Direct Connect connections. For more information, see Step 4: Configure Redundant Connections with AWS Direct Connect in the AWS Direct Connect User Guide.

To ensure continuous availability between your application and Amazon EFS, we recommend that your application be designed to recover from potential connection interruptions. In general, there are two scenarios for on-premises applications connected to an Amazon EFS file system; highly available and not highly available.

If your application is Highly Available (HA) and uses multiple on-premises servers in its HA cluster, ensure that each on-premises server in the HA cluster connects to a mount target in a different Availability Zone (AZ) in your Amazon VPC. If your on-premises server can't access the mount target because the AZ in which the mount target exists becomes unavailable, your application should failover to a server with an available mount target.

If your application is not highly available, and your on-premises server can't access the mount target because the AZ in which the mount target exists becomes unavailable, your application should implement restart logic and connect to a mount target in a different AZ.

Amazon EFS Performance Tips

When using Amazon EFS, keep the following performance tips in mind:

- **Average I/O Size** – The distributed nature of Amazon EFS enables high levels of availability, durability, and scalability. This distributed architecture results in a small latency overhead for each file operation. Due to this per-operation latency, overall throughput generally increases as the average I/O size increases, because the overhead is amortized over a larger amount of data.
- **Simultaneous Connections** – Amazon EFS file systems can be mounted on up to thousands of Amazon EC2 instances concurrently. If you can parallelize your application across more instances, you can drive higher throughput levels on your file system in aggregate across instances.

- **Request Model** – By enabling asynchronous writes to your file system, pending write operations are buffered on the Amazon EC2 instance before they are written to Amazon EFS asynchronously. Asynchronous writes typically have lower latencies. When performing asynchronous writes, the kernel uses additional memory for caching. A file system that has enabled synchronous writes, or one that opens files using an option that bypasses the cache (for example, O_DIRECT), will issue synchronous requests to Amazon EFS and every operation will go through a round trip between the client and Amazon EFS. **Note**
  Your chosen request model will have tradeoffs in consistency (if you're using multiple Amazon EC2 instances) and speed.
- **NFS Client Mount Settings** – Verify that you're using the recommended mount options as outlined in Mounting File Systems and in Additional Mounting Considerations. Amazon EFS supports the Network File System versions 4.0 and 4.1 (NFSv4) and NFSv4.0 protocols when mounting your file systems on Amazon EC2 instances. NFSv4.1 provides better performance. **Note**
  You might want to increase the size of the read and write buffers for your NFS client to 1 MB when you mount your file system.
- **Amazon EC2 Instances** – Applications that perform a large number of read and write operations likely need more memory or computing capacity than applications that don't. When launching your Amazon EC2 instances, choose instance types that have the amount of these resources that your application needs. Note that the performance characteristics of Amazon EFS file systems are not dependent on the use of EBS-optimized instances.
- **Encryption** – Amazon EFS supports two forms of encryption, encryption in transit and encryption at rest. This option is for encryption at rest. Choosing to enable either or both types of encryption for your file system has a minimal effect on I/O latency and throughput.

For information about the Amazon EFS limits for total file system throughput, per-instance throughput, and operations per second in General Purpose performance mode, see Amazon EFS Limits.

Related Topics

- Metering – How Amazon EFS Reports File System and Object Sizes
- Troubleshooting Amazon EFS

Security

Following, you can find a description of security considerations for working with Amazon EFS. There are four levels of access control to consider for Amazon EFS file systems, with different mechanisms used for each.

Topics

- AWS Identity and Access Management (IAM) Permissions for API Calls
- Security Groups for Amazon EC2 Instances and Mount Targets
- Read, Write, and Execute Permissions for EFS Files and Directories
- Source Ports for Working with EFS
- Encrypting Data and Metadata in EFS

AWS Identity and Access Management (IAM) Permissions for API Calls

You create, manage, and delete file systems with calls to the Amazon EFS API. If the caller is using credentials for an AWS Identity and Access Management (IAM) user or assumed role, each API call requires that the caller have permissions for the action being called in its IAM policy. Some API actions support policy permissions specific to the file system that is the object of the call (that is, resource-level permissions). API calls made with an account's root credentials have permissions for all API actions on file systems owned by the account.

As an example of IAM permissions, IAM user Alice might have permissions to retrieve descriptions of all file systems in her parent AWS account. However, she might be allowed to manage the security groups for only one of them, file system ID `fs-12345678`.

For more information about IAM permissions with the Amazon EFS API, see Authentication and Access Control for Amazon EFS.

Security Groups for Amazon EC2 Instances and Mount Targets

When using Amazon EFS, you specify Amazon EC2 security groups for your EC2 instances and security groups for the EFS mount targets associated with the file system. Security groups act as a firewall, and the rules you add define the traffic flow. In the Getting Started exercise, you created one security group when you launched the EC2 instance. You then associated another with the EFS mount target (that is, the default security group for your default VPC). That approach works for the Getting Started exercise. However, for a production system, you should set up security groups with minimal permissions for use with EFS.

You can authorize inbound and outbound access to your EFS file system. To do so, you add rules that allow your EC2 instance to connect to your Amazon EFS file system through the mount target using the Network File System (NFS) port. Take the following steps to create and update your security groups.

To create security groups for EC2 instances and mount targets

1. Create two security groups in your VPC.

   For instructions, see the procedure "To create a security group" in Creating a Security Group in the *Amazon VPC User Guide.*

2. Open the Amazon VPC Management Console at https://console.aws.amazon.com/vpc/, and verify the default rules for these security groups. Both security groups should have only an outbound rule that allows traffic to leave.

To update the necessary access for your security groups

1. Open the Amazon VPC console at https://console.aws.amazon.com/vpc/.

2. Add a rule for your EC2 security group to allow inbound access using Secure Shell (SSH) from any host. Optionally, restrict the **Source** address.

You don't need to add an outbound rule, because the default outbound rule allows all traffic to leave. If this were not the case, you'd need to add an outbound rule to open the TCP connection on the NFS port, identifying the mount target security group as the destination.

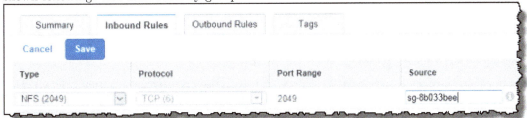

For instructions, see Adding and Removing Rules in the *Amazon VPC User Guide*.

3. Add a rule for the mount target security group to allow inbound access from the EC2 security group as shown following. The EC2 security group is identified as the source.

Type	Protocol	Port Range	Source
NFS (2049)	TCP (6)	2049	sg-8b033bee

4. Verify that both security groups now authorize inbound and outbound access.

For more information about security groups, see Security Groups for EC2-VPC in the *Amazon EC2 User Guide for Linux Instances*.

Security Considerations for Mounting an Amazon EFS File System

An NFSv4.1 client can only mount a file system if it can make a network connection to the NFS port of one of the file system's mount targets. Similarly, an NFSv4.1 client can only assert a user and group ID when accessing a file system if it can make this network connection.

The ability to make this network connection is governed by a combination of the following:

- **Network isolation provided by the mount targets' VPC** – File system mount targets can't have public IP addresses associated with them. Only Amazon EC2 instances in the Amazon VPC or on-premises servers connected to the Amazon VPC by using AWS Direct Connect can mount Amazon EFS file systems.

   You can't currently use other mechanisms for connecting to a VPC's private IP addresses from outside the VPC to mount Amazon EFS file systems. For example, you can't use VPN connections or VPC peering to do so. Don't rely on such other methods for file system access control.

- **Network access control lists (ACLs) for the VPC subnets of the client and mount targets, for access from outside the mount target's subnets** – To mount a file system, the client must be able to make a TCP connection to the NFS port of a mount target and receive return traffic.

- **Rules of the client's and mount targets' VPC security groups, for all access** – For an EC2 instance to mount a file system, the following security group rules must be in effect:

   - The file system must have a mount target whose network interface has a security group with a rule that enables inbound connections on the NFS port from the instance. You can enable inbound connections either by IP address (CIDR range) or security group. The source of the security group rules for the inbound NFS port on mount target network interfaces is a key element of file system access control.

Inbound rules other than the one for the NFS port, and any outbound rules, aren't used by network interfaces for file system mount targets.
- The mounting instance must have a network interface with a security group rule that enables outbound connections to the NFS port on one of the file system's mount targets. You can enable outbound connections either by IP address (CIDR range) or security group.

For more information, see Creating Mount Targets.

Read, Write, and Execute Permissions for EFS Files and Directories

Files and directories in an EFS file system support standard Unix-style read, write, and execute permissions based on the user and group ID asserted by the mounting NFSv4.1 client. For more information, see Network File System (NFS)–Level Users, Groups, and Permissions.

Note
This layer of access control depends on trusting the NFSv4.1 client in its assertion of the user and group ID. There is no authentication of the identity of the NFSv4.1 client when establishing a mount connection. Thus, any NFSv4.1 client that can make a network connection to the NFS port of a file system's mount target IP address can read and write the file system as the root user ID.

As an example of read, write, and execute permissions for files and directories, Alice might have permissions to read and write to any files that she wants to in her personal directory on a file system, /alice. However, in this example Alice is not allowed to read or write to any files in Mark's personal directory on the same file system, /mark. Both Alice and Mark are allowed to read but not write files in the shared directory /share.

Source Ports for Working with EFS

To support a broad set of NFS clients, Amazon EFS allows connections from any source port. If you require that only privileged users can access Amazon EFS, we recommend using the following client firewall rule.

```
1 iptables -I OUTPUT 1 -m owner --uid-owner 1-4294967294 -m tcp -p tcp --dport 2049 -j DROP
```

This command inserts a new rule at the start of the OUTPUT chain (-I OUTPUT 1). The rule prevents any unprivileged, nonkernel process (-m owner --uid-owner 1-4294967294) from opening a connection to the NFS port (-m tcp -p tcp dport 2049).

Encrypting Data and Metadata in EFS

Amazon EFS supports two forms of encryption for file systems, encryption of data in transit and encryption at rest. You can enable encryption of data at rest when creating an Amazon EFS file system. You can enable encryption of data in transit when you mount the file system.

When to Use Encryption

If your organization is subject to corporate or regulatory policies that require encryption of data and metadata at rest, we recommend creating an encrypted file system mounting your file system using encryption of data in transit.

Encrypting Data in Transit

You can encrypt data in transit using an Amazon EFS file system, without needing to modify your applications.

Encrypting Data in Transit with TLS

Enabling encryption of data in transit for your Amazon EFS file system is done by enabling Transport Layer Security (TLS) when you mount your file system using the Amazon EFS mount helper. For more information, see Mounting with the EFS Mount Helper.

When encryption of data in transit is declared as a mount option for your Amazon EFS file system, the mount helper initializes a client stunnel process. Stunnel is an open source multipurpose network relay. The client stunnel process listens on a local port for inbound traffic, and the mount helper redirects NFS client traffic to this local port. The mount helper uses a Transport Layer Security (TLS) version 1.2 to communicate with your file system.

Mounting your Amazon EFS file system with the mount helper with encryption of data in transit enabled

1. Access the terminal for your instance through Secure Shell (SSH), and log in with the appropriate user name. For more information on how to do this, see Connecting to Your Linux Instance Using SSH in the Amazon EC2 User Guide for Linux Instances.

2. Run the following command to mount your file system.

```
1 sudo mount -t efs -o tls fs-12345678:/ /mnt/efs
```

How Encrypting in Transit Works

Encryption of data in transit is enabled by connecting to Amazon EFS using TLS. We recommend using the mount helper because it's the simplest option.

If you're not using the mount helper, you can still enable encryption of data in transit. At a high level, the following are the steps to do so.

To enable encryption of data in transit without the mount helper

1. Download and install stunnel, and note the port that the application is listening on.

2. Run stunnel to connect to your Amazon EFS file system on port 2049 using TLS.

3. Using the NFS client, mount `localhost:port`, where `port` is the port that you noted in the first step.

Because encryption of data in transit is configured on a per-connection basis, each configured mount has a dedicated stunnel process running on the instance. By default, the stunnel process used by the mount helper listens on local ports 20049 and 20449, and it connects to Amazon EFS on port 2049.

Note
By default, when using the Amazon EFS mount helper with TLS, it enforces the use of the Online Certificate Status Protocol (OCSP) and certificate hostname checking. The Amazon EFS mount helper uses the stunnel program for its TLS functionality. Note that some versions of Linux don't include a version of stunnel that supports these TLS features by default. When using one of those Linux versions, mounting an Amazon EFS file system using TLS fails.
After you've installed the amazon-efs-utils package, to upgrade your system's version of stunnel, see Upgrading Stunnel.
For issues with encryption, see Troubleshooting Encryption.

When using encryption of data in transit, your NFS client setup is changed. When you inspect your actively mounted file systems, you see one mounted to 127.0.0.1, or localhost, as in the following example.

```
1 $ mount | column -t
2 127.0.0.1:/  on  /home/ec2-user/efs       type  nfs4        (rw,relatime,vers=4.1,rsize
    =1048576,wsize=1048576,namlen=255,hard,proto=tcp,port=20127,timeo=600,retrans=2,sec=sys,
    clientaddr=127.0.0.1,local_lock=none,addr=127.0.0.1)
```

When mounting with TLS and the Amazon EFS mount helper, you are reconfiguring your NFS client to mount to a local port. The mount helper starts a client stunnel process that is listening on this local port, and stunnel is opening an encrypted connection to EFS using TLS. The EFS mount helper is responsible for setting up and maintaining this encrypted connection and associated configuration.

To determine which Amazon EFS file system ID corresponds to which local mount point, you can use the following command. Remember to replace *efs-mount-point* with the local path where you've mounted your file system.

```
1 grep -E "Successfully mounted.*efs-mount-point" /var/log/amazon/efs/mount.log | tail -1
```

When you use the mount helper for encryption of data in transit, it also creates a process called **amazon-efs-mount-watchdog**. This process ensures that each mount's stunnel process is running, and stops the stunnel when the Amazon EFS file system is unmounted. If for some reason a stunnel process is terminated unexpectedly, the watchdog process restarts it.

Encrypting Data at Rest

As with unencrypted file systems, you can create encrypted file systems through the AWS Management Console, the AWS CLI, or programmatically through the Amazon EFS API or one of the AWS SDKs. Your organization might require the encryption of all data that meets a specific classification or is associated with a particular application, workload, or environment.

You can enforce data encryption policies for Amazon EFS file systems by using Amazon CloudWatch and AWS CloudTrail to detect the creation of a file system and verify that encryption is enabled. For more information, see Walkthrough 6: Enforcing Encryption on an Amazon EFS File System at Rest.

Note
The AWS key management infrastructure uses Federal Information Processing Standards (FIPS) 140-2 approved cryptographic algorithms. The infrastructure is consistent with National Institute of Standards and Technology (NIST) 800-57 recommendations.

Encrypting a File System at Rest Using the Console

You can choose to enable encryption at rest for a file system when you create it. The following procedure describes how to enable encryption for a new file system when you create it from the console.

To encrypt a new file system on the console

1. Open the Amazon Elastic File System console at https://console.aws.amazon.com/efs/.

2. Choose **Create file system** to open the file system creation wizard.

3. For **Step 1: Configure file system access**, choose your VPC, create your mount targets, and then choose **Next Step**.

4. For **Step 2: Configure optional settings**, add any tags, choose your performance mode, check the box to encrypt your file system, and then choose **Next Step**.

5. For **Step 3: Review and create**, review your settings, and choose **Create File System**.

You now have a new encrypted-at-rest file system.

How Encryption at Rest Works

In an encrypted-at-rest file system, data and metadata are automatically encrypted before being written to the file system. Similarly, as data and metadata are read, they are automatically decrypted before being presented to the application. These processes are handled transparently by Amazon EFS, so you don't have to modify your applications.

Amazon EFS uses an industry-standard AES-256 encryption algorithm to encrypt EFS data and metadata at rest. For more information, see Cryptography Basics in the *AWS Key Management Service Developer Guide*.

How Amazon EFS Uses AWS KMS

Amazon EFS integrates with AWS Key Management Service (AWS KMS) for key management. Amazon EFS uses customer master keys (CMKs) to encrypt your file system in the following way:

- **Encrypting metadata at rest** – An EFS-managed key is used to encrypt and decrypt file system metadata (that is, file names, directory names, and directory contents).
- **Encrypting file data at rest** – You choose the CMK used to encrypt and decrypt file data (that is, the contents of your files). You can enable, disable, or revoke grants on this CMK. This CMK can be one of the two following types:
    - **AWS-managed CMK** – This is the default CMK, and it's free to use.
    - **Customer-managed CMK** – This is the most flexible master key to use, because you can configure its key policies and grants for multiple users or services. For more information on creating CMKs, see Creating Keys in the* AWS Key Management Service Developer Guide.*
      If you use a customer-managed CMK as your master key for file data encryption and decryption, you can enable key rotation. When you enable key rotation, AWS KMS automatically rotates your key once per year. Additionally, with a customer-managed CMK, you can choose when to disable, re-enable, delete, or revoke access to your CMK at any time. For more information, see Disabling, Deleting, or Revoking Access to the CMK for a File System.

Data encryption and decryption at rest are handled transparently. However, AWS account IDs specific to Amazon EFS appear in your AWS CloudTrail logs related to AWS KMS actions. For more information, see Amazon EFS Log File Entries for Encrypted-at-Rest File Systems.

Amazon EFS Key Policies for AWS KMS

Key policies are the primary way to control access to CMKs. For more information on key policies, see Using Key Policies in AWS KMS in the *AWS Key Management Service Developer Guide. *The following list describes all the AWS KMS-related permissions supported by Amazon EFS for encrypted at rest file systems:

- **kms:Encrypt** – (Optional) Encrypts plaintext into ciphertext. This permission is included in the default key policy.
- **kms:Decrypt** – (Required) Decrypts ciphertext. Ciphertext is plaintext that has been previously encrypted. This permission is included in the default key policy.
- **kms:ReEncrypt** – (Optional) Encrypts data on the server side with a new customer master key (CMK), without exposing the plaintext of the data on the client side. The data is first decrypted and then re-encrypted. This permission is included in the default key policy.
- **kms:GenerateDataKeyWithoutPlaintext** – (Required) Returns a data encryption key encrypted under a CMK. This permission is included in the default key policy under **kms:GenerateDataKey***.
- **kms:CreateGrant** – (Required) Adds a grant to a key to specify who can use the key and under what conditions. Grants are alternate permission mechanisms to key policies. For more information on grants, see Using Grants in the *AWS Key Management Service Developer Guide.* This permission is included in the default key policy.
- **kms:DescribeKey** – (Required) Provides detailed information about the specified customer master key. This permission is included in the default key policy.
- **kms:ListAliases** – (Optional) Lists all of the key aliases in the account. When you use the console to create an encrypted file system, this permission populates the **Select KMS master key** list. We recommend using this permission to provide the best user experience. This permission is included in the default key policy.

Related Topics

For more information on encryption with Amazon EFS, see these related topics:

- Creating Resources for Amazon EFS
- Managing Access to Encrypted File Systems
- Amazon EFS Performance Tips
- Amazon EFS API Permissions: Actions, Resources, and Conditions Reference
- Amazon EFS Log File Entries for Encrypted-at-Rest File Systems
- Troubleshooting Encryption

Amazon EFS Limits

Following, you can find out about limitations when working with Amazon EFS.

Topics

- Amazon EFS Limits That You Can Increase
- Resource Limits
- Limits for Client EC2 Instances
- Limits for Amazon EFS File Systems
- Limits for EFS File Sync
- Unsupported NFSv4 Features
- Additional Considerations

Amazon EFS Limits That You Can Increase

Following are the limits for Amazon EFS that can be increased by contacting AWS Support.

Resource	Default Limit
Total throughput for each file system for all connected clients	US East (Ohio) Region – 3 GB/s US East (N. Virginia) Region – 3 GB/s US West (N. California) Region – 1 GB/s US West (Oregon) Region – 3 GB/s Asia Pacific (Seoul) 1 GB/s EU (Frankfurt) Region – 1 GB/s EU (Ireland) Region – 3 GB/s Asia Pacific (Sydney) Region – 3 GB/s

You can take the following steps to request an increase for these limits. These increases are not granted immediately, so it might take a couple of days for your increase to become effective.

To request a limit increase

1. Open the AWS Support Center page, sign in, if necessary, and then choose **Create Case**.

2. Under **Regarding**, choose **Service Limit Increase**.

3. Under **Limit Type**, choose the type of limit to increase, fill in the necessary fields in the form, and then choose your preferred method of contact.

Resource Limits

Following are the limits on Amazon EFS resources for each customer account in an AWS Region.

Resource	Limit
Number of file systems	US East (Ohio) Region – 125 US East (N. Virginia) Region – 70 US West (N. California) Region – 125 US West (Oregon) Region – 125 Asia Pacific (Seoul) 125 EU (Frankfurt) Region – 125 EU (Ireland) Region – 125 Asia Pacific (Sydney) Region – 125

Resource	Limit
Number of mount targets for each file system in an Availability Zone	1
Number of security groups for each mount target	5
Number of tags for each file system	50
Number of VPCs for each file system	1

Limits for Client EC2 Instances

The following limits for client EC2 instances apply, assuming a Linux NFSv4.1 client:

- The maximum throughput you can drive for each Amazon EC2 instance is 250 MB/s.
- Up to 128 active user accounts for each instance can have files open at the same time. Each user account represents one local user logged in to the instance.
- Up to 32,768 files open at the same time on the instance.
- Each unique mount on the instance can acquire up to a total of 8,192 locks across a maximum of 256 unique file/process pairs. For example, a single process can acquire one or more locks on 256 separate files, or 8 processes can each acquire one or more locks on 32 files.
- Using Amazon EFS with Microsoft Windows Amazon EC2 instances is not supported.

Limits for Amazon EFS File Systems

The following are limits specific to the Amazon EFS file systems:

- Maximum name length: 255 bytes.
- Maximum symbolic link (symlink) length: 4080 bytes.
- Maximum number of hard links to a file: 177.
- Maximum size of a single file: 52,673,613,135,872 bytes (47.9 TiB).
- Maximum directory depth: 1000 levels deep.
- Any one particular file can have up to 87 locks across all users of the file system. You can mount a file system on one or more Amazon EC2 instances, but the maximum 87-lock limit for a file applies.
- In General Purpose mode, there is a limit of 7000 file system operations per second. This operations limit is calculated for all clients connected to a single file system.

Limits for EFS File Sync

Following are the limits on EFS File Sync resources for each customer account in an AWS Region.

Resource	Limit
Maximum number of sync tasks	10
Maximum number of files for each sync task	35,000,000
Maximum file ingest rate for each sync task	500 files per second
Maximum data throughput for each sync task	1 Gbps

Unsupported NFSv4 Features

Although Amazon Elastic File System does not support NFSv2, or NFSv3, Amazon EFS supports both NFSv4.1 and NFSv4.0, except for the following features:

- pNFS
- Client delegation or callbacks of any type
  - Operation OPEN always returns `OPEN_DELEGATE_NONE` as the delegation type.
  - The operation OPEN returns `NFSERR_NOTSUPP` for the `CLAIM_DELEGATE_CUR` and `CLAIM_DELEGATE_PREV` claim types.
- Mandatory locking

  All locks in Amazon EFS are advisory, which means that READ and WRITE operations do not check for conflicting locks before the operation is executed.
- Deny share

  NFS supports the concept of a share deny, primarily used by Windows clients for users to deny others access to a particular file that has been opened. Amazon EFS does not support this, and returns the NFS error `NFS4ERR_NOTSUPP` for any OPEN commands specifying a share deny value other than `OPEN4_SHARE_DENY_NONE`. Linux NFS clients do not use anything other than `OPEN4_SHARE_DENY_NONE`.
- Access control lists (ACL)
- Amazon EFS does not update the `time_access` attribute on file reads. Amazon EFS updates `time_access` in the following events:
  - When a file is created (an inode is created).
  - When an NFS client makes an explicit `setattr` call.
  - On a write to the inode caused by, for example, file size changes or file metadata changes.
  - Any inode attribute is updated.
- Namespaces
- Persistent reply cache
- Kerberos based security
- NFSv4.1 data retention
- SetUID on directories
- Unsupported file types when using the CREATE operation: Block devices (NF4BLK), character devices (NF4CHR), attribute directory (NF4ATTRDIR), and named attribute (NF4NAMEDATTR).
- Unsupported attributes: FATTR4_ARCHIVE, FATTR4_FILES_AVAIL, FATTR4_FILES_FREE, FATTR4_FILES_TOTAL, FATTR4_FS_LOCATIONS, FATTR4_MIMETYPE, FATTR4_QUOTA_AVAIL_HARD, FATTR4_QUOTA_AVAIL_SOFT, FATTR4_QUOTA_USED, FATTR4_TIME_BACKUP, and FATTR4_ACL.

  An attempt to set these attributes results in an `NFS4ERR_ATTRNOTSUPP` error that is sent back to the client.

Additional Considerations

In addition, note the following:

- For a list of AWS Regions where you can create Amazon EFS file systems, see the AWS General Reference.
- Some AWS accounts created before 2012 might have access to Availability Zones in us-east-1 that don't support creating mount targets. If you can't create a mount target in one of these AWS Regions, try a different Availability Zone in that AWS Region. However, there are cost considerations for mounting a file system on an EC2 instance in an Availability Zone through a mount target created in another Availability Zone.
- You mount your file system from EC2 instances in your VPC by using the mount targets you create in the VPC. You can also mount your file system on your EC2-Classic instances (which are not in the VPC), but

you must first link them to your VPC by using ClassicLink. For more information about using ClassicLink, see ClassicLink in the *Amazon EC2 User Guide for Linux Instances.*

- You can mount an Amazon EFS file system from on-premises data center servers using AWS Direct Connect.
- VPC peering within a single AWS Region when using C5 or M5 instances is supported. However, other VPC private connectivity mechanisms such as a VPN connection, interregion VPC peering, and intraregion VPC peering using other instance types are not supported.

Troubleshooting Amazon EFS

Following, you can find information on how to troubleshoot issues for Amazon Elastic File System (Amazon EFS).

Topics

- Troubleshooting Amazon EFS: General Issues
- Troubleshooting File Operation Errors
- Troubleshooting AMI and Kernel Issues
- Troubleshooting Mount Issues
- Troubleshooting Encryption

Troubleshooting Amazon EFS: General Issues

Following, you can find information about general troubleshooting issues related to Amazon EFS. For information on performance, see Amazon EFS Performance.

In general, if you encounter issues with Amazon EFS that you have trouble resolving, confirm that you're using a recent Linux kernel. If you are using an enterprise Linux distribution, we recommend the following:

- Amazon Linux 2015.09 or newer
- RHEL 7.3 or newer
- RHEL 6.9 with kernel 2.6.32-704 or newer
- All versions of Ubuntu 16.04
- Ubuntu 14.04 with kernel 3.13.0-83 or newer
- SLES 12 Sp2 or later

If you are using another distribution or a custom kernel, we recommend kernel version 4.3 or newer.

Topics

- Amazon EC2 Instance Hangs
- Application Writing Large Amounts of Data Hangs
- Open and Close Operations Are Serialized
- Custom NFS Settings Causing Write Delays
- Creating Backups with Oracle Recovery Manager Is Slow

Amazon EC2 Instance Hangs

An Amazon EC2 instance can hang because you deleted a file system mount target without first unmounting the file system.

Action to Take
Before you delete a file system mount target, unmount the file system. For more information about unmounting your Amazon EFS file system, see Unmounting File Systems.

Application Writing Large Amounts of Data Hangs

An application that writes a large amount of data to Amazon EFS hangs and causes the instance to reboot.

Action to Take

If an application takes too long to write all of its data to Amazon EFS, Linux might reboot because it appears that the process has become unresponsive. Two kernel configuration parameters define this behavior, `kernel.hung_task_panic` and `kernel.hung_task_timeout_secs`.

In the example following, the state of the hung process is reported by the `ps` command with `D` before the instance reboot, indicating that the process is waiting on I/O.

```
1 $ ps aux | grep large_io.py
2 root 33253 0.5 0.0 126652 5020 pts/3 D+ 18:22 0:00 python large_io.py
3 /efs/large_file
```

To prevent a reboot, increase the timeout period or disable kernel panics when a hung task is detected. The following command disables hung task kernel panics on most Linux systems.

```
1 $ sudo sysctl -w kernel.hung_task_panic=0
```

Open and Close Operations Are Serialized

Open and close operations that are performed on a file system by a user on a single Amazon EC2 instance are serialized.

Action to Take

To resolve this issue, use NFS protocol version 4.1 and one of the suggested Linux kernels. By using NFSv4.1 when mounting your file systems, you enable parallelized open and close operations on files. We recommend using **Amazon Linux AMI 2016.03.0** as the AMI for the Amazon EC2 instance that you mount your file system to.

If you can't use NFSv4.1, be aware that the Linux NFSv4.0 client serializes open and close requests by user ID and group IDs. This serialization happens even if multiple processes or multiple threads issue requests at the same time. The client only sends one open or close operation to an NFS server at a time, when all of the IDs match.

In addition, you can perform any of the following actions to resolve this issue:

- You can run each process from a different user ID on the same Amazon EC2 instance.
- You can leave the user IDs the same across all open requests, and modify the set of group IDs instead.
- You can run each process from a separate Amazon EC2 instance.

Custom NFS Settings Causing Write Delays

You have custom NFS client settings, and it takes up to three seconds for an Amazon EC2 instance to see a write operation performed on a file system from another Amazon EC2 instance.

Action to Take

If you encounter this issue, you can resolve it in one of the following ways:

- If the NFS client on the Amazon EC2 instance that's reading data has attribute caching activated, unmount your file system. Then remount it with the **noac** option to disable attribute caching. Attribute caching in NFSv4.1 is enabled by default. **Note**
  Disabling client-side caching can potentially reduce your application's performance.

- You can also clear your attribute cache on demand by using a programming language compatible with the NFS procedures. To do this, you can send an **ACCESS** procedure request immediately before a read request.

  For example, using the Python programming language, you can construct the following call.

```
1 # Does an NFS ACCESS procedure request to clear the attribute cache, given a path to the
    file
2 import os
3 os.access(path, os.W_OK)
```

Creating Backups with Oracle Recovery Manager Is Slow

Creating backups with Oracle Recovery Manager can be slow if Oracle Recovery Manager pauses for 120 seconds before starting a backup job.

Action to Take

If you encounter this issue, disable Oracle Direct NFS, as described in Enabling and Disabling Direct NFS Client Control of NFS in the Oracle Help Center.

Note
Amazon EFS doesn't support Oracle Direct NFS.

Troubleshooting File Operation Errors

When you access Amazon EFS file systems, certain limits on the files in the file system apply. Exceeding these limits causes file operation errors. For more information on client and file-based limits in Amazon EFS, see Limits for Client EC2 Instances . Following, you can find some common file operation errors and the limits associated with each error.

Command Fails with "Disk quota exceeded" Error

Amazon EFS doesn't currently support user disk quotas. This error can occur if any of the following limits have been exceeded:

- Up to 128 active user accounts can have files open at once for an instance.
- Up to 32,768 files can be open at once for an instance.
- Each unique mount on the instance can acquire up to a total of 8,192 locks across 256 unique file-process pairs. For example, a single process can acquire one or more locks on 256 separate files, or eight processes can each acquire one or more locks on 32 files.

Action to Take
If you encounter this issue, you can resolve it by identifying which of the preceding limits you are exceeding, and then making changes to meet that limit.

Command Fails with "I/O error"

This error occurs when more than 128 active user accounts for each instance have files open at once.

Action to Take
If you encounter this issue, you can resolve it by meeting the supported limit of open files on your instances. To do so, reduce the number of active users that have files from your Amazon EFS file system open simultaneously on your instances.

Command Fails with "File name is too long" Error

This error occurs when the size of a file name or its symbolic link (symlink) is too long. File names have the following limits:

- A name can be up to 255 bytes long.
- A symlink can be up to 4080 bytes in size.

Action to Take
If you encounter this issue, you can resolve it by reducing the size of your file name or symlink length to meet the supported limits.

Command Fails with "Too many links" Error

This error occurs when there are too many hard links to a file. You can have up to 177 hard links in a file.

Action to Take
If you encounter this issue, you can resolve it by reducing the number of hard links to a file to meet the supported limit.

Command Fails with "File too large" Error

This error occurs when a file is too large. A single file can be up to 52,673,613,135,872 bytes (47.9 TiB) in size.

Action to Take
If you encounter this issue, you can resolve it by reducing the size of a file to meet the supported limit.

Command Fails with "Try again" Error

This error occurs when too many users or applications try to access a single file. When an application or user accesses a file, a lock is placed on the file. Any one particular file can have up to 87 locks among all users and applications of the file system. You can mount a file system on one or more Amazon EC2 instances, but the 87-lock limit for a file still applies.

Action to Take
If you encounter this issue, you can resolve it by reducing the number of applications or users accessing the file until that number meets the number of allowed locks or lower.

Troubleshooting AMI and Kernel Issues

Following, you can find information about troubleshooting issues related to certain Amazon Machine Image (AMI) or kernel versions when using Amazon EFS from an Amazon EC2 instance.

Topics

- Unable to chown
- File System Keeps Performing Operations Repeatedly Due to Client Bug
- Deadlocked Client
- Listing Files in a Large Directory Takes a Long Time

Unable to chown

You're unable to change the ownership of a file/directory using the Linux chown command.

Kernel Versions with This Bug
2.6.32

Action to Take

You can resolve this error by doing the following:

- If you're performing chown for the one-time setup step necessary to change ownership of the EFS root directory, you can run the chown command from an instance running a newer kernel. For example, use the newest version of Amazon Linux.
- If chown is part of your production workflow, you must update the kernel version to use chown.

File System Keeps Performing Operations Repeatedly Due to Client Bug

A file system gets stuck performing repeated operations due to a client bug.

Action to Take
Update the client software to the latest version.

Deadlocked Client

A client becomes deadlocked.

Kernel Versions with This Bug

- CentOS-7 with kernel Linux 3.10.0-229.20.1.el7.x86_64
- Ubuntu 15.10 with kernel Linux 4.2.0-18-generic

Action to Take
Do one of the following:

- Upgrade to a newer kernel version. For CentOS-7, kernel version **Linux 3.10.0-327** or later contains the fix.
- Downgrade to an older kernel version.

Listing Files in a Large Directory Takes a Long Time

This can happen if the directory is changing while your NFS client iterates through the directory to finish the list operation. Whenever the NFS client notices that the contents of the directory changed during this iteration, the NFS client restarts iterating from the beginning. As a result, the ls command can take a long time to complete for a large directory with frequently changing files.

Kernel Versions with This Bug
CentOS kernel versions lower than 2.6.32-696.1.1.el6

Action to Take
To resolve this issue, upgrade to a newer kernel version.

Troubleshooting Mount Issues

Topics

- File System Mount on Windows Instance Fails
- Automatic Mounting Fails and the Instance Is Unresponsive
- Mounting Multiple Amazon EFS File Systems in /etc/fstab Fails
- Mount Command Fails with "wrong fs type" Error Message
- Mount Command Fails with "incorrect mount option" Error Message
- File System Mount Fails Immediately After File System Creation
- File System Mount Hangs and Then Fails with Timeout Error
- File System Mount Using DNS Name Fails
- Mount Target Lifecycle State Is Stuck
- Mount Does Not Respond
- Operations on Newly Mounted File System Return "bad file handle" Error
- Unmounting a File System Fails

File System Mount on Windows Instance Fails

A file system mount on an Amazon EC2 instance on Microsoft Windows fails.

Action to Take
Don't use Amazon EFS with Windows EC2 instances, which isn't supported.

Automatic Mounting Fails and the Instance Is Unresponsive

This issue can occur if the file system was mounted automatically on an instance and the _netdev option wasn't declared. If _netdev is missing, your EC2 instance might stop responding. This result is because network file systems need to be initialized after the compute instance starts its networking.

Action to Take
If this issue occurs, contact AWS Support.

Mounting Multiple Amazon EFS File Systems in /etc/fstab Fails

For instances that use the systemd init system with two or more Amazon EFS entries at /etc/fstab, there might be times where some or all of these entries are not mounted. In this case, the dmesg output shows one or more lines similar to the following.

```
1 NFS: nfs4_discover_server_trunking unhandled error -512. Exiting with error EIO
```

Action to Take
In this case, we recommend that you create a new systemd service file in /etc/systemd/system/mount-nfs-sequentially.service with the following contents.

```
1 [Unit]
2 Description=Workaround for mounting NFS file systems sequentially at boot time
3 After=remote-fs.target
4
5 [Service]
6 Type=oneshot
7 ExecStart=/bin/mount -avt nfs4
8 RemainAfterExit=yes
9
```

```
10 [Install]
11 WantedBy=multi-user.target
```

After you do so, run the following two commands:

1. `sudo systemctl daemon-reload`

2. `sudo systemctl enable mount-nfs-sequentially.service`

Then restart your Amazon EC2 instance. The file systems are mounted on demand, generally within a second.

Mount Command Fails with "wrong fs type" Error Message

The mount command fails with the following error message.

```
1 mount: wrong fs type, bad option, bad superblock on 10.1.25.30:/,
2 missing codepage or helper program, or other error (for several filesystems
3 (e.g. nfs, cifs) you might need a /sbin/mount.<type> helper program)
4 In some cases useful info is found in syslog - try dmesg | tail or so.
```

Action to Take
If you receive this message, install the `nfs-utils` (or `nfs-common` on Ubuntu) package. For more information, see Installing the NFS Client.

Mount Command Fails with "incorrect mount option" Error Message

The mount command fails with the following error message.

```
1 mount.nfs: an incorrect mount option was specified
```

Action to Take
This error message most likely means that your Linux distribution doesn't support Network File System versions 4.0 and 4.1 (NFSv4). To confirm this is the case, you can run the following command.

```
1 $ grep CONFIG_NFS_V4_1 /boot/config*
```

If the preceding command returns `# CONFIG_NFS_V4_1 is not set`, NFSv4.1 is not supported on your Linux distribution. For a list of the Amazon Machine Images (AMIs) for Amazon Elastic Compute Cloud (Amazon EC2) that support NFSv4.1, see NFS Support.

File System Mount Fails Immediately After File System Creation

It can take up to 90 seconds after creating a mount target for the Domain Name Service (DNS) records to propagate fully in an AWS Region.

Action to Take
If you're programmatically creating and mounting file systems, for example with an AWS CloudFormation template, we recommend that you implement a wait condition.

File System Mount Hangs and Then Fails with Timeout Error

The file system mount command hangs for a minute or two, and then fails with a timeout error. The following code shows an example.

```
1 $ sudo mount -t nfs -o nfsvers=4.1,rsize=1048576,wsize=1048576,hard,timeo=600,retrans=2,
    noresvport mount-target-ip:/ mnt
2
3 [2+ minute wait here]
4 mount.nfs: Connection timed out
5 $Ã
```

Action to Take

This error can occur because either the Amazon EC2 instance or the mount target security groups are not configured properly. For more information, see Creating Security Groups.

Verify that the mount target IP address that you specified is valid. If you specify the wrong IP address and there is nothing else at that IP address to reject the mount, you might experience this issue.

File System Mount Using DNS Name Fails

A file system mount that is using a DNS name fails. The following code shows an example.

```
1 $ sudo mount -t nfs -o nfsvers=4.1,rsize=1048576,wsize=1048576,hard,timeo=600,retrans=2,
    noresvport file-system-id.efs.aws-region.amazonaws.com:/ mnt
2 mount.nfs: Failed to resolve server file-system-id.efs.aws-region.amazonaws.com:
3   Name or service not known.
4
5 $
```

Action to Take

Check your VPC configuration. If you are using a custom VPC, make sure that DNS settings are enabled. For more information, see Using DNS with Your VPC in the *Amazon VPC User Guide*.

To specify a DNS name in the mount command, you must do the following:

- Ensure that there's an Amazon EFS mount target in the same Availability Zone as the Amazon EC2 instance.
- Connect your Amazon EC2 instance inside an Amazon VPC configured to use the DNS server provided by Amazon. For more information, see DHCP Options Sets in the *Amazon VPC User Guide*.
- Ensure that the Amazon VPC of the connecting Amazon EC2 instance has DNS hostnames enabled. For more information, see Updating DNS Support for Your VPC in the *Amazon VPC User Guide*.

Mount Target Lifecycle State Is Stuck

The mount target lifecycle state is stuck in the **creating** or **deleting** state.

Action to Take
Retry the CreateMountTarget or DeleteMountTarget call.

Mount Does Not Respond

An Amazon EFS mount appears unresponsive. For example, commands like ls hang.

Action to Take

This error can occur if another application is writing large amounts of data to the file system. Access to the files that are being written might be blocked until the operation is complete. In general, any commands or applications that attempt to access files that are being written to might appear to hang. For example, the ls command might hang when it gets to the file that is being written. This result is because some Linux distributions alias the ls command so that it retrieves file attributes in addition to listing the directory contents.

To resolve this issue, verify that another application is writing files to the Amazon EFS mount, and that it is in the Uninterruptible sleep (D) state, as in the following example:

```
1 $ ps aux | grep large_io.py
2 root 33253 0.5 0.0 126652 5020 pts/3 D+ 18:22 0:00 python large_io.py /efs/large_file
```

After you've verified that this is the case, you can address the issue by waiting for the other write operation to complete, or by implementing a workaround. In the example of ls, you can use the /bin/ls command directly, instead of an alias. Doing this allows the command to proceed without hanging on the file being written. In general, if the application writing the data can force a data flush periodically, perhaps by using fsync(2), doing so can help improve the responsiveness of your file system for other applications. However, this improvement might be at the expense of performance when the application writes data.

Operations on Newly Mounted File System Return "bad file handle" Error

Operations performed on a newly mounted file system return a bad file handle error.

This error can happen if an Amazon EC2 instance was connected to one file system and one mount target with a specified IP address, and then that file system and mount target were deleted. If you create a new file system and mount target to connect to that Amazon EC2 instance with the same mount target IP address, this issue can occur.

Action to Take
You can resolve this error by unmounting the file system, and then remounting the file system on the Amazon EC2 instance. For more information about unmounting your Amazon EFS file system, see Unmounting File Systems.

Unmounting a File System Fails

If your file system is busy, you can't unmount it.

Action to Take
You can resolve this issue in the following ways:

- Wait for all read and write operations to finish, and then attempt the umount command again.
- Force the umount command to finish with the -f option. **Warning**
  Forcing an unmount interrupts any data read or write operations that are currently in process for the file system.

Troubleshooting Encryption

Topics

- Mounting with Encryption of Data in Transit Fails
- Mounting with Encryption of Data in Transit is Interrupted
- Encrypted-at-Rest File System Can't Be Created
- Unusable Encrypted File System

Mounting with Encryption of Data in Transit Fails

By default, when using the Amazon EFS mount helper with TLS, it enforces use of the Online Certificate Status Protocol (OCSP) and certificate hostname checking. If your system doesn't support either of these features (for example, when using Red Hat Enterprise Linux or CentOS), mounting an EFS file system using TLS fails.

Action to Take
We recommend upgrading the version of stunnel on your client to support these features. For more information, see Upgrading Stunnel.

Mounting with Encryption of Data in Transit is Interrupted

It's possible, however unlikely, that your encrypted connection to your Amazon EFS file system can hang or be interrupted by client-side events.

Action to Take
If your connection to your Amazon EFS file system with encryption of data in transit is interrupted, take the following steps:

1. Ensure that the stunnel service is running on the client.

2. Confirm that the watchdog application `amazon-efs-mount-watchdog` is running on the client. You can find out whether this application is running with the following command:

```
1 ps aux | grep [a]mazon-efs-mount-watchdog
```

3. Check your support logs. For more information, see Getting Support Logs.

4. Optionally, you can enable your stunnel logs and check the information in those as well. You can change the configuration of your logs in `/etc/amazon/efs/amazon-efs-utils.conf` to enable the stunnel logs. However, doing so requires unmounting and then remounting the file system with the mount helper for the changes to take effect. **Important**
Enabling the stunnel logs can use up a nontrivial amount of space on your file system.

If the interruptions continue, contact AWS Support.

Encrypted-at-Rest File System Can't Be Created

You've tried to create a new encrypted-at-rest file system. However, you get an error message saying that AWS KMS is unavailable.

Action to Take
This error can occur in the rare case that AWS KMS becomes temporarily unavailable in your AWS Region. If this happens, wait until AWS KMS returns to full availability, and then try again to create the file system.

Unusable Encrypted File System

An encrypted file system consistently returns NFS server errors. These errors can occur when EFS can't retrieve your master key from AWS KMS for one of the following reasons:

- The key was disabled.
- The key was deleted.
- Permission for Amazon EFS to use the key was revoked.
- AWS KMS is temporarily unavailable.

Action to Take

First, confirm that the AWS KMS key is enabled. You can do so by viewing the keys in the console. For more information, see Viewing Keys in the *AWS Key Management Service Developer Guide*.

If the key is not enabled, enable it. For more information, see Enabling and Disabling Keys in the *AWS Key Management Service Developer Guide*.

If the key is pending deletion, then this status disables the key. You can cancel the deletion, and re-enable the key. For more information, see Scheduling and Canceling Key Deletion in the *AWS Key Management Service Developer Guide*.

If the key is enabled, and you're still experiencing an issue, or if you encounter an issue re-enabling your key, contact AWS Support.

Troubleshooting EFS File Sync

Following, you can find information on how to troubleshoot issues with EFS File Sync.

Topics

- Your On-Premises Source File System Is Stuck in Mounting Status
- Your Amazon EC2 Source File System Is Stuck in Mounting Status
- Your Sync Task Is Stuck in Starting Status
- Your Sync Task Failed with Permission Denied Error Message
- How Long Does the Preparing Status of a Sync Task Take to Complete?
- How Long Does the Verifying Status of a Sync Task Take to Complete?
- Enabling AWS Support to Help Troubleshoot Your EFS File Sync Running On-Premises
- Enabling AWS Support to Help Troubleshoot Your EFS File Sync Running on Amazon EC2

Your On-Premises Source File System Is Stuck in Mounting Status

Your on-premises source file system can become stuck in **Mounting** status when the sync agent that you chose can't mount the location that you specified during configuration.

Action to Take

First, make sure that the NFS server and export that you specified are both valid. If they aren't, delete the sync set, create a new one using the correct NFS server, and then export.

If the NFS server and export are both valid, it generally indicates one of two things. Either a firewall is preventing the sync agent from mounting the NFS server, or the NFS server is not configured to allow the sync agent to mount it.

Make sure that there is no firewall between the sync agent and the NFS server. Then make sure that the NFS server is configured to allow the sync agent to mount the export specified in the sync set.

If you perform these actions and the sync agent still can't mount the NFS server and export, open a support channel and engage AWS customer support. For information about how to open a support channel, see Enabling AWS Support to Help Troubleshoot Your EFS File Sync Running On-Premises or Enabling AWS Support to Help Troubleshoot Your EFS File Sync Running on Amazon EC2.

Your Amazon EC2 Source File System Is Stuck in Mounting Status

Your Amazon EC2 source file system can become stuck in **Mounting** status when the sync agent that you chose can't mount the location that you specified during configuration.

Action to Take

First, make sure that the NFS server and export that you specified are both valid. If they aren't, delete the sync set, create a new one using the correct NFS server, and then export.

If the NFS server and export are both valid, it generally indicates one of two things. Either a firewall is preventing the sync agent from mounting the NFS server, or the NFS server is not configured to allow the sync agent to mount it.

Make sure that the VPC in which your NFS server resides has a security group inbound rule that allows all traffic to the sync agent that you created for your source file system. Then make sure that the VPC in which your sync agent is running in has a security group outbound rule that allows all traffic from the sync agent.

If you perform these actions and the sync agent still can't mount the NFS server and export, open a support channel and engage AWS customer support. For information about how to open a support channel, see Enabling AWS Support to Help Troubleshoot Your EFS File Sync Running On-Premises or Enabling AWS Support to Help Troubleshoot Your EFS File Sync Running on Amazon EC2.

Your Sync Task Is Stuck in Starting Status

Your sync task can become stuck in **Starting** status when EFS File Sync can't instruct the specified source sync agent to begin a sync task. This issue usually occurs because the sync agent either is powered off or has lost network connectivity.

Action to Take
Make sure that the source sync agent is connected and the status is **Running**. If the status is **Offline**, then the agent is not connected.

Next, make sure that your sync agent is powered on. If it isn't, power it on.

If the sync agent is powered on and the sync task is still stuck in **Starting** status, then a network connectivity problem between the sync agent and EFS File Sync is the most likely issue. Check your network and firewall settings to make sure that the sync agent can connect to EFS File Sync.

If you perform these actions and the issue isn't resolved, open a support channel and engage AWS customer support. For information about how to open a support channel, see Enabling AWS Support to Help Troubleshoot Your EFS File Sync Running On-Premises or Enabling AWS Support to Help Troubleshoot Your EFS File Sync Running on Amazon EC2.

Your Sync Task Failed with Permission Denied Error Message

You can get a permissions denied error message if you configure your NFS server with root_squash or all_squash enabled, and your files don't have all read access.

Action to Take
To fix this issue, either configure the NFS export with no_root_squash, or ensure that the permissions for all of the files you want to sync allow read access for all users. Doing either enables the sync agent to read the files. For the sync agent to access directories, you must additionally enable all execute access. For information about NFS export configuration, see 18.7. The /etc/exports Configuration File in the Centos documentation.

If you perform these actions and the issue isn't resolved, contact AWS customer support.

How Long Does the Preparing Status of a Sync Task Take to Complete?

The time EFS File Sync spends in the **Preparing** status depends on the number of files in both the source and destination file systems, and the performance of these file systems. When a sync task starts, EFS File Sync performs a recursive directory listing to discover all files and file metadata in the source and destination file system. These listings are used to identify differences and determine what to copy.

Action to take
You don't need to take any action. Wait for the **Preparing** status to complete and status changes to **Syncing**. If the status doesn't change to **Syncing** status, contact AWS customer support.

How Long Does the Verifying Status of a Sync Task Take to Complete?

The time EFS File Sync spends in the **Verifying** status depends on the number of files, the total size of all files in both the source and destination file systems, and the performance of these file systems. By default, **Verification mode** is enabled in the sync setting. The verification EFS File Sync performs includes a SHA256 checksum on all file content and an exact comparison of all file metadata.

Action to take
You don't need to take any action. Wait for the **Verifying** status to complete. If the **Verifying** status doesn't complete, contact AWS customer support.

Enabling AWS Support to Help Troubleshoot Your EFS File Sync Running On-Premises

EFS File Sync provides a local console you can use to perform several maintenance tasks, including enabling AWS Support to access your EFS File Sync to assist you with troubleshooting EFS File Sync issues. By default, AWS Support access to your EFS File Sync is disabled. You enable this access through the host's local console. To give AWS Support access to your EFS File Sync, you first log in to the local console for the host then connect to the support server.

To enable AWS Support access to EFS File Sync

1. Log in to your host's local console. use user name: admin and password: password

   The local console looks like the following.

```
AWS Appliance Activation - Configuration

############################################################
##   Currently connected network adapters:
##
##   eth0:
############################################################

1: Network Configuration
2: View System Resource Check (0 Errors)
3: System Time Management
4: Command Prompt

Press "x" to exit session

Enter command: _
```

2. At the prompt, type **4** to open the help menu.

3. Type **h** to open the **AVAILABLE COMMANDS** window.

4. In the **AVAILABLE COMMANDS** window, type **open-support-channel** to connect to customer support. You must allow TCP port 22 to initiate a support channel to AWS. When you connect to customer support, EFS File Sync assigns you a support number. Make a note of your support number.

```
AVAILABLE COMMANDS
ip                      Show / manipulate routing, devices, and tunnels
save-routing-table      Save newly added routing table entry
ifconfig                View or configure network interfaces
iptables                Administration tool for IPv4 packet filtering and NAT
save-iptables           Persist IP tables
passwd                  Update authentication tokens
open-support-channel    Connect to AWS Support
h                       Display available command list
exit                    Return to Configuration menu

Command: _
```

Note

The channel number is not a Transmission Control Protocol/User Datagram Protocol (TCP/UDP) port

134

number. Instead, it makes a Secure Shell (SSH) (TCP 22) connection to servers and provides the support channel for the connection.

5. Once the support channel is established, provide your support service number to AWS Support so AWS Support can provide troubleshooting assistance.

6. When the support session is completed, type **q** to end it.

7. Type **exit** to log out of the EFS File Sync local console.

8. Follow the prompts to exit the local console.

Enabling AWS Support to Help Troubleshoot Your EFS File Sync Running on Amazon EC2

EFS File Sync provides a local console you can use to perform several maintenance tasks, including enabling AWS Support to access your EFS File Sync to assist you with troubleshooting EFS File Sync issues. By default, AWS Support access to your EFS File Sync is disabled. You enable this access through the Amazon EC2 local console. You log in to the Amazon EC2 local console through a Secure Shell (SSH). To successfully log in through SSH, your instance's security group must have a rule that opens TCP port 22.

Note
If you add a new rule to an existing security group, the new rule applies to all instances that use that security group. For more information about security groups and how to add a security group rule, see Amazon EC2 Security Groups in the *Amazon EC2 User Guide*.

To let AWS Support connect to your EFS File Sync, you first log in to the local console for the Amazon EC2 instance, navigate to the EFS File Sync's console, and then provide the access.

To enable AWS support access to an EFS File Sync deployed on an Amazon EC2 instance

1. Log in to the local console for your Amazon EC2 instance. For instructions, go to Connect to Your Instance in the *Amazon EC2 User Guide*.

   You can use the following command to log in to the EC2 instance's local console. the user name is **admin**.

   ```
   1 ssh -i PRIVATE-KEY admin@INSTANCE-PUBLIC-DNS-NAME
   ```

Note
The *PRIVATE-KEY* is the .pen file containing the private certificate of the EC2 key pair that you used to launch the Amazon EC2 instance. For more information, see Retrieving the Public Key for Your Key Pair in the *Amazon EC2 User Guide*.
The *INSTANCE-PUBLIC-DNS-NAME* is the public Domain Name System (DNS) name of your Amazon EC2 instance that your EFS File Sync is running on. You obtain this public DNS name by selecting the Amazon EC2 instance in the EC2 console and clicking the **Description** tab.

```
1 The local console looks like the following\.
```

```
AWS Appliance Activation - Configuration

#####################################################
##   Currently connected network adapters:
##
##   eth0:
#####################################################

1: View System Resource Check (0 Errors)
2: Command Prompt

Press "x" to exit session

Enter command: █
```

1. At the prompt, type **2** to open the help menu.

2. Type **h** to open the **AVAILABLE COMMANDS** window.

3. In the **AVAILABLE COMMANDS** window, type **open-support-channel** to connect to customer
   support for EFS File Sync. You must allow TCP port 22 to initiate a support channel to AWS. When you
   connect to customer support, EFS File Sync assigns you a support number. Make a note of your support
   number.

```
AVAILABLE COMMANDS
ip                     Show / manipulate routing, devices, and tunnels
save-routing-table     Save newly added routing table entry
ifconfig               View or configure network interfaces
iptables               Administration tool for IPv4 packet filtering and NAT
save-iptables          Persist IP tables
open-support-channel   Connect to AWS Support
h                      Display available command list
exit                   Return to Configuration menu

Command: █
```

Note
The channel number is not a Transmission Control Protocol/User Datagram Protocol (TCP/UDP) port
number. Instead, the EFS File Sync makes a Secure Shell (SSH) (TCP 22) connection to EFS File Sync
servers and provides the support channel for the connection.

4. Once the support channel is established, provide your support service number to AWS Support so AWS
   Support can provide troubleshooting assistance.

5. When the support session is completed, type **q** to end it.

6. Type **exit** to exit the EFS File Sync console.

7. Follow the console menus to log out of the EFS File Sync instance.

Amazon Elastic File System Walkthroughs

This section provides walkthroughs that you can use to explore Amazon EFS and test the end-to-end setup.

Topics

- Walkthrough 1: Create Amazon EFS File System and Mount It on an EC2 Instance Using the AWS CLI
- Walkthrough 2: Set Up an Apache Web Server and Serve Amazon EFS Files
- Walkthrough 3: Create Writable Per-User Subdirectories and Configure Automatic Remounting on Reboot
- Walkthrough 4: Backup Solutions for Amazon EFS File Systems
- Walkthrough 5: Create and Mount a File System On-Premises with AWS Direct Connect
- Walkthrough 6: Enforcing Encryption on an Amazon EFS File System at Rest
- Walkthrough 7: Sync Files from an On-Premises File System to Amazon EFS by Using EFS File Sync
- Walkthrough 8: Sync a File System from Amazon EC2 to Amazon EFS Using EFS File Sync

Walkthrough 1: Create Amazon EFS File System and Mount It on an EC2 Instance Using the AWS CLI

This walkthrough uses the AWS CLI to explore the Amazon EFS API. In this walkthrough, you create an Amazon EFS file system, mount it on an EC2 instance in your VPC, and test the setup.

Note
This walkthrough is similar to the Getting Started exercise. In the Getting Started exercise, you use the console to create EC2 and Amazon EFS resources. In this walkthrough, you use the AWS CLI to do the same—primarily to familiarize yourself with the Amazon EFS API.

In this walkthrough, you create the following AWS resources in your account:

- Amazon EC2 resources:
  - Two security groups (for your EC2 instance and Amazon EFS file system).
    You add rules to these security groups to authorize appropriate inbound/outbound access to allow your EC2 instance to connect to the file system via the mount target using a standard NFSv4.1 TCP port.
  - An Amazon EC2 instance in your VPC.
- Amazon EFS resources:
  - A file system.
  - A mount target for your file system.
    To mount your file system on an EC2 instance you need to create a mount target in your VPC. You can create one mount target in each of the Availability Zones in your VPC. For more information, see Amazon EFS: How It Works.

Then, you test the file system on your EC2 instance. The cleanup step at the end of the walkthrough provides information for you to remove these resources.

The walkthrough creates all these resources in the US West (Oregon) Region (`us-west-2`). Whichever AWS Region you use, be sure to use it consistently. All of your resources—your VPC, EC2 resources, and Amazon EFS resources—must be in the same AWS Region.

Before You Begin

- You can use the root credentials of your AWS account to sign in to the console and try the Getting Started exercise. However, AWS Identity and Access Management (IAM) recommends that you do not use the root credentials of your AWS account. Instead, create an administrator user in your account and use those credentials to manage resources in your account. For more information, see Setting Up.
- You can use a default VPC or a custom VPC that you have created in your account. For this walkthrough, the default VPC configuration works. However, if you use a custom VPC, verify the following:
  - DNS hostnames are enabled. For more information, see Updating DNS Support for Your VPC in the *Amazon VPC User Guide*.
  - The Internet gateway is attached to your VPC. For more information, see Internet Gateways in the *Amazon VPC User Guide*.
  - The VPC subnets are configured to request public IP addresses for instances launched in the VPC subnets. For more information, see IP Addressing in Your VPC in the *Amazon VPC User Guide*.
  - The VPC route table includes a rule to send all Internet-bound traffic to the Internet gateway.
- You need to set up the AWS CLI and add the adminuser profile.

Setting Up AWS CLI

Use the following instructions to set up the AWS CLI and user profile.

To set up the AWS CLI

1. Download and configure the AWS CLI. For instructions, see the following topics in the *AWS Command Line Interface User Guide*.

   Getting Set Up with the AWS Command Line Interface

   Installing the AWS Command Line Interface

   Configuring the AWS Command Line Interface

2. Set profiles.

   You store user credentials in the AWS CLI `config` file. The example CLI commands in this walkthrough specify the adminuser profile. Create the adminuser profile in the `config` file. You can also set the administrator user profile as the default in the `config` file as shown.

```
1 [profile adminuser]
2 aws_access_key_id = admin user access key ID
3 aws_secret_access_key = admin user secret access key
4 region = us-west-2
5
6 [default]
7 aws_access_key_id = admin user access key ID
8 aws_secret_access_key = admin user secret access key
9 region = us-west-2
```

   The preceding profile also sets the default AWS Region. If you don't specify a region in the CLI command, the us-west-2 region is assumed.

3. Verify the setup by entering the following command at the command prompt. Both of these commands don't provide credentials explicitly, so the credentials of the default profile are used.

   - Try the help command

     You can also specify the user profile explicitly by adding the `--profile` parameter.

```
1 aws help
```

```
1 aws help \
2 --profile adminuser
```

Next Step
Step 1: Create Amazon EC2 Resources

Step 1: Create Amazon EC2 Resources

In this step, you do the following:

- Create two security groups.
- Add rules to the security groups to authorize additional access.
- Launch an EC2 instance. You create and mount an Amazon EFS file system on this instance in the next step.

Topics

- Step 1.1: Create Two Security Groups
- Step 1.2: Add Rules to the Security Groups to Authorize Inbound/Outbound Access
- Step 1.3: Launch an EC2 instance

Step 1.1: Create Two Security Groups

In this section, you create security groups in your VPC for your EC2 instance and Amazon EFS mount target. Later in the walkthrough, you assign these security groups to an EC2 instance and an Amazon EFS mount target. For information about security groups, see Security Groups for EC2-VPC in the *Amazon EC2 User Guide for Linux Instances*.

To create security groups

1. Create two security groups using the `create-security-group` CLI command.

   1. Create a security group (`efs-walkthrough1-ec2-sg`) for your EC2 instance. You will need to provide your VPC ID.

   ```
   $ aws ec2 create-security-group \
   --region us-west-2 \
   --group-name efs-walkthrough1-ec2-sg \
   --description "Amazon EFS walkthrough 1, SG for EC2 instance" \
   --vpc-id vpc-id-in-us-west-2 \
   --profile adminuser
   ```

   Write down the security group ID. The following is an example response:

   ```
   {
       "GroupId": "sg-aexample"
   }
   ```

   You can find the VPC ID using the following command:

   ```
   $ aws  ec2 describe-vpcs
   ```

   2. Create a security group (`efs-walkthrough1-mt-sg`) for your Amazon EFS mount target. You need to provide your VPC ID.

   ```
   $ aws ec2 create-security-group \
   --region us-west-2 \
   --group-name efs-walkthrough1-mt-sg \
   --description "Amazon EFS walkthrough 1, SG for mount target" \
   --vpc-id vpc-id-in-us-west-2 \
   --profile adminuser
   ```

   Write down the security group ID. The following is an example response:

```
1 {
2     "GroupId": "sg-aexample"
3 }
```

2. Verify the security groups.

```
1 aws ec2 describe-security-groups \
2 --group-ids list of security group IDs separated by space \
3 --profile adminuser \
4 --region us-west-2
```

Both should have only one outbound rule that allows all traffic to leave.

In the next section, you authorize additional access that enable the following:

- Enable you to connect to your EC2 instance.
- Enable traffic between an EC2 instance and an Amazon EFS mount target (to which you will associate these security groups later in this walkthrough).

Step 1.2: Add Rules to the Security Groups to Authorize Inbound/Outbound Access

In this step, you add rules to the security groups to authorize inbound/outbound access.

To add rules

1. Authorize incoming SSH connections to the security group for your EC2 instance (efs-walkthrough1-ec2-sg) so you can connect to your EC2 instance using SSH from any host.

```
1 $ aws ec2 authorize-security-group-ingress \
2 --group-id id of the security group created for EC2 instance \
3 --protocol tcp \
4 --port 22 \
5 --cidr 0.0.0.0/0 \
6 --profile adminuser \
7 --region us-west-2
```

Verify that the security group has the inbound and outbound rule you added.

```
1 aws ec2 describe-security-groups \
2 --region us-west-2 \
3 --profile adminuser \
4 --group-id security-group-id
```

2. Authorize inbound access to the security group for the Amazon EFS mount target (efs-walkthrough1-mt-sg).

At the command prompt, run the following AWS CLI authorize-security-group-ingress command using the adminuser profile to add the inbound rule.

```
1 $ aws ec2 authorize-security-group-ingress \
2 --group-id ID of the security group created for Amazon EFS mount target \
3 --protocol tcp \
4 --port 2049 \
5 --source-group ID of the security group created for EC2 instance \
6 --profile adminuser \
7 --region us-west-2
```

3. Verify that both security groups now authorize inbound access.

```
1 aws ec2 describe-security-groups \
2 --group-names efs-walkthrough1-ec2-sg   efs-walkthrough1-mt-sg \
3 --profile adminuser \
4 --region us-west-2
```

Step 1.3: Launch an EC2 instance

In this step, you launch an EC2 instance.

To launch an EC2 instance

1. Gather the following information that you need to provide when launching an EC2 instance:

    1. Key pair name.

        - For introductory information, see Setting Up with Amazon EC2 in the *Amazon EC2 User Guide for Linux Instances*.
        - For instructions to create a .pem file, see Create a Key Pair in the *Amazon EC2 User Guide for Linux Instances*.

    2. The AMI ID you want to launch.

        The AWS CLI command you will use to launch an EC2 instance requires an AMI ID (that you want to deploy) as a parameter. The exercise uses the Amazon Linux HVM AMI. **Note**
        You can use most general purpose Linux-based AMIs. If you use another Linux API, keep in mind that you will use yum to install NFS client on the instance and you might need to add software packages as you need them.

        For the Amazon Linux HVM AMI, you can find the latest IDs at Amazon Linux AMI. You choose the ID value from the Amazon Linux AMI IDs table as follows:

        - Choose the **US West Oregon** region. This walkthrough assumes you are creating all resources in the US West (Oregon) Region (us-west-2).
        - Choose the **EBS-backed HVM 64-bit** type (because in the CLI command you specify the `t2.micro` instance type, which does not support instance store).

    3. ID of the security group you created for an EC2 instance.

    4. AWS Region. This walkthrough uses the us-west-2 region.

    5. Your VPC subnet ID where you want to launch the instance. You can get list of subnets using the `describe-subnets` command.

        ```
        1 $ aws ec2 describe-subnets \
        2 --region us-west-2 \
        3 --filters "Name=vpc-id,Values=vpc-id" \
        4 --profile adminuser
        ```

        After you choose subnet ID, write down the following values from the `describe-subnets` result:

        - **subnet ID** – You need this value when you create a mount target. In this exercise, you create a mount target in the same subnet where you launch an EC2 instance.
        - **Availability Zone of the subnet** – You need this to construct your mount target DNS name, which you use to mount a file system on the EC2 instance.

2. Run the following AWS CLI `run-instances` command to launch an EC2 instance.

```
1 $ aws ec2 run-instances \
2 --image-id AMI ID \
```

```
3 --count 1 \
4 --instance-type t2.micro \
5 --associate-public-ip-address \
6 --key-name key-pair-name \
7 --security-group-ids ID of the security group created for EC2 instance \
8 --subnet-id VPC subnet ID \
9 --region us-west-2 \
10 --profile adminuser
```

3. Write down the instance ID returned by the **run-instances** command.

4. The EC2 instance you created must have a public DNS name that you use to connect to the EC2 instance and mount the file system on it. The public DNS name is of the form:

```
1 ec2-xx-xx-xx-xxx.compute-1.amazonaws.com
```

Run the following CLI command and write down the public DNS name.

```
1 aws ec2 describe-instances \
2 --instance-ids EC2 instance ID \
3 --region us-west-2 \
4 --profile adminuser
```

If you don't find the public DNS name, check the configuration of the VPC in which you launched the EC2 instance. For more information, see Before You Begin.

5. You can assign a name to the EC2 instance you created by adding a tag with the key Name and value set to the name you want to assign to the instance. Run the following AWS CLI **create-tags** command.

```
1 $ aws ec2 create-tags \
2 --resources EC2-instance-ID \
3 --tags Key=Name,Value=Provide-instance-name \
4 --region us-west-2 \
5 --profile adminuser
```

Next Step
Step 2: Create Amazon EFS Resources

Step 2: Create Amazon EFS Resources

In this step, you do the following:

- Create an Amazon EFS file system.
- Create a mount target in the Availability Zone where you have your EC2 instance launched.

Topics

- Step 2.1: Create Amazon EFS File System
- Step 2.2: Create a Mount Target

Step 2.1: Create Amazon EFS File System

In this step, you create an Amazon EFS file system. Write down the `FileSystemId` to use later when you create mount targets for the file system in the next step.

To create a file system

1. Create a file system and add the optional `Name` tag.

   1. At the command prompt, run the following AWS CLI `create-file-system` command.

   ```
   1 $ aws efs create-file-system \
   2 --creation-token FileSystemForWalkthrough1 \
   3 --region us-west-2 \
   4 --profile adminuser
   ```

   2. Verify the file system creation by calling the `describe-file-systems` CLI command.

   ```
   1 $ aws efs describe-file-systems \
   2 --region us-west-2 \
   3 --profile adminuser
   ```

   Here's an example response:

   ```
   1  {
   2      "FileSystems": [
   3          {
   4              "SizeInBytes": {
   5                  "Timestamp": 1418062014.0,
   6                  "Value": 1024
   7              },
   8              "CreationToken": "FileSystemForWalkthrough1",
   9              "CreationTime": 1418062014.0,
   10             "FileSystemId": "fs-cda54064",
   11             "PerformanceMode" : "generalPurpose",
   12             "NumberOfMountTargets": 0,
   13             "LifeCycleState": "available",
   14             "OwnerId": "account-id"
   15         }
   16     ]
   17 }
   ```

   3. Note the `FileSystemId` value. You need this value when you create a mount target for this file system in the next step.

2. (Optional) Add a tag to the file system you created using the `create-tag` CLI command.

   You don't need to create a tag for your file system to complete this walkthrough. But you are exploring the Amazon EFS API, so let's test the Amazon EFS API for creating and managing tags. For more information, see CreateTags.

   1. Add a tag.

   ```
   1 $ aws efs create-tags \
   2 --file-system-id File-System-ID \
   3 --tags Key=Name,Value=SomeExampleNameValue \
   4 --region us-west-2 \
   5 --profile adminuser
   ```

   2. Retrieve a list of tags added to the file system by using the `describe-tags` CLI command.

   ```
   1 $ aws efs describe-tags \
   2 --file-system-id File-System-ID \
   3 --region us-west-2 \
   4 --profile adminuser
   ```

   Amazon EFS returns tags list in the response body.

   ```
   1 {
   2     "Tags": [
   3         {
   4             "Value": "SomeExampleNameValue",
   5             "Key": "Name"
   6         }
   7     ]
   8 }
   ```

Step 2.2: Create a Mount Target

In this step, you create a mount target for your file system in the Availability Zone where you have your EC2 instance launched.

1. Make sure you have the following information:

   - ID of the file system (for example, `fs-example`) for which you are creating the mount target.

   - VPC subnet ID where you launched the EC2 instance in Step 1.

     For this walkthrough, you create the mount target in the same subnet in which you launched the EC2 instance, so you need the subnet ID (for example, `subnet-example`).

   - ID of the security group you created for the mount target in the preceding step.

2. At the command prompt, run the following AWS CLI `create-mount-target` command.

   ```
   1 $ aws efs create-mount-target \
   2 --file-system-id file-system-id \
   3 --subnet-id  subnet-id \
   4 --security-group ID-of-the security-group-created-for-mount-target \
   5 --region us-west-2 \
   6 --profile adminuser
   ```

   You get this response:

```
1  {
2      "MountTargetId": "fsmt-example",
3      "NetworkInterfaceId": "eni-example",
4      "FileSystemId": "fs-example",
5      "PerformanceMode" : "generalPurpose",
6      "LifeCycleState": "available",
7      "SubnetId": "fs-subnet-example",
8      "OwnerId": "account-id",
9      "IpAddress": "xxx.xx.xx.xxx"
10 }
```

3. You can also use the `describe-mount-targets` command to get descriptions of mount targets you created on a file system.

```
1  $ aws efs describe-mount-targets \
2  --file-system-id file-system-id \
3  --region us-west-2 \
4  --profile adminuser
```

Next Step
Step 3: Mount the Amazon EFS File System on the EC2 Instance and Test

Step 3: Mount the Amazon EFS File System on the EC2 Instance and Test

In this step, you do the following:

Topics

- Step 3.1: Gather Information
- Step 3.2: Install the NFS Client on Your EC2 Instance
- Step 3.3: Mount File System on Your EC2 Instance and Test
- Next Step
- Install an NFS client on your EC2 instance.
- Mount the file system on your EC2 instance and test the setup.

Step 3.1: Gather Information

Make sure you have the following information as you follow the steps in this section:

- Public DNS name of your EC2 instance in the following format:

```
1 ec2-xx-xxx-xxx-xx.aws-region.compute.amazonaws.com
```

- DNS name of your file system. You can construct this DNS name using the following generic form:

```
1 file-system-id.efs.aws-region.amazonaws.com
```

The EC2 instance on which you mount the file system by using the mount target can resolve the file system's DNS name to the mount target's IP address.

Note
Amazon EFS doesn't require that your Amazon EC2 instance have either a public IP address or public DNS name. The requirements listed preceding are just for this walkthrough example to ensure that you'll be able to connect by using SSH into the instance from outside the VPC.

Step 3.2: Install the NFS Client on Your EC2 Instance

You can connect to your EC2 instance from Windows or from a computer running Linux, or Mac OS X, or any other Unix variant.

To install an NFS client

1. Connect to your EC2 instance:

    - To connect to your instance from a computer running Mac OS or Linux, you specify the .pem file to your ssh command with the -i option and the path to your private key.
    - To connect to your instance from a computer running Windows, you can use either MindTerm or PuTTY. If you plan to use PuTTY, you need to install it and use the following procedure to convert the .pem file to a .ppk file.

    For more information, see the following topics in the *Amazon EC2 User Guide for Linux Instances*:

    - Connecting to Your Linux Instance from Windows Using PuTTY
    - Connecting to Your Linux Instance Using SSH

2. Execute the following commands on the EC2 instance by using the SSH session:

    1. (Optional) Get updates and reboot.

```
1 $  sudo yum -y update
2 $  sudo reboot
```

After the reboot, reconnect to your EC2 instance.

2. Install the NFS client.

```
1 $ sudo yum -y install nfs-utils
```

Note
If you choose the **Amazon Linux AMI 2016.03.0** Amazon Linux AMI when launching your Amazon EC2 instance, you won't need to install `nfs-utils` because it is already included in the AMI by default.

Step 3.3: Mount File System on Your EC2 Instance and Test

Now you mount the file system on your EC2 instance.

1. Make a directory ("efs-mount-point").

```
1 $  mkdir ~/efs-mount-point
```

2. Mount the Amazon EFS file system.

```
1 $ sudo mount -t nfs -o nfsvers=4.1,rsize=1048576,wsize=1048576,hard,timeo=600,retrans=2,
    noresvport mount-target-DNS:/   ~/efs-mount-point
```

The EC2 instance can resolve the mount target DNS name to the IP address. You can optionally specify the IP address of the mount target directly.

```
1 $ sudo mount -t nfs -o nfsvers=4.1,rsize=1048576,wsize=1048576,hard,timeo=600,retrans=2,
    noresvport mount-target-ip:/   ~/efs-mount-point
```

3. Now that you have the Amazon EFS file system mounted on your EC2 instance, you can create files.

   1. Change the directory.

   ```
   1 $  cd ~/efs-mount-point
   ```

   2. List the directory contents.

   ```
   1 $  ls -al
   ```

   It should be empty.

   ```
   1 drwxr-xr-x 2 root     root     4096 Dec 29 22:33 .
   2 drwx------ 4 ec2-user ec2-user 4096 Dec 29 22:54 ..
   ```

   3. The root directory of a file system, upon creation, is owned by and is writable by the root user, so you need to change permissions to add files.

   ```
   1 $  sudo chmod go+rw .
   ```

   Now, if you try the `ls -al` command you see that the permissions have changed.

   ```
   1 drwxrwxrwx 2 root     root     4096 Dec 29 22:33 .
   2 drwx------ 4 ec2-user ec2-user 4096 Dec 29 22:54 ..
   ```

   4. Create a text file.

   ```
   1 $  touch test-file.txt
   ```

5. List directory content.

```
1 $ ls -l
```

You now have successfully created and mounted an Amazon EFS file system on your EC2 instance in your VPC.

The file system you mounted will not persist across reboots. To automatically remount the directory you can use the `fstab` file. For more information, see Automatic Remounting on Reboot. If you are using an Auto Scaling group to launch EC2 instances, you can also set scripts in a launch configuration. For an example, see Walkthrough 2: Set Up an Apache Web Server and Serve Amazon EFS Files.

Next Step

Step 4: Clean Up

Step 4: Clean Up

If you no longer need the resources you created, you should remove them. You can do this with the CLI.

- Remove EC2 resources (the EC2 instance and the two security groups). Amazon EFS deletes the network interface when you delete the mount target.
- Remove Amazon EFS resources (file system, mount target).

To delete AWS resources created in this walkthrough

1. Terminate the EC2 instance you created for this walkthrough.

```
1 $ aws ec2 terminate-instances \
2 --instance-ids instance-id \
3 --profile adminuser
```

   You can also delete EC2 resources using the console. For instructions, see Terminating an Instance in the *Amazon EC2 User Guide for Linux Instances*.

2. Delete the mount target.

   You must delete the mount targets created for the file system before deleting the file system. You can get a list of mount targets by using the `describe-mount-targets` CLI command.

```
1 $  aws efs describe-mount-targets \
2 --file-system-id file-system-ID \
3 --profile adminuser \
4 --region aws-region
```

   Then delete the mount target by using the `delete-mount-target` CLI command.

```
1 $ aws efs delete-mount-target \
2 --mount-target-id ID-of-mount-target-to-delete \
3 --profile adminuser \
4 --region aws-region
```

3. (Optional) Delete the two security groups you created. You don't pay for creating security groups.

   You must delete the mount target's security group first, before deleting the EC2 instance's security group. The mount target's security group has a rule that references the EC2 security group. Therefore, you cannot first delete the EC2 instance's security group.

   For instructions, see Deleting a Security Group in the *Amazon EC2 User Guide for Linux Instances*.

4. Delete the file system by using the `delete-file-system` CLI command. You can get a list of your file systems by using the `describe-file-systems` CLI command. You can get the file system ID from the response.

```
1 aws efs describe-file-systems \
2 --profile adminuser \
3 --region aws-region
```

   Delete the file system by providing the file system ID.

```
1 $ aws efs delete-file-system \
2 --file-system-id ID-of-file-system-to-delete \
3 --region aws-region \
4 --profile adminuser
```

Walkthrough 2: Set Up an Apache Web Server and Serve Amazon EFS Files

You can have EC2 instances running the Apache web server serving files stored on your Amazon EFS file system. It can be one EC2 instance, or if your application needs, you can have multiple EC2 instances serving files from your Amazon EFS file system. The following procedures are described.

- Set up an Apache web server on an EC2 instance.
- Set up an Apache web server on multiple EC2 instances by creating an Auto Scaling group. You can create multiple EC2 instances using Amazon EC2 Auto Scaling, an AWS service that allows you to increase or decrease the number of EC2 instances in a group according to your application needs. When you have multiple web servers, you also need a load balancer to distribute request traffic among them.

Note
For both procedures, you create all resources in the US West (Oregon) Region (`us-west-2`).

Single EC2 Instance Serving Files

Follow the steps to set up an Apache web server on one EC2 instance to serve files you create in your Amazon EFS file system.

1. Follow the steps in the Getting Started exercise so that you have a working configuration consisting of the following:

   - Amazon EFS file system
   - EC2 instance
   - File system mounted on the EC2 instance

   For instructions, see Getting Started with Amazon Elastic File System. As you follow the steps, write down the following:

   - Public DNS name of the EC2 instance.
   - Public DNS name of the mount target created in the same Availability Zone where you launched the EC2 instance.

2. (Optional) You may choose to unmount the file system from the mount point you created in the Getting Started exercise.

```
1 $ sudo umount  ~/efs-mount-point
```

   In this walkthrough, you create another mount point for the file system.

3. On your EC2 instance, install the Apache web server and configure it as follows:

   1. Connect to your EC2 instance and install the Apache web server.

   ```
   1 $ sudo yum -y install httpd
   ```

   2. Start the service.

   ```
   1 $ sudo service httpd start
   ```

   3. Create a mount point.

      First note that the `DocumentRoot` in the `/etc/httpd/conf/httpd.conf` file points to `/var/www/html` (`DocumentRoot "/var/www/html"`).

      You will mount your Amazon EFS file system on a subdirectory under the document root.

      1. Create a subdirectory efs-mount-point under /var/www/html.

```
1 $ sudo mkdir /var/www/html/efs-mount-point
```

2. Mount your Amazon EFS file system. You need to update the following command by providing your file system ID and AWS region (if you followed the Getting Started exercise to create a file system, the getting started assumes us-west-2 AWS Region).

```
1 $ sudo mount -t nfs -o nfsvers=4.1,rsize=1048576,wsize=1048576,hard,timeo=600,
     retrans=2,noresvport file-system-id.efs.aws-region.amazonaws.com:/ /var/www/
     html/efs-mount-point
```

Here you dynamically construct DNS name of the mount target from the EC2 instance you are on. For more information, see Mounting on Amazon EC2 with a DNS Name.

4. Test the setup.

1. Add a rule in the EC2 instance security group, which you created in the Getting Started exercise, to allow HTTP traffic on TCP port 80 from anywhere.

After you add the rule, the EC2 instance security group will have the following inbound rules.

For instructions, see Creating Security Groups Using the AWS Management Console.

2. Create a sample html file.

1. Change directory.

```
1 $ cd /var/www/html/efs-mount-point
```

2. Make a subdirectory for sampledir and change the ownership. And change directory so you can create files in the sampledir subdirectory.

```
1 $ sudo mkdir sampledir
2 $ sudo chown  ec2-user sampledir
3 $ sudo chmod -R o+r sampledir
4 $ cd sampledir
```

1. Create a sample hello.html file.

```
1 $ echo "<html><h1>Hello from Amazon EFS</h1></html>" > hello.html
```

3. Open a browser window and enter the URL to access the file (it is the public DNS name of the EC2 instance followed by the file name). For example:

```
1 http://EC2-instance-public-DNS/efs-mount-point/sampledir/hello.html
```

Now you are serving web pages stored on an Amazon EFS file system.

Note

This setup does not configure the EC2 instance to automatically start httpd (web server) on boot, and also does not mount the file system on boot. In the next walkthrough, you create a launch configuration to set this up.

Multiple EC2 Instances Serving Files

Follow the steps to serve the same content in your Amazon EFS file system from multiple EC2 instances for improved scalability or availability.

1. Follow the steps in the Getting Started exercise so that you have an Amazon EFS file system created and tested. **Important**
   For this walkthrough, you don't use the EC2 instance that you created in the Getting Started exercise. Instead, you launch new EC2 instances.

2. Create a load balancer in your VPC using the following steps.

   1. Define a load balancer

      In the **Basic Configuration** section, select your VPC where you also create the EC2 instances on which you mount the file system.

      In the **Select Subnets** section, you can select all of the available subnets or select . For details, see the `cloud-config` script in the next section.

   2. Assign security groups

      Create a new security group for the load balancer to allow HTTP access from port 80 from anywhere, as shown following:

      - Type: HTTP
      - Protocol: TCP
      - Port Range: 80
      - Source: Anywhere (0.0.0.0/0) **Note**
        When everything works, you can also update the EC2 instance security group inbound rule access to allow HTTP traffic only from the load balancer.

   3. Configure a health check

      Set the **Ping Path** value to `/efs-mount-point/test.html`. The `efs-mount-point` is the subdirectory where you have the file system mounted. You add `test.html` page in it later in this procedure. **Note**
      Don't add any EC2 instances. Later, you create an Auto Scaling Group in which you launch EC2 instance and specify this load balancer.

   For instructions to create a load balancer, see Getting Started with Elastic Load Balancing in the *Elastic Load Balancing User Guide*.

3. Create an Auto Scaling group with two EC2 instances. First, you create a launch configuration describing the instances. Then, you create an Auto Scaling group by specifying the launch configuration. The following steps provide configuration information that you specify to create an Auto Scaling group from the Amazon EC2 console.

   1. Choose **Launch Configurations** under **AUTO SCALING** from the left hand navigation.

   2. Choose **Create Auto Scaling group** to launch the wizard.

   3. Choose **Create launch configuration**.

   4. From **Quick Start**, select the latest version of the **Amazon Linux (HVM)** AMI. This is same AMI you used in Step 1: Create Your EC2 Resources and Launch Your EC2 Instance of the Getting Started exercise.

5. In the **Advanced** section, do the following:

- For **IP Address Type**, choose **Assign a public IP address to every instance.**

- Copy/paste the following script in the **User data** box.

  You must update the script by providing values for the *file-system-id* and *aws-region* (if you followed the Getting Started exercise, you created the file system in the us-west-2 region).

  In the script, note the following:

  - The script installs the NFS client and the Apache web server.

  - The echo command writes the following entry in the /etc/fstab file identifying the file system's DNS name and subdirectory on which to mount it. This entry ensures that the file gets mounted after each system reboot. Note that the file system's DNS name is dynamically constructed. For more information, see Mounting on Amazon EC2 with a DNS Name.

  ```
  1 file-system-ID.efs.aws-region.amazonaws.com:/ /var/www/html/efs-mount-point
        nfs4    defaults
  ```

  - Creates efs-mount-point subdirectory and mounts the file system on it.

  - Creates a test.html page so ELB health check can find the file (when creating a load balancer you specified this file as the ping point).

  For more information about user data scripts, see Adding User Data in the *Amazon EC2 User Guide for Linux Instances*.

  ```
  1  #cloud-config
  2  package_upgrade: true
  3  packages:
  4  - nfs-utils
  5  - httpd
  6  runcmd:
  7  - echo "$(curl -s http://169.254.169.254/latest/meta-data/placement/availability-
        zone).file-system-id.efs.aws-region.amazonaws.com:/    /var/www/html/efs-mount-
        point    nfs4    defaults" >> /etc/fstab
  8  - mkdir /var/www/html/efs-mount-point
  9  - mount -a
  10 - touch /var/www/html/efs-mount-point/test.html
  11 - service httpd start
  12 - chkconfig httpd on
  ```

6. For **Assign a security group**, choose **Select an existing security group**, and then choose the security group you created for the EC2 instance.

When configuring the Auto Scaling group details, use the following information:

1. For **Group size**, choose **Start with 2 instances**. You will create two EC2 instances.

2. Select your VPC from the **Network** list.

3. Select a subnet in the same Availability Zone that you used when specifying the mount target ID in the User Data script when creating the launch configuration in the preceding step.

4. In the Advanced Details section

   1. For **Load Balancing**, choose **Receive traffic from Elastic Load Balancer(s)**, and then select the load balancer you created for this exercise.

   2. For **Health Check Type**, choose **ELB**.

Follow the instructions to create an Auto Scaling group at Set Up a Scaled and Load-Balanced Application in the *Amazon EC2 Auto Scaling User Guide*. Use the information in the preceding tables where applicable.

4. Upon successful creation of the Auto Scaling group, you have two EC2 instances with `nfs-utils` and the Apache web server installed. On each instance, verify that you have the `/var/www/html/efs-mount-point` subdirectory with your Amazon EFS file system mounted on it. For instructions to connect to an EC2 instance, see Step 3: Connect to Your Amazon EC2 Instance and Mount the Amazon EFS File System.
   Note
   If you choose the **Amazon Linux AMI 2016.03.0** Amazon Linux AMI when launching your Amazon EC2 instance, you won't need to install `nfs-utils` because it is already included in the AMI by default.

5. Create a sample page (index.html).

   1. Change directory.

   ```
   1 $ cd /var/www/html/efs-mount-point
   ```

   2. Make a subdirectory for `sampledir` and change the ownership. And change directory so you can create files in the `sampledir` subdirectory. If you followed the preceding Single EC2 Instance Serving Files, you already created the `sampledir` subdirectory, so you can skip this step.

   ```
   1 $  sudo mkdir sampledir
   2 $  sudo chown  ec2-user sampledir
   3 $  sudo chmod -R o+r sampledir
   4 $  cd sampledir
   ```

   1. Create a sample `index.html` file.

   ```
   1 $ echo "<html><h1>Hello from Amazon EFS</h1></html>" > index.html
   ```

6. Now you can test the setup. Using the load balancer's public DNS name, access the index.html page.

```
1 http://load balancer public DNS Name/efs-mount-point/sampledir/index.html
```

The load balancer sends a request to one of the EC2 instances running the Apache web server. Then, the web server serves the file that is stored in your Amazon EFS file system.

Walkthrough 3: Create Writable Per-User Subdirectories and Configure Automatic Remounting on Reboot

After you create an Amazon EFS file system and mount it locally on your EC2 instance, it exposes an empty directory called the *file system root*. One common use case is to create a "writable" subdirectory under this file system root for each user you create on the EC2 instance, and mount it on the user's home directory. All files and subdirectories the user creates in their home directory are then created on the Amazon EFS file system.

In this walkthrough, you first create a user "mike" on your EC2 instance. You then mount an Amazon EFS subdirectory onto user mike's home directory. The walkthrough also explains how to configure automatic remounting of subdirectories if the system reboots.

Suppose you have an Amazon EFS file system created and mounted on a local directory on your EC2 instance. Let's call it *EFSroot*.

Note
You can follow the Getting Started exercise to create and mount an Amazon EFS file system on your EC2 instance.

In the following steps, you create a user (mike), create a subdirectory for the user (*EFSroot*/mike), make user mike the owner of the subdirectory, granting him full permissions, and finally mount the Amazon EFS subdirectory on the user's home directory (/home/mike).

1. Create user mike:

    1. Log in to your EC2 instance. Using root privileges (in this case, using the sudo command), create user mike and assign a password.

    ```
    1 $ sudo useradd -c "Mike Smith" mike
    2 $ sudo passwd mike
    ```

    This also creates a home directory, /home/mike, for the user.

2. Create a subdirectory under *EFSroot* for user mike:

    1. Create subdirectory mike under *EFSroot*.

    ```
    1 $  sudo mkdir /EFSroot/mike
    ```

    You will need to replace *EFSroot* with your local directory name.

    2. The root user and root group are the owners of the /mike subdirectory (you can verify this by using the ls -l command). To enable full permissions for user mike on this subdirectory, grant mike ownership of the directory.

    ```
    1 $ sudo chown mike:mike /EFSroot/mike
    ```

```
drwxr-xr-x  4 root     root     4096 Feb  5 22:37 .
dr-xr-xr-x 25 root     root     4096 Feb  5 22:20 ..
drwxr-xr-x  2 mike     mike     4096 Feb  4 01:18 mike
```

    1. Use the mount command to mount the *EFSroot*/mike subdirectory onto mike's home directory.

    ```
    1 $  sudo mount -t nfs -o nfsvers=4.1,rsize=1048576,wsize=1048576,hard,timeo=600,retrans=2,
          noresvport mount-target-DNS:/mike  /home/mike
    ```

    The *mount-target-DNS* address identifies the remote Amazon EFS file system root.

Now user mike's home directory is a subdirectory, writable by mike, in the Amazon EFS file system. If you unmount this mount target, the user can't access their EFS directory without remounting, which requires root permissions.

Automatic Remounting on Reboot

You can use the file `fstab` to automatically remount your file system after any system reboots. For more information, see Mounting Your Amazon EFS File System Automatically.

Walkthrough 4: Backup Solutions for Amazon EFS File Systems

If you need to be able to recover from unintended changes or deletions in your Amazon EFS file systems, we recommend that you use the EFS-to-EFS Backup Solution.

The EFS-to-EFS backup solution is suitable for all Amazon EFS file systems in all AWS Regions. It includes an AWS CloudFormation template that launches, configures, and runs the AWS services required to deploy this solution. This solution follows AWS best practices for security and availability.

For more information on the EFS-to-EFS backup solution, see EFS-to-EFS Backup Solution in AWS Answers.

Note
Before the EFS-to-EFS backup solution was available, we recommended an alternative backup solution that is only suitable in AWS Regions that have AWS Data Pipeline support. For more information on that previous solution, see Backing Up Amazon EFS File Systems Using AWS Data Pipeline.

Walkthrough 5: Create and Mount a File System On-Premises with AWS Direct Connect

This walkthrough uses the AWS Management Console to create and mount a file system on an on-premises client using an AWS Direct Connect connection.

In this walkthrough, we assume that you already have an AWS Direct Connect connection. If you don't have one, you can begin the connection process now and come back to this walkthrough when your connection is established. For more information, see AWS Direct Connect Product Details.

When you have an AWS Direct Connect connection, you create an Amazon EFS file system and a mount target in your Amazon VPC. After that, you download and install the amazon-efs-utils tools. Then, you test the file system from your on-premises client. Finally, the clean-up step at the end of the walkthrough provides information for you to remove these resources.

The walkthrough creates all these resources in the US West (Oregon) Region (`us-west-2`). Whichever AWS Region you use, be sure to use it consistently. All of your resources—your VPC, your mount target, and your Amazon EFS file system—must be in the same AWS Region.

Note
If your local application needs to know if the EFS file system is available, your application should be able to point to a different mount point IP address if the first mount point becomes temporarily unavailable. In this scenario, we recommend that you have two on-premises clients connected to your file system through different Availability Zones (AZs) for higher availability.

Before You Begin

You can use the root credentials of your AWS account to sign in to the console and try this exercise. However, AWS Identity and Access Management (IAM) best practices recommend that you don't use the root credentials of your AWS account. Instead, create an administrator user in your account and use those credentials to manage resources in your account. For more information, see Setting Up.

You can use a default VPC or a custom VPC that you have created in your account. For this walkthrough, the default VPC configuration works. However, if you use a custom VPC, verify the following:

- The internet gateway is attached to your VPC. For more information, see Internet Gateways in the *Amazon VPC User Guide*.
- The VPC route table includes a rule to send all internet-bound traffic to the Internet gateway.

Step 1: Create Your Amazon Elastic File System Resources

In this step, you create your Amazon EFS file system and mount targets.

To create your Amazon EFS file system

1. Open the Amazon EFS console at https://console.aws.amazon.com/efs/.
2. Choose **Create File System**.
3. Choose your default VPC from the **VPC** list.
4. Select the check boxes for all of the Availability Zones. Make sure that they all have the default subnets, automatic IP addresses, and the default security groups chosen. These are your mount targets. For more information, see Creating Mount Targets.
5. Choose **Next Step**.

159

6. Name your file system, keep **general purpose** selected as your default performance mode, and choose **Next Step**.

7. Choose **Create File System**.

8. Choose your file system from the list and make a note of the **Security group** value. You need this value for the next step.

The file system you just created has mount targets, created in step 1.4. Each mount target has an associated security group. The security group acts as a virtual firewall that controls network traffic. If you didn't provide a security group when creating a mount target, Amazon EFS associates the default security group of the VPC with it. If you followed the preceding steps exactly, then your mount targets are using the default security group.

Next, you add a rule to the mount target's security group to allow inbound traffic to the NFS port (2049). You can use the AWS Management Console to add the rule to your mount target's security groups in your VPC.

To allow inbound traffic to the NFS port

1. Sign in to the AWS Management Console and open the Amazon EC2 console at https://console.aws.amazon.com/ec2/.

2. Under **NETWORK & SECURITY**, choose **Security Groups**.

3. Choose the security group associated with your file system. You made a note of this at the end of Step 1: Create Your Amazon Elastic File System Resources.

4. In the tabbed pane that appears below the list of security groups, choose the **Inbound** tab.

5. Choose **Edit**.

6. Choose **Add Rule**, and choose a rule of the following type:

   - **Type – NFS**
   - **Source – Anywhere**

   We recommend that you only use the **Anywhere** source for testing. You can create a custom source set to the IP address of the on-premises client, or use the console from the client itself, and choose **My IP**. **Note** You don't need to add an outbound rule, because the default outbound rule allows all traffic to leave. If you don't have this default outbound rule, add an outbound rule to open a TCP connection on the NFS port, identifying the mount target security group as the destination.

Step 2: Download and Install amazon-efs-utils

The amazon-efs-utils package is an open-source collection of Amazon EFS tools, and comes with a mount helper and tooling that makes it easier to perform encryption of data in transit for Amazon EFS. For more information, see Using the amazon-efs-utils Tools. This package is available as a free download from GitHub, which you can get by cloning the package's repository.

To clone amazon-efs-utils from GitHub

1. Access the terminal for your on-premises client.

2. From the terminal, clone the amazon-efs-utils tool from GitHub to a directory of your choice, with the following command.

```
1 git clone https://github.com/aws/efs-utils
```

Now that you have the package, you can install it. This installation is handled differently depending on the Linux distribution of your on-premises client. The following distributions are supported:

- Amazon Linux 2
- Amazon Linux
- Red Hat Enterprise Linux (and derivatives such as CentOS) version 7 and newer

- Ubuntu 16.04 LTS and newer

To build and install amazon-efs-utils as an RPM package

1. Open a terminal on your client and navigate to the directory that has the cloned amazon-efs-utils package from GitHub.

2. Build the package with the following command:

```
1 make rpm
```

Note

If you haven't already, you'll need to install the rpm-builder package with the following command:

```
1 sudo yum -y install rpm-build
```

1. Install the package with the following command:

```
1 sudo yum -y install build/amazon-efs-utils*rpm
```

To build and install amazon-efs-utils as an deb package

1. Open a terminal on your client and navigate to the directory that has the cloned amazon-efs-utils package from GitHub.

2. Build the package with the following command:

```
1 ./build-deb.sh
```

3. Install the package with the following command:

```
1 sudo apt-get install build/amazon-efs-utils*deb
```

After the package is installed, configure amazon-efs-utils for use in your AWS Region with AWS Direct Connect.

To configure amazon-efs-utils for use in your AWS Region

1. Using your text editor of choice, open /etc/amazon/efs/amazon-efs-utils.conf for editing.

2. Find the line dns_name_format = {fs_id}.efs.{region}.amazonaws.com.

3. Change {region} with the ID for your AWS Region, for example us-west-2.

Now that the amazon-efs-utils package is installed and configured, you can mount your file system to your on-premises client.

Step 3: Mount the Amazon EFS File System on Your On-Premises Client

To mount the EFS file system on your on-premises client, first open a terminal on your on-premises Linux client. To mount the system, you need the file system ID, the mount target IP address for one of your mount targets, and the file system's AWS Region. If you created multiple mount targets for your file system, then you can choose any one of these.

When you have that information, you can mount your file system in three steps:

1. Choose your preferred IP address of the mount target in the Availability Zone. You can measure the latency from your on-premises Linux clients. To do so, use a terminal-based tool like **ping** against the IP address of your EC2 instances in different Availability Zones to find the one with the lowest latency.

2. Add an entry to your local **/etc/hosts** file with the file system ID and the mount target IP address, in the following format.

```
1 mount-target-IP-Address file-system-ID.efs.region.amazonaws.com
```

Example

```
1 192.0.2.0 fs-12345678.efs.us-west-2.amazonaws.com
```

1. Create a local directory to mount the file system to.
   Example

   ```
   1 mkdir ~/efs
   ```

2. Run the mount command to mount the file system.
   Example

   ```
   1 sudo mount -t efs fs-12345678 ~/efs
   ```

   If you want to use encryption of data in transit, your mount command looks something like the following.
   Example

   ```
   1 sudo mount -t efs -o tls fs-12345678 ~/efs
   ```

Now that you've mounted your Amazon EFS file system, you can test it out with the following procedure.

To test the Amazon EFS file system connection

1. Change directories to the new directory that you created with the following command.

   ```
   1 $ cd ~/efs
   ```

2. Make a subdirectory and change the ownership of that subdirectory to your EC2 instance user. Then, navigate to that new directory with the following commands.

   ```
   1 $ sudo mkdir getting-started
   2 $ sudo chown ec2-user getting-started
   3 $ cd getting-started
   ```

3. Create a text file with the following command.

   ```
   1 $ touch test-file.txt
   ```

4. List the directory contents with the following command.

   ```
   1 $ ls -al
   ```

As a result, the following file is created.

```
1 -rw-rw-r-- 1 username username 0 Nov 15 15:32 test-file.txt
```

You can also mount your file system automatically by adding an entry to the /etc/fstab file. For more information, see Mounting Your Amazon EFS File System Automatically.

Warning
Use the _netdev option, used to identify network file systems, when mounting your file system automatically. If _netdev is missing, your EC2 instance might stop responding. This result is because network file systems need to be initialized after the compute instance starts its networking. For more information, see Automatic Mounting Fails and the Instance Is Unresponsive.

Step 4: Clean Up Resources and Protect Your AWS Account

After you have finished this walkthrough, or if you don't want to explore the walkthroughs, you should follow these steps to clean up your resources and protect your AWS account.

To clean up resources and protect your AWS account

1. Unmount the Amazon EFS file system with the following command.

```
1 $ sudo umount ~/efs
```

2. Open the Amazon EFS console at https://console.aws.amazon.com/efs/.

3. Choose the Amazon EFS file system that you want to delete from the list of file systems.

4. For **Actions**, choose **Delete file system**.

5. In the **Permanently delete file system** dialog box, type the file system ID for the Amazon EFS file system that you want to delete, and then choose **Delete File System**.

6. Open the Amazon EC2 console at https://console.aws.amazon.com/ec2/.

7. In the navigation pane, choose **Security Groups**.

8. Select the name of the security group that you added the rule to for this walkthrough. **Warning** Don't delete the default security group for your VPC.

9. For **Actions**, choose **Edit inbound rules**.

10. Choose the X at the end of the inbound rule you added, and choose **Save**.

Walkthrough 6: Enforcing Encryption on an Amazon EFS File System at Rest

Following, you can find details about how to enforce encryption at rest using Amazon CloudWatch and AWS CloudTrail. This walkthrough is based upon the AWS whitepaper Encrypt Data at Rest with Amazon EFS Encrypted File Systems.

Note
Currently, you can't enforce encryption in transit.

Enforcing Encryption at Rest

Your organization might require the encryption at rest of all data that meets a specific classification or that is associated with a particular application, workload, or environment. You can enforce policies for data encryption at rest for Amazon EFS file systems by using detective controls. These controls detect the creation of a file system and verify that encryption at rest is enabled.

If a file system that doesn't have encryption at rest is detected, you can respond in a number of ways. These range from deleting the file system and mount targets to notifying an administrator.

If you want to delete an unencrypted-at-rest file system but want to retain the data, first create a new encrypted-at-rest file system. Next, copy the data over to the new encrypted-at-rest file system. After the data is copied over, you can delete the unencrypted-at-rest file system.

Detecting Files Systems That Are Unencrypted at Rest

You can create an CloudWatch alarm to monitor CloudTrail logs for the `CreateFileSystem` event. You can then trigger the alarm to notify an administrator if the file system that was created was unencrypted at rest.

Create a Metric Filter

To create a CloudWatch alarm that is triggered when an unencrypted Amazon EFS file system is created, use the following procedure.

Before you begin, you must have an existing trail created that is sending CloudTrail logs to a CloudWatch Logs log group. For more information, see Sending Events to CloudWatch Logs in the *AWS CloudTrail User Guide*.

To create a metric filter

1. Open the CloudWatch console at https://console.aws.amazon.com/cloudwatch/.

2. In the navigation pane, choose **Logs**.

3. In the list of log groups, choose the log group that you created for CloudTrail log events.

4. Choose **Create Metric Filter**.

5. On the** Define Logs Metric Filter** page, choose **Filter Pattern** and then type the following:

```
1 { ($.eventName = CreateFileSystem) && ($.responseElements.encrypted IS FALSE) }
```

6. Choose **Assign Metric**.

7. For **Filter Name**, type **UnencryptedFileSystemCreated**.

8. For **Metric Namespace**, type **CloudTrailMetrics**.

9. For **Metric Name**, type **UnencryptedFileSystemCreatedEventCount**.

10. Choose **Show advanced metric settings**.

11. For **Metric Value**, type **1**.

12. Choose **Create Filter**.

Create an Alarm

After you create the metric filter, use the following procedure to create an alarm.

To create an alarm

1. On the **Filters** for the **Log_Group_Name** page, next to the **UnencryptedFileSystemCreated** filter name, choose **Create Alarm**.

2. On the **Create Alarm** page, set the following parameters:

   - For **Name**, type **Unencrypted File System Created**
   - For **Whenever**, do the following:
     - Set **is** to > = *1*
     - Set **for:** to *1* consecutive period(s).
   - For **Treat missing data as**, choose **good (not breaching threshold)**.
   - For **Actions**, do the following:
     - For **Whenever this alarm**, choose **State is ALARM**.
     - For **Send notification to**, choose **NotifyMe**, choose **New list**, and then type a unique topic name for this list.
     - For **Email list**, type in the email address where you want notifications sent. You should receive an email at this address to confirm that you created this alarm.
   - For **Alarm Preview**, do the following:
     - For **Period**, choose **1 Minute**.
     - For **Statistic**, choose **Standard** and **Sum**.

3. Choose **Create Alarm**.

Test the Alarm for the Creation of Unencrypted File Systems

You can test the alarm by creating an unencrypted-at-rest file system, as follows.

To test the alarm by creating an unencrypted-at-rest file system

1. Open the Amazon EFS console at https://console.aws.amazon.com/efs.

2. Choose **Create File System**.

3. From the **VPC** list, choose your default VPC.

4. Choose all the Availability Zones. Ensure that the default subnets, automatic IP addresses, and the default security groups are chosen. These are your mount targets.

5. Choose **Next Step**.

6. Name your file system and keep **Enable encryption** unchecked to create an unencrypted file system.

7. Choose **Next Step**.

8. Choose **Create File System**.

Your trail logs the `CreateFileSystem` operation and delivers the event to your CloudWatch Logs log group. The event triggers your metric alarm and CloudWatch Logs sends you a notification about the change.

Walkthrough 7: Sync Files from an On-Premises File System to Amazon EFS by Using EFS File Sync

This walkthrough shows the steps how to sync files from an on-premises file system to Amazon EFS using EFS File Sync.

Topics

- Before You Begin
- Step 1: Create a Sync Agent
- Step 2: Create a Sync Task
- Step 3: Sync Your Source File System to Amazon EFS
- Step 4: Access Your Files
- Step 5: Clean Up

Before You Begin

In this walkthrough, we assume the following:

- You have a Network File System (NFS) file server in your on-premises data center.
- You have a VMware ESXi Hypervisor host in your on-premises data center.
- You have created an Amazon EFS file system. If you don't have an Amazon EFS file system, create one now and come back to this walkthrough when you are done. For more information about how to create an Amazon EFS file system, see Getting Started with Amazon Elastic File System.

You can securely and efficiently copy your files over the Internet or use AWS Direct Connect. For information about how to use AWS Direct Connect , see Walkthrough 5: Create and Mount a File System On-Premises with AWS Direct Connect.

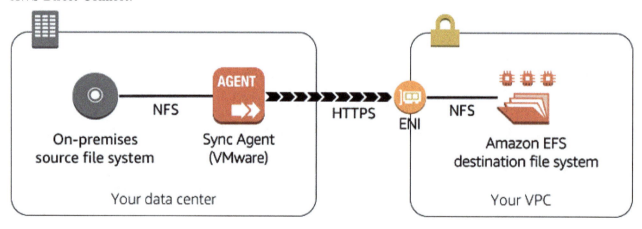

Step 1: Create a Sync Agent

To create a sync agent, you download a virtual machine (VM) image and deploy it into your on-premises environment so that it can mount your source file system. Once deployed, you activate the agent to securely associate it with your AWS account.

To create a sync agent for on-premises data

1. Open the Amazon EFS Management Console at https://console.aws.amazon.com/efs/.

2. Choose **File syncs**. If you haven't yet used EFS File Sync in this AWS Region, you see an introductory page. Choose **Get started** to open the **Select a host platform** page.

If you have previously used EFS File Sync in this AWS Region, choose **Agents** from the left navigation, and then choose **Create sync agent** to open the **Select a host platform** page.

3. From the **Select host platform** page, choose **VMware ESXi**, and then choose **Download image**. The virtual machine (VM) image will begin downloading.

4. When the download completes, deploy the VM to your VMware ESXi hypervisor and, use the VMware client to configure the VM. We recommend a VM with 4 vCPUs, 32 GB of memory, 10 Gigabit networking, and an 80 GB root volume.

5. Start the VM, and then take note of the VM IP address. This VM must be able to mount your source file system using NFS. **Note**
Although it's not required, we recommend that you use paravirtualized network controllers for your VMware ESXi VM.
You don't need to add additional disks to the VM. EFS File Sync uses only the root disk.

6. On the Amazon EFS Console, choose **Next: Connect to agent**

7. For** IP address**, type the VM's IP address, and then choose **Next: Activate agent**. Your browser will connect to this IP address to get a unique activation key from your sync agent. This key securely associates your sync agent with your AWS account. This IP address doesn't need to be accessible from outside your network, but must be accessible from your browser.

8. On the** Activate agent** page, type a name for your sync agent, and then choose **Activate agent**.

At this point, you should see your activated sync agent on the Amazon EFS console.

Step 2: Create a Sync Task

Create a sync task and configure the source and destination file systems.

To create a sync task

1. Choose **Create sync task**. The **Configure source location** page appears.

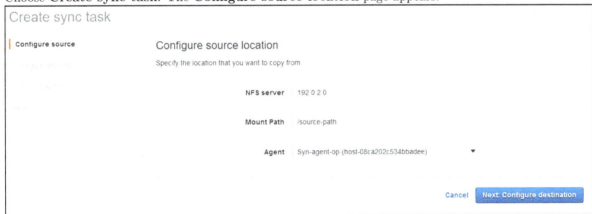

2. Provide the following information for the source file system:

- For **NFS server**, type the domain name or IP address of the source NFS server.
- For **Mount Path**, type the mount path for your source file system.
- For **Agent**, choose the sync agent that you created earlier.

3. Choose **Next: Configure destination**. The **Configure destination location** page appears.

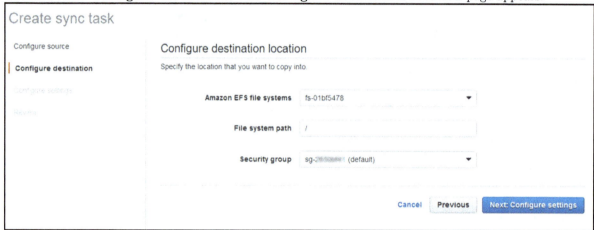

4. Provide the following information for the destination file system:

- For **Amazon EFS file system**, choose the EFS file system you want to sync to. If you don't have an Amazon EFS file system, create one now and restart this walkthrough when you are done. For more information about how to create an Amazon EFS file system, see Getting Started with Amazon Elastic File System.
- For **File system path**, type the path of the file system that you want to write data to. This path must exist in the destination file system.
- For **Security group**, choose a security group that allows access to the destination Amazon EFS file system you selected.

5. Choose **Next: Configure settings**. The **Configure sync settings** page appears.

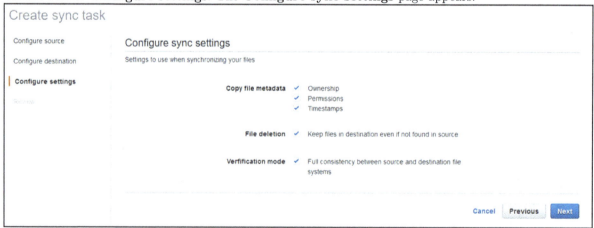

6. Configure the default settings that you want this sync task to use for synchronizing your files: **Note** You can override these settings later when you start a sync task.

- Choose **Ownership (User/Group ID)** to copy the user and group IDs from the source files.
- Choose **Permissions** to copy the source files permissions.
- Choose **Timestamps** to copy time stamps from the source files.
- Choose **File deletion** to keep all files in the destination that are not found in the source file system. If this box is cleared, all files in the destination that are not found in the source file system will be deleted.

- Choose **Verification mode** to check that the destination file system is an exact copy of the source file system after the sync task completes. If you do not choose this option, only the data that is transferred is verified. Changes made to files while they are being actively transferred and changes made to files that are not actively being transferred, will not be discovered. We recommend choosing full verification.

7. Choose **Next: Review and Create**, and then review your sync task settings. When you are ready, choose **Create sync task**.

Your sync task is created. The status of the task show as **Available** when the source and destination file systems have been mounted.

The **Details** tab shows the status and settings for your source and destination file systems.

Step 3: Sync Your Source File System to Amazon EFS

Now that you have a sync task, you can start your sync task to begin syncing files from the source file system to the destination Amazon EFS file system.

To sync the source file system

1. On the Tasks page, choose the sync task you just created. The Details tab shows the status of your sync task.

2. In the **Actions** menu, choose **Start**.

3. In the **Start sync task** dialog box, you can modify the settings for your sync task and choose** Start**.

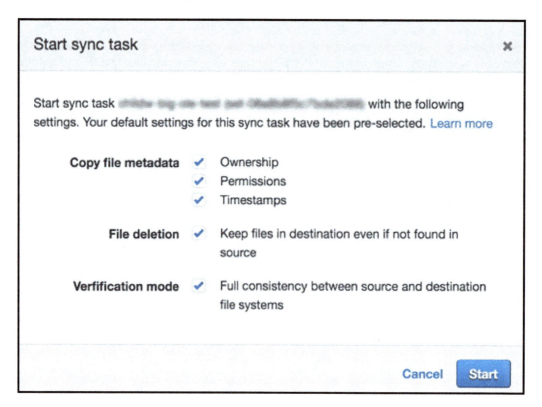

4. Choose **Start** to start syncing files.

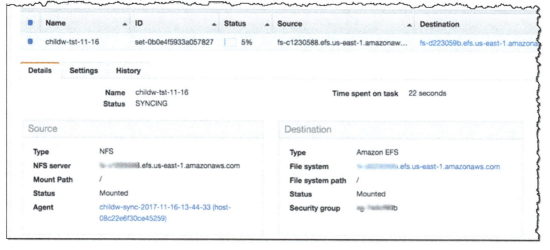

5. When the sync task starts, the **Status** column shows the progress of the sync task. As the sync task begins preparation, the status changes from **Starting** to **Preparing**. When the task starts to sync files, the status changes from **Preparing** to **Syncing**. When file consistency verification starts, the status changes to **Verifying**. When the sync task is done, the status changes to **Success**.

Step 4: Access Your Files

To access your files, you connect to the Amazon EFS file system from an Amazon EC2 instance or use AWS Direct Connect.

For information about how to connect using Amazon EC2, see Connect to Your Amazon EC2 Instance and Mount the Amazon EFS File System.

For information about how to connect using AWS Direct Connect, see Walkthrough 5: Create and Mount a File System On-Premises with AWS Direct Connect.

Step 5: Clean Up

If you no longer need the resources you created, you should remove them:

- Delete the task you created. For more information, see Deleting a Sync Task.
- Delete the sync agent you created. This will not delete the VM you deployed to your on-premises hypervisor.
- Clean up the Amazon EFS resources you created. For more information, see Step 5: Clean Up Resources and Protect Your AWS Account.

Walkthrough 8: Sync a File System from Amazon EC2 to Amazon EFS Using EFS File Sync

This walkthrough shows the steps how to sync files from a file system that is in AWS to Amazon EFS using EFS File Sync.

Topics

- Before You Begin
- Step 1: Create a Sync Agent
- Step 2: Create a Sync Task
- Step 3: Sync Your Source File System to Amazon EFS
- Step 4: Access Your Files
- Step 4: Clean Up

Before You Begin

In this walkthrough, we assume the following:

- You have a Network File System (NFS) file server on an Amazon EC2 instance.
- You have created an Amazon EFS file system. If you don't have an Amazon EFS file system, create one now and come back to this walkthrough when you are done. For more information about how to create an Amazon EFS file system, see Getting Started with Amazon Elastic File System.

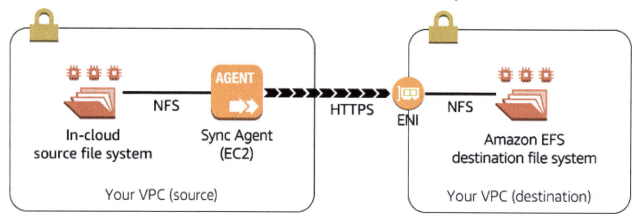

Step 1: Create a Sync Agent

To create a sync agent in Amazon EC2, you will use the AMI provided to create an Amazon EC2 instance that can mount the source file system in your AWS environment. This Amazon EC2 instance will run in the same AWS Region as your source file system. Once deployed, you will activate the agent to securely associate it with your AWS account.

To create a sync agent for data in AWS

1. Open the Amazon EFS Management Console at https://console.aws.amazon.com/efs/ and choose the AWS Region where you created your source file system.

2. Choose **File syncs**. If you haven't used EFS File Sync in this AWS Region, you see an introductory page. Choose **Get started** to open the **Select a host platform** page.

   If you have previously used EFS File Sync in this AWS Region, choose **Agents** from the left navigation, and then choose **Create sync agent** to open the **Select a host platform** page.

3. From **Select a host platform** page, choose **Amazon EC2**, choose the AWS Region where your source file system is located and then choose **Launch instance**. You will be redirected to the **Choose an Instance Type** page in the Amazon EC2 Management Console in that AWS Region, where you can choose an instance type. **Note**
A sync agent syncs files to EFS file systems in the AWS region where the sync agent is activated. Standard Amazon EC2 rates apply to the instance.

4. On the **Choose an Instance Type** page, choose the hardware configuration of your instance. When deploying your sync agent on Amazon EC2, we recommend choosing one of the **Memory optimized** instance types for your sync agent. The instance size you choose must be at least **xlarge**.

5. Choose **Next: Configure Instance Details**.

6. On the **Configure Instance Details** page, choose a value for **Auto-assign Public IP**. If you want your instance to be accessible from the public internet, set **Auto-assign Public IP** to **Enable**. Otherwise, set **Auto-assign Public IP** to **Disable**.

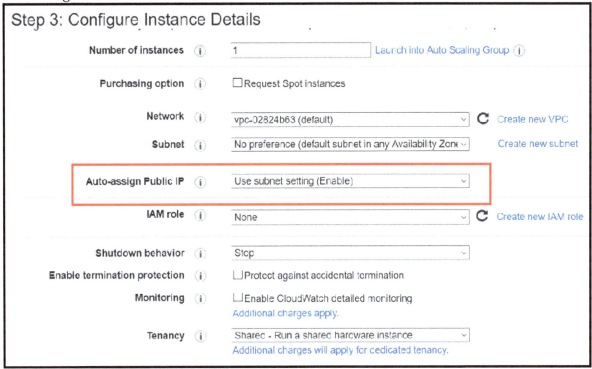

7. Choose Next: **Add Storage** and choose **Next: Add tags**. The EFS File Sync agent uses the root volume and doesn't require additional storage.

8. On the **Add Tags** page, you can optionally add tags to your instance. Then choose **Next: Configure Security Group**.

9. On the **Configure Security Group** page, add firewall rules for specific traffic to reach your instance. You can create a new security group or choose an existing security group. **Important**
At a minimum, your security group must allow inbound access to HTTP port 80 from your web browser to activate your sync agent.

10. Choose **Review and Launch** to review your configuration, then choose **Launch** to launch your instance. We recommend selecting an existing key pair or creating a new key pair for your instance. This key pair is not needed for normal operation of EFS File Sync, but it may be needed if you contact AWS to get support.

A confirmation page appears to say that your instance is launching.

11. Choose **View Instances** to close the confirmation page and return to the console. On the **Instances**

screen, you can view the status of your instance. It takes a short time for an instance to launch. When you launch an instance, its initial state is **pending**. After the instance starts, its state changes to **running**, and it's assigned a public DNS name and IP address.

12. Choose your instance and take note of the public IP address in the **Description** tab. You use this IP address to connect to your sync agent. **Note**
The IP address doesn't need to be accessible from outside your network. **Important**
If your source file system and destination Amazon EFS file system are in different AWS Regions, you open the Amazon EFS Console in the AWS Region where your destination Amazon EFS file system is located to connect.

13. Choose **File syncs**, choose **Create sync agent**, and then choose **Next: Connect to agent** on the **Select host platform** page.

14. For **IP address**, type the Amazon EC2 instance IP address, and then choose **Next: Activate agent**. Your browser will connect to this IP address to get a unique activation key from your sync agent. This key securely associates your sync agent with your AWS account. This IP address doesn't need to be accessible from outside your network, but must be accessible from your browser.

15. On the **Activate agent** page, type a name for your sync agent and choose **Activate agent**.

At this point, you should see your activated sync agent on the Amazon EFS console.

Step 2: Create a Sync Task

Create a sync task and configure the source and destination file systems.

To create a sync task

1. Choose **Create sync task**. The **Configure source location** page appears.

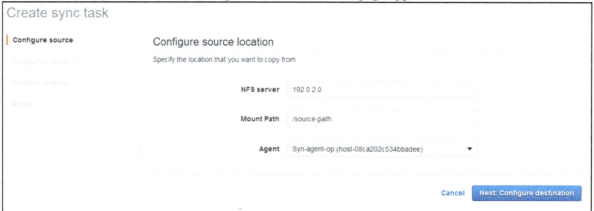

2. Provide the following information for the source file system:

   - For **NFS server**, type the domain name or IP address of the source NFS server.
   - For **Mount Path**, type the mount path for your source file system.
   - For **Agent**, choose the sync agent that you created earlier.

3. Choose **Next: Configure destination**. The **Configure destination location** page appears.

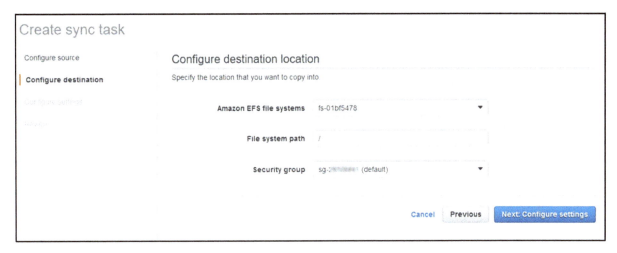

4. Provide the following information for the destination file system:

- For **Amazon EFS file system**, choose the EFS file system you want to sync to. If you don't have an Amazon EFS file system, create one now and restart this walkthrough when you are done. For more information about how to create an Amazon EFS file system, see Getting Started with Amazon Elastic File System.
- For **File system path**, type the path of the file system that you want to write data to. This path must exist in the destination file system.
- For **Security group**, choose a security group that allows access to the destination Amazon EFS file system you selected.

5. Choose **Next: Configure settings**. The **Configure sync settings** page appears.

6. Configure the default settings that you want this sync task to use for synchronizing your files: **Note** You can override these settings later when you start a sync task.

- Choose **Ownership (User/Group ID)** to copy the user and group IDs from the source files.
- Choose **Permissions** to copy the source files permissions.
- Choose **Timestamps** to copy time stamps from the source files.
- Choose **File deletion** to keep all files in the destination that are not found in the source file system. If this box is cleared, all files in the destination that are not found in the source file system will be deleted.
- Choose **Verification mode** to check that the destination file system is an exact copy of the source file system after the sync task completes. If you do not choose this option, only the data that is transferred is verified. Changes made to files while they are being actively transferred and changes made to files that are not actively being transferred, will not be discovered. We recommend choosing full verification.

7. Choose **Next: Review and Create**, and then review your sync task settings. When you are ready, choose **Create sync task**.

Your sync task is created. The status of the task will show as **Available** when the source and destination file systems have been mounted.

The **Details** tab shows the status and settings for your source and destination file systems.

Step 3: Sync Your Source File System to Amazon EFS

Now that you have a sync task, you can start your sync task to begin syncing files from the source file system to the destination EFS File Sync file system.

To sync the source file system

1. On the Tasks page, choose the sync task you just created. The Details tab shows the status of your sync task.

2. In the **Actions** menu, choose **Start**.

3. In the **Start sync task** dialog box, you can modify the settings for your sync task and choose** Start**.

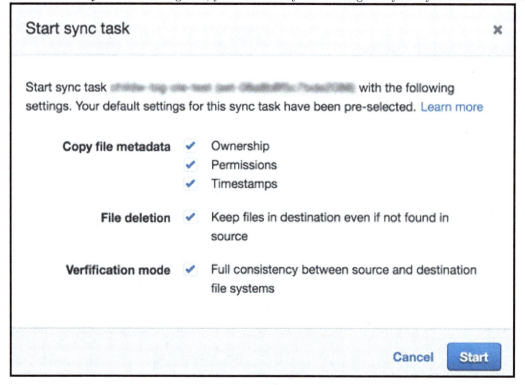

4. Choose **Start** to start syncing files.

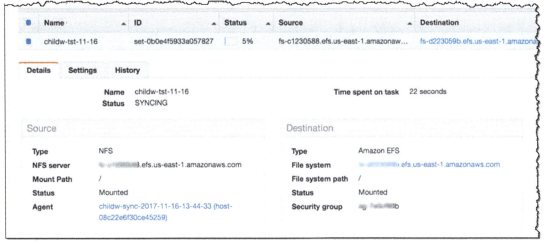

5. When the sync task starts, the **Status** column shows the progress of the sync task. As the sync task begins preparation, the status changes from **Starting** to **Preparing**. When the task starts to sync files, the status changes from **Preparing** to **Syncing**. When file consistency verification starts, the status changes to **Verifying**. When the sync task is done, the status changes to **Success**.

Step 4: Access Your Files

To access your files, connect to the Amazon EFS file system from an Amazon EC2 instance or use AWS Direct Connect.

For information about how to connect using Amazon EC2, see Connect to Your Amazon EC2 Instance and Mount the Amazon EFS File System.

For information about how to connect using AWS Direct Connect, see Walkthrough 5: Create and Mount a File System On-Premises with AWS Direct Connect.

Step 4: Clean Up

If you no longer need the resources you created, you should remove them to protect your account:

If you no longer need the resources you created, you should remove them:

- Delete the task you created. For more information, see Deleting a Sync Task.
- Delete the sync agent you created. This will not delete the Amazon EC2 instance you launched. .
- Clean up the Amazon EFS resources you created. For more information, see Step 5: Clean Up Resources and Protect Your AWS Account.
- Clean up your instance if you created your EFS File Sync on Amazon EC2. For more information, see Step 3: Clean Up Your Instance in the *Amazon EC2 User Guide for Linux Instances*.

Authentication and Access Control for Amazon EFS

Access to Amazon EFS or Amazon EFS File Sync requires credentials that AWS can use to authenticate your requests. Those credentials must have permissions to access AWS resources, such an Amazon EFS file system or an Amazon Elastic Compute Cloud (Amazon EC2) instance. The following sections provide details on how you can use AWS Identity and Access Management (IAM) and Amazon EFS to help secure your resources by controlling who can access them.

- Authentication
- Access Control

Authentication

You can access AWS as any of the following types of identities:

- **AWS account root user** – When you sign up for AWS, you provide an email address and password that is associated with your AWS account. This is your *AWS account root user*. Its credentials provide complete access to all of your AWS resources. **Important**
  For security reasons, we recommend that you use the root user only to create an *administrator*, which is an *IAM user* with full permissions to your AWS account. You can then use this administrator user to create other IAM users and roles with limited permissions. For more information, see IAM Best Practices and Creating an Admin User and Group in the *IAM User Guide*.

- **IAM user** – An IAM user is simply an identity within your AWS account that has specific custom permissions (for example, permissions to create a file system in Amazon EFS). You can use an IAM user name and password to sign in to secure AWS webpages like the AWS Management Console, AWS Discussion Forums, or the AWS Support Center.

  In addition to a user name and password, you can also generate access keys for each user. You can use these keys when you access AWS services programmatically, either through one of the several SDKs or by using the AWS Command Line Interface (CLI). The SDK and CLI tools use the access keys to cryptographically sign your request. If you don't use the AWS tools, you must sign the request yourself. Amazon EFS supports *Signature Version 4*, a protocol for authenticating inbound API requests. For more information about authenticating requests, see Signature Version 4 Signing Process in the *AWS General Reference*.

- **IAM role** – An IAM role is another IAM identity that you can create in your account that has specific permissions. It is similar to an *IAM user*, but it is not associated with a specific person. An IAM role enables you to obtain temporary access keys that can be used to access AWS services and resources. IAM roles with temporary credentials are useful in the following situations:

  - **Federated user access** – Instead of creating an IAM user, you can use preexisting user identities from AWS Directory Service, your enterprise user directory, or a web identity provider. These are known as *federated users*. AWS assigns a role to a federated user when access is requested through an identity provider. For more information about federated users, see Federated Users and Roles in the *IAM User Guide*.

  - **Cross-account administration** – You can use an IAM role in your account to grant another AWS account permissions to administer your account's Amazon EFS resources. For an example, see Tutorial: Delegate Access Across AWS Accounts Using IAM Roles in the *IAM User Guide*. Note that you can't mount Amazon EFS file systems from across VPCs or accounts. For more information, see Managing File System Network Accessibility

- **AWS service access** – You can use an IAM role in your account to grant an AWS service permissions to access your account's resources. For example, you can create a role that allows Amazon Redshift to access an Amazon S3 bucket on your behalf and then load data from that bucket into an Amazon Redshift cluster. For more information, see Creating a Role to Delegate Permissions to an AWS Service in the *IAM User Guide*.

- **Applications running on Amazon EC2** – You can use an IAM role to manage temporary credentials for applications running on an EC2 instance and making AWS API requests. This is preferable to storing access keys within the EC2 instance. To assign an AWS role to an EC2 instance and make it available to all of its applications, you create an instance profile that is attached to the instance. An instance profile contains the role and enables programs running on the EC2 instance to get temporary credentials. For more information, see Using Roles for Applications on Amazon EC2 in the *IAM User Guide*.

Access Control

You can have valid credentials to authenticate your requests, but unless you have permissions you cannot create or access Amazon Elastic File System resources. For example, you must have permissions to create an Amazon EFS file system.

The following sections describe how to manage permissions for Amazon Elastic File System. We recommend that you read the overview first.

- Overview of Managing Access Permissions to Your Amazon EFS Resources
- Using Identity-Based Policies (IAM Policies) for Amazon Elastic File System

Overview of Managing Access Permissions to Your Amazon EFS Resources

Every AWS resource is owned by an AWS account, and permissions to create or access a resource are governed by permissions policies. An account administrator can attach permissions policies to IAM identities (that is, users, groups, and roles), and some services (such as AWS Lambda) also support attaching permissions policies to resources.

Note

An *account administrator* (or administrator user) is a user with administrator privileges. For more information, see IAM Best Practices in the *IAM User Guide*.

When granting permissions, you decide who is getting the permissions, the resources they get permissions for, and the specific actions that you want to allow on those resources.

Topics

- Amazon Elastic File System Resources and Operations
- Understanding Resource Ownership
- Managing Access to Resources
- Specifying Policy Elements: Actions, Effects, and Principals
- Specifying Conditions in a Policy

Amazon Elastic File System Resources and Operations

In Amazon Elastic File System, the primary resource is a *file system*. Amazon Elastic File System also supports additional resource types, the *mount target* and *tags*. However, for Amazon EFS, you can create mount targets and tags only in the context of an existing file system. Mount targets and tags are referred to as *subresource*.

These resources and subresources have unique Amazon Resource Names (ARNs) associated with them as shown in the following table.

Resource Type	ARN Format
File system	arn:aws:elasticfilesystem:region:account-id:file-system/file-system-id

Amazon EFS provides a set of operations to work with Amazon EFS resources. For a list of available operations, see Amazon Elastic File System Actions.

Understanding Resource Ownership

The AWS account owns the resources that are created in the account, regardless of who created the resources. Specifically, the resource owner is the AWS account of the principal entity (that is, the root account, an IAM user, or an IAM role) that authenticates the resource creation request. The following examples illustrate how this works:

- If you use the root account credentials of your AWS account to create a file system, your AWS account is the owner of the resource (in Amazon EFS, the resource is the file system).
- If you create an IAM user in your AWS account and grant permissions to create a file system to that user, the user can create a file system. However, your AWS account, to which the user belongs, owns the file system resource.

- If you create an IAM role in your AWS account with permissions to create a file system, anyone who can assume the role can create a file system. Your AWS account, to which the role belongs, owns the file system resource.

Managing Access to Resources

A *permissions policy* describes who has access to what. The following section explains the available options for creating permissions policies.

Note
This section discusses using IAM in the context of Amazon Elastic File System. It doesn't provide detailed information about the IAM service. For complete IAM documentation, see What Is IAM? in the *IAM User Guide*. For information about IAM policy syntax and descriptions, see AWS IAM Policy Reference in the *IAM User Guide*.

Policies attached to an IAM identity are referred to as *identity-based* policies (IAM polices) and policies attached to a resource are referred to as *resource-based* policies. Amazon Elastic File System supports only identity-based policies (IAM policies).

Topics

- Identity-Based Policies (IAM Policies)
- Resource-Based Policies

Identity-Based Policies (IAM Policies)

You can attach policies to IAM identities. For example, you can do the following:

- **Attach a permissions policy to a user or a group in your account** – To grant a user permissions to create an Amazon EFS resource, such as a file system, you can attach a permissions policy to a user or group that the user belongs to.

- **Attach a permissions policy to a role (grant cross-account permissions)** – You can attach an identity-based permissions policy to an IAM role to grant cross-account permissions. For example, the administrator in Account A can create a role to grant cross-account permissions to another AWS account (for example, Account B) or an AWS service as follows:

  1. Account A administrator creates an IAM role and attaches a permissions policy to the role that grants permissions on resources in Account A.

  2. Account A administrator attaches a trust policy to the role identifying Account B as the principal who can assume the role.

  3. Account B administrator can then delegate permissions to assume the role to any users in Account B. Doing this allows users in Account B to create or access resources in Account A. The principal in the trust policy can also be an AWS service principal if you want to grant an AWS service permissions to assume the role.

  For more information about using IAM to delegate permissions, see Access Management in the *IAM User Guide*.

The following is an example policy that allows a user to perform the `CreateFileSystem` action for your AWS account.

```
1  {
2    "Version": "2012-10-17",
3    "Statement": [
4      {
5        "Sid" : "Stmt1EFSpermissions",
```

```
6      "Effect": "Allow",
7      "Action": [
8        "elasticfilesystem:CreateFileSystem",
9        "elasticfilesystem:CreateMountTarget"
10     ],
11     "Resource": "arn:aws:elasticfilesystem:us-west-2:account-id:file-system/*"
12   },
13   {
14   "Sid" : "Stmt2EC2permissions",
15   "Effect": "Allow",
16   "Action": [
17     "ec2:DescribeSubnets",
18     "ec2:CreateNetworkInterface",
19     "ec2:DescribeNetworkInterfaces"
20   ],
21     "Resource": "*"
22   }
23 ]
```

For more information about using identity-based policies with Amazon EFS, see Using Identity-Based Policies (IAM Policies) for Amazon Elastic File System. For more information about users, groups, roles, and permissions, see Identities (Users, Groups, and Roles) in the *IAM User Guide*.

Resource-Based Policies

Other services, such as Amazon S3, also support resource-based permissions policies. For example, you can attach a policy to an S3 bucket to manage access permissions to that bucket. Amazon Elastic File System doesn't support resource-based policies.

Specifying Policy Elements: Actions, Effects, and Principals

For each Amazon Elastic File System resource (see Amazon Elastic File System Resources and Operations), the service defines a set of API operations (see Actions). To grant permissions for these API operations, Amazon EFS defines a set of actions that you can specify in a policy. For example, for the Amazon EFS file system resource, the following actions are defined: `CreateFileSystem`, `DeleteFileSystem`, and `DescribeFileSystems`. Note that, performing an API operation can require permissions for more than one action.

The following are the most basic policy elements:

- **Resource** – In a policy, you use an Amazon Resource Name (ARN) to identify the resource to which the policy applies. For more information, see Amazon Elastic File System Resources and Operations.
- **Action** – You use action keywords to identify resource operations that you want to allow or deny. For example, depending on the specified `Effect`, `elasticfilesystem:CreateFileSystem` either allows or denies the user permissions to perform the Amazon Elastic File System `CreateFileSystem` operation.
- **Effect** – You specify the effect when the user requests the specific action—this can be either allow or deny. If you don't explicitly grant access to (allow) a resource, access is implicitly denied. You can also explicitly deny access to a resource, which you might do to make sure that a user cannot access it, even if a different policy grants access.
- **Principal** – In identity-based policies (IAM policies), the user that the policy is attached to is the implicit principal. For resource-based policies, you specify the user, account, service, or other entity that you want to receive permissions (applies to resource-based policies only). Amazon EFS doesn't support resource-based policies.

To learn more about IAM policy syntax and descriptions, see AWS IAM Policy Reference in the *IAM User Guide*.

For a table showing all of the Amazon Elastic File System API actions, see Amazon EFS API Permissions: Actions, Resources, and Conditions Reference.

Specifying Conditions in a Policy

When you grant permissions, you can use the IAM policy language to specify the conditions when a policy should take effect. For example, you might want a policy to be applied only after a specific date. For more information about specifying conditions in a policy language, see Condition in the *IAM User Guide*.

To express conditions, you use predefined condition keys. There are no condition keys specific to Amazon Elastic File System. However, there are AWS-wide condition keys that you can use as appropriate. For a complete list of AWS-wide keys, see Available Keys for Conditions in the *IAM User Guide*.

Note
Do not use the `aws:SourceIp` AWS-wide condition for the `CreateMountTarget`, `DeleteMountTarget`, or `ModifyMountTargetSecurityGroup` actions. Amazon EFS provisions mount targets by using its own IP address, not the IP address of the originating request.

Using Identity-Based Policies (IAM Policies) for Amazon Elastic File System

This topic provides examples of identity-based policies that demonstrate how an account administrator can attach permissions policies to IAM identities (that is, users, groups, and roles) and thereby grant permissions to perform operations on Amazon EFS resources.

Important
We recommend that you first review the introductory topics that explain the basic concepts and options available for you to manage access to your Amazon Elastic File System resources. For more information, see Overview of Managing Access Permissions to Your Amazon EFS Resources.

The sections in this topic cover the following:

- Permissions Required to Use the Amazon EFS Console
- AWS Managed (Predefined) Policies for Amazon EFS
- Customer Managed Policy Examples

The following shows an example of a permissions policy.

```
1  {
2    "Version": "2012-10-17",
3    "Statement": [
4      {
5        "Sid" : "AllowFileSystemPermissions",
6        "Effect": "Allow",
7        "Action": [
8          "elasticfilesystem:CreateFileSystem",
9          "elasticfilesystem:CreateMountTarget"
10       ],
11       "Resource": "arn:aws:elasticfilesystem:us-west-2:account-id:file-system/*"
12     },
13     {
14       "Sid" : "AllowEC2Permissions",
15       "Effect": "Allow",
16       "Action": [
17         "ec2:DescribeSubnets",
18         "ec2:CreateNetworkInterface",
19         "ec2:DescribeNetworkInterfaces"
20       ],
21       "Resource": "*"
22     }
23   ]
24 }
```

The policy has two statements:

- The first statement grants permissions for two Amazon EFS actions (`elasticfilesystem:CreateFileSystem` and `elasticfilesystem:CreateMountTarget`) on a resource using the *Amazon Resource Name (ARN)* for the file system. The ARN specifies a wildcard character (*) because you don't know the file system ID until after you create a file system.
- The second statement grants permissions for some of the Amazon EC2 actions because the `elasticfilesystem:CreateMountTarget` action in the first statement requires permissions for specific Amazon EC2 actions. Because these Amazon EC2 actions don't support resource-level permissions, the policy specifies the wildcard character (*) as the `Resource` value instead of specifying a file system ARN.

The policy doesn't specify the `Principal` element because in an identity-based policy you don't specify the principal who gets the permission. When you attach policy to a user, the user is the implicit principal. When you attach a permissions policy to an IAM role, the principal identified in the role's trust policy gets the permissions.

For a table showing all of the Amazon Elastic File System API actions and the resources that they apply to, see Amazon EFS API Permissions: Actions, Resources, and Conditions Reference.

Permissions Required to Use the Amazon EFS Console

The permissions reference table lists the Amazon EFS API operations and shows the required permissions for each operation. For more information about Amazon EFS API operations, see Amazon EFS API Permissions: Actions, Resources, and Conditions Reference.

To use the Amazon EFS console, you need to grant permissions for additional actions as shown in the following permissions policy:

```
1  {
2    "Version": "2012-10-17",
3    "Statement": [
4      {
5        "Sid" : "Stmt1AddtionalEC2PermissionsForConsole",
6        "Effect": "Allow",
7        "Action": [
8          "ec2:DescribeAvailabilityZones",
9          "ec2:DescribeSecurityGroups",
10         "ec2:DescribeVpcs",
11         "ec2:DescribeVpcAttribute"
12
13       ],
14       "Resource": "*"
15     }
16     {
17       "Sid" : "Stmt2AdditionalKMSPermissionsForConsole",
18       "Effect": "Allow",
19       "Action": [
20         "kms:ListAliases",
21         "kms:DescribeKey"
22       ],
23       "Resource": "*"
24     }
25   ]
26 }
```

The Amazon EFS console needs these additional permissions for the following reasons:

- Permissions for the Amazon EFS actions enable the console to display Amazon EFS resources in the account.
- The console needs permissions for the `ec2` actions to query Amazon EC2 so it can display Availability Zones, VPCs, security groups, and account attributes.
- The console needs permissions for the `kms` actions to create an encrypted file system. For more information on encrypted file systems, see Encrypting Data and Metadata in EFS.

AWS Managed (Predefined) Policies for Amazon EFS

AWS addresses many common use cases by providing standalone IAM policies that are created and administered by AWS. Managed policies grant necessary permissions for common use cases so you can avoid having to investigate what permissions are needed. For more information, see AWS Managed Policies in the *IAM User Guide*.

The following AWS managed policies, which you can attach to users in your account, are specific to Amazon EFS:

- **AmazonElasticFileSystemReadOnlyAccess** – Grants read-only access to Amazon EFS resources.
- **AmazonElasticFileSystemFullAccess** – Grants full access to Amazon EFS resources.

Note

You can review these permissions policies by signing in to the IAM console and searching for specific policies there.

You can also create your own custom IAM policies to allow permissions for Amazon EFS API actions. You can attach these custom policies to the IAM users or groups that require those permissions.

Customer Managed Policy Examples

In this section, you can find example user policies that grant permissions for various Amazon EFS actions. These policies work when you are using AWS SDKs or the AWS CLI. When you are using the console, you need to grant additional permissions specific to the console, which is discussed in Permissions Required to Use the Amazon EFS Console.

Note

All examples use the us-west-2 region and contain fictitious account IDs.

Topics

- Example 1: Allow a User to Create a Mount Target and Tags on an Existing File System
- Example 2: Allow a User to Perform All Amazon EFS Actions

Example 1: Allow a User to Create a Mount Target and Tags on an Existing File System

The following permissions policy grants the user permissions to create mount targets and tags on a particular file system in the `us-west-2` region. To create mount targets, permissions for specific Amazon EC2 actions are also required and are included in the permissions policy.

```
1  {
2    "Version": "2012-10-17",
3    "Statement": [
4      {
5        "Sid" : "Stmt1CreateMountTargetAndTag",
6        "Effect": "Allow",
7        "Action": [
8          "elasticfilesystem:CreateMountTarget",
9          "elasticfilesystem:DescribeMountTargets",
10         "elasticfilesystem:CreateTags",
11         "elasticfilesystem:DescribeTags"
12       ],
13       "Resource": "arn:aws:elasticfilesystem:us-west-2:123456789012:file-system/file-system-ID"
14     },
15     {
16       "Sid" : "Stmt2AdditionalEC2PermissionsToCreateMountTarget",
```

```
17        "Effect": "Allow",
18        "Action": [
19          "ec2:DescribeSubnets",
20          "ec2:CreateNetworkInterface",
21          "ec2:DescribeNetworkInterfaces"
22        ],
23        "Resource": "*"
24      }
25    ]
26 }
```

Example 2: Allow a User to Perform All Amazon EFS Actions

The following permissions policy uses a wildcard character ("elasticfilesystem:*") to allow all Amazon EFS actions in the us-west-2 region. Because some of the Amazon EFS actions also require permissions for Amazon EC2 actions, the policy also grants permissions for all those actions.

```
1  {
2    "Version": "2012-10-17",
3    "Statement": [
4      {
5        "Sid" : "Stmt1PermissionForAllEFSActions",
6        "Effect": "Allow",
7        "Action": "elasticfilesystem:*",
8        "Resource": "arn:aws:elasticfilesystem:us-west-2:123456789012:file-system/*"
9      },
10     {
11       "Sid" : "Stmt2RequiredEC2PermissionsForAllEFSActions",
12       "Effect": "Allow",
13       "Action": [
14         "ec2:DescribeSubnets",
15         "ec2:CreateNetworkInterface",
16         "ec2:DescribeNetworkInterfaces",
17         "ec2:DeleteNetworkInterface",
18         "ec2:ModifyNetworkInterfaceAttribute",
19         "ec2:DescribeNetworkInterfaceAttribute"
20       ],
21       "Resource": "*"
22     }
23
24   ]
25 }
```

Amazon EFS API Permissions: Actions, Resources, and Conditions Reference

When you are setting up Access Control and writing a permissions policy that you can attach to an IAM identity (identity-based policies), you can use the following table as a reference. The table lists each Amazon EFS API operation, the corresponding actions for which you can grant permissions to perform the action, and the AWS resource for which you can grant the permissions. You specify the actions in the policy's `Action` field, and you specify the resource value in the policy's `Resource` field.

You can use AWS-wide condition keys in your Amazon EFS policies to express conditions. For a complete list of AWS-wide keys, see Available Keys in the *IAM User Guide.*

Note

To specify an action, use the `elasticfilesystem:` prefix followed by the API operation name (for example, `elasticfilesystem:CreateFileSystem`).

If you see an expand arrow () in the upper-right corner of the table, you can open the table in a new window. To close the window, choose the close button (**X**) in the lower-right corner.

Amazon EFS API and Required Permissions for Actions

Amazon EFS API Operations	Required Permissions (API Actions)	Resources
CreateFileSystem	elasticfilesystem:CreateFileSystem For information about KMS-related permissions for encrypted file systems, see Amazon EFS Key Policies for AWS KMS.	`arn:aws:` `elasticfilesystem:region` `:account-id:file-system` `/*`
CreateMountTarget	`elasticfilesystem:` `CreateMountTarget ec2` `:DescribeSubnets ec2:` `DescribeNetworkInterfaces` `ec2:` `CreateNetworkInterface`	arn:aws:elasticfilesystem:region:account-id:file-system/file-system-id
CreateTags	elasticfilesystem:CreateTags	arn:aws:elasticfilesystem:region:account-id:file-system/filesystem-id
DeleteFileSystem	elasticfilesystem:DeleteFileSystem	arn:aws:elasticfilesystem:region:account-id:file-system/filesystem-id
DeleteMountTarget	`elasticfilesystem:` `DeleteMountTarget ec2` `:DeleteNetworkInterface`	arn:aws:elasticfilesystem:region:account-id:file-system/filesystem-id
DeleteTags	elasticfilesystem:DeleteTags	arn:aws:elasticfilesystem:region:account-id:file-system/filesystem-id
DescribeFileSystems	elasticfilesystem:DescribeFileSystems	`arn:aws:` `elasticfilesystem:region` `:account-id:file-system/` `filesystem-id` or `arn:aws:` `elasticfilesystem:region` `:account-id:file-system` `/*`

Amazon EFS API Operations	Required Permissions (API Actions)	Resources
DescribeMountTargetSecurityGroups	`elasticfilesystem: DescribeMountTargetSecurit` `ec2: DescribeNetworkInterfaceAt`	arn:aws:elasticfilesystem:region:account-id:filesystem/filesystem-id
DescribeMountTargets	elasticfilesystem:DescribeMountTargets	arn:aws:elasticfilesystem:region:account-id:filesystem/filesystem-id
DescribeTags	elasticfilesystem:DescribeTags	arn:aws:elasticfilesystem:region:account-id:filesystem/filesystem-id
ModifyMountTargetSecurityGroups	`elasticfilesystem: ModifyMountTargetSecurityG` `ec2: ModifyNetworkInterfaceAttr`	arn:aws:elasticfilesystem:region:account-id:filesystem/filesystem-id

Amazon EFS API

The Amazon EFS API is a network protocol based on HTTP (RFC 2616). For each API call, you make an HTTP request to the region-specific Amazon EFS API endpoint for the AWS Region where you want to manage file systems. The API uses JSON (RFC 4627) documents for HTTP request/response bodies.

The Amazon EFS API is an RPC model, in which there is a fixed set of operations and the syntax for each operation is known to clients without any prior interaction. This section describes each API operation using an abstract RPC notation, with an operation name that does not appear on the wire. For each operation, the topic specifies the mapping to HTTP request elements.

The specific Amazon EFS operation to which a given request maps is determined by a combination of the request's method (GET, PUT, POST, or DELETE) and which of the various patterns its Request-URI matches. If the operation is PUT or POST, Amazon EFS extracts call arguments from the Request-URI path segment, query parameters, and the JSON object in the request body.

Note

Although the operation name, such as `CreateFileSystem`, does not appear on the wire these names are meaningful in IAM policies. For more information, see Authentication and Access Control for Amazon EFS. The operation name is also used to name commands in command-line tools and elements of the AWS SDK APIs. For example, there is a CLI command `create-file-system` that maps to the `CreateFileSystem` operation. It also appears in CloudTrail logs for Amazon EFS API calls.

API Endpoint

The API endpoint is the DNS name used as a host in the HTTP URI for the API calls. These API endpoints are region-specific and take the following form:

```
1 elasticfilesystem.aws-region.amazonaws.com
```

For example, the Amazon EFS API endpoint for the US West (Oregon) Region is:

```
1 elasticfilesystem.us-west-2.amazonaws.com
```

For a list of AWS Regions that Amazon EFS supports (where you can create and manage file systems), see Amazon Elastic File System in the *AWS General Reference*.

The region-specific API endpoint defines the scope of the Amazon EFS resources that are accessible when you make an API call. For example, when you call the `DescribeFileSystems` operation using the preceding endpoint, you get a list of file systems in the US West (Oregon) Region that have been created in your account.

API Version

The version of the API being used for a call is identified by the first path segment of the request URI, and its form is a ISO 8601 date. For example, see CreateFileSystem.

The documentation describes API version 2015-02-01.

Related Topics

The following sections provide descriptions of the API operations, how to create a signature for request authentication, and how to grant permissions for these API operations using the IAM policies.

- Authentication and Access Control for Amazon EFS
- Actions
- Data Types

Actions

The following actions are supported:

- CreateFileSystem
- CreateMountTarget
- CreateTags
- DeleteFileSystem
- DeleteMountTarget
- DeleteTags
- DescribeFileSystems
- DescribeMountTargets
- DescribeMountTargetSecurityGroups
- DescribeTags
- ModifyMountTargetSecurityGroups

CreateFileSystem

Creates a new, empty file system. The operation requires a creation token in the request that Amazon EFS uses to ensure idempotent creation (calling the operation with same creation token has no effect). If a file system does not currently exist that is owned by the caller's AWS account with the specified creation token, this operation does the following:

- Creates a new, empty file system. The file system will have an Amazon EFS assigned ID, and an initial lifecycle state `creating`.
- Returns with the description of the created file system.

Otherwise, this operation returns a `FileSystemAlreadyExists` error with the ID of the existing file system.

Note

For basic use cases, you can use a randomly generated UUID for the creation token.

The idempotent operation allows you to retry a `CreateFileSystem` call without risk of creating an extra file system. This can happen when an initial call fails in a way that leaves it uncertain whether or not a file system was actually created. An example might be that a transport level timeout occurred or your connection was reset. As long as you use the same creation token, if the initial call had succeeded in creating a file system, the client can learn of its existence from the `FileSystemAlreadyExists` error.

Note

The `CreateFileSystem` call returns while the file system's lifecycle state is still `creating`. You can check the file system creation status by calling the DescribeFileSystems operation, which among other things returns the file system state.

This operation also takes an optional `PerformanceMode` parameter that you choose for your file system. We recommend `generalPurpose` performance mode for most file systems. File systems using the `maxIO` performance mode can scale to higher levels of aggregate throughput and operations per second with a tradeoff of slightly higher latencies for most file operations. The performance mode can't be changed after the file system has been created. For more information, see Amazon EFS: Performance Modes.

After the file system is fully created, Amazon EFS sets its lifecycle state to `available`, at which point you can create one or more mount targets for the file system in your VPC. For more information, see CreateMountTarget. You mount your Amazon EFS file system on an EC2 instances in your VPC via the mount target. For more information, see Amazon EFS: How it Works.

This operation requires permissions for the `elasticfilesystem:CreateFileSystem` action.

Request Syntax

```
1 POST /2015-02-01/file-systems HTTP/1.1
2 Content-type: application/json
3
4 {
5    "[CreationToken](#efs-CreateFileSystem-request-CreationToken)": "string",
6    "[Encrypted](#efs-CreateFileSystem-request-Encrypted)": boolean,
7    "[KmsKeyId](#efs-CreateFileSystem-request-KmsKeyId)": "string",
8    "[PerformanceMode](#efs-CreateFileSystem-request-PerformanceMode)": "string"
9 }
```

URI Request Parameters

The request does not use any URI parameters.

Request Body

The request accepts the following data in JSON format.

** CreationToken ** String of up to 64 ASCII characters. Amazon EFS uses this to ensure idempotent creation.
Type: String
Length Constraints: Minimum length of 1. Maximum length of 64.
Required: Yes

** Encrypted ** A Boolean value that, if true, creates an encrypted file system. When creating an encrypted file system, you have the option of specifying a CreateFileSystem:KmsKeyId for an existing AWS Key Management Service (AWS KMS) customer master key (CMK). If you don't specify a CMK, then the default CMK for Amazon EFS, /aws/elasticfilesystem, is used to protect the encrypted file system.
Type: Boolean
Required: No

** KmsKeyId ** The ID of the AWS KMS CMK to be used to protect the encrypted file system. This parameter is only required if you want to use a non-default CMK. If this parameter is not specified, the default CMK for Amazon EFS is used. This ID can be in one of the following formats:

- Key ID - A unique identifier of the key, for example, `1234abcd-12ab-34cd-56ef-1234567890ab`.
- ARN - An Amazon Resource Name (ARN) for the key, for example, `arn:aws:kms:us-west -2:111122223333:key/1234abcd-12ab-34cd-56ef-1234567890ab`.
- Key alias - A previously created display name for a key. For example, `alias/projectKey1`.
- Key alias ARN - An ARN for a key alias, for example, `arn:aws:kms:us-west-2:444455556666:alias/ projectKey1`. If KmsKeyId is specified, the CreateFileSystem:Encrypted parameter must be set to true.
  Type: String
  Length Constraints: Minimum length of 1. Maximum length of 2048.
  Required: No

** PerformanceMode ** The `PerformanceMode` of the file system. We recommend `generalPurpose` performance mode for most file systems. File systems using the `maxIO` performance mode can scale to higher levels of aggregate throughput and operations per second with a tradeoff of slightly higher latencies for most file operations. This can't be changed after the file system has been created.
Type: String
Valid Values:`generalPurpose` | `maxIO`
Required: No

Response Syntax

```
1 HTTP/1.1 201
2 Content-type: application/json
3
4 {
5     "[CreationTime](#efs-CreateFileSystem-response-CreationTime)": number,
6     "[CreationToken](#efs-CreateFileSystem-response-CreationToken)": "string",
7     "[Encrypted](#efs-CreateFileSystem-response-Encrypted)": boolean,
8     "[FileSystemId](#efs-CreateFileSystem-response-FileSystemId)": "string",
9     "[KmsKeyId](#efs-CreateFileSystem-response-KmsKeyId)": "string",
10    "[LifeCycleState](#efs-CreateFileSystem-response-LifeCycleState)": "string",
11    "[Name](#efs-CreateFileSystem-response-Name)": "string",
12    "[NumberOfMountTargets](#efs-CreateFileSystem-response-NumberOfMountTargets)": number,
13    "[OwnerId](#efs-CreateFileSystem-response-OwnerId)": "string",
14    "[PerformanceMode](#efs-CreateFileSystem-response-PerformanceMode)": "string",
15    "[SizeInBytes](#efs-CreateFileSystem-response-SizeInBytes)": {
16        "[Timestamp](API_FileSystemSize.md#efs-Type-FileSystemSize-Timestamp)": number,
```

```
17      "[Value](API_FileSystemSize.md#efs-Type-FileSystemSize-Value)": number
18    }
19 }
```

Response Elements

If the action is successful, the service sends back an HTTP 201 response.

The following data is returned in JSON format by the service.

** CreationTime ** Time that the file system was created, in seconds (since 1970-01-01T00:00:00Z).
Type: Timestamp

** CreationToken ** Opaque string specified in the request.
Type: String
Length Constraints: Minimum length of 1. Maximum length of 64.

** Encrypted ** A Boolean value that, if true, indicates that the file system is encrypted.
Type: Boolean

** FileSystemId ** ID of the file system, assigned by Amazon EFS.
Type: String

** KmsKeyId ** The ID of an AWS Key Management Service (AWS KMS) customer master key (CMK) that was used to protect the encrypted file system.
Type: String
Length Constraints: Minimum length of 1. Maximum length of 2048.

** LifeCycleState ** Lifecycle phase of the file system.
Type: String
Valid Values:`creating | available | deleting | deleted`

** Name ** You can add tags to a file system, including a `Name` tag. For more information, see CreateTags. If the file system has a `Name` tag, Amazon EFS returns the value in this field.
Type: String
Length Constraints: Maximum length of 256.

** NumberOfMountTargets ** Current number of mount targets that the file system has. For more information, see CreateMountTarget.
Type: Integer
Valid Range: Minimum value of 0.

** OwnerId ** AWS account that created the file system. If the file system was created by an IAM user, the parent account to which the user belongs is the owner.
Type: String

** PerformanceMode ** The `PerformanceMode` of the file system.
Type: String
Valid Values:`generalPurpose | maxIO`

** SizeInBytes ** Latest known metered size (in bytes) of data stored in the file system, in bytes, in its `Value` field, and the time at which that size was determined in its `Timestamp` field. The `Timestamp` value is the integer number of seconds since 1970-01-01T00:00:00Z. Note that the value does not represent the size of a consistent snapshot of the file system, but it is eventually consistent when there are no writes to the file system. That is, the value will represent actual size only if the file system is not modified for a period longer than a couple of hours. Otherwise, the value is not the exact size the file system was at any instant in time.
Type: FileSystemSize object

Errors

BadRequest
Returned if the request is malformed or contains an error such as an invalid parameter value or a missing required parameter.
HTTP Status Code: 400

FileSystemAlreadyExists
Returned if the file system you are trying to create already exists, with the creation token you provided.
HTTP Status Code: 409

FileSystemLimitExceeded
Returned if the AWS account has already created maximum number of file systems allowed per account.
HTTP Status Code: 403

InternalServerError
Returned if an error occurred on the server side.
HTTP Status Code: 500

Example

Create a file system

The following example sends a POST request to create a file system in the us-west-2 region. The request specifies myFileSystem1 as the creation token.

Sample Request

```
1 POST /2015-02-01/file-systems HTTP/1.1
2 Host: elasticfilesystem.us-west-2.amazonaws.com
3 x-amz-date: 20140620T215117Z
4 Authorization: <...>
5 Content-Type: application/json
6 Content-Length: 42
7
8 {
9 "CreationToken" : "myFileSystem1",
10 "PerformanceMode" : "generalPurpose"
11 }
```

Sample Response

```
1 HTTP/1.1 201 Created
2 x-amzn-RequestId: 7560489e-8bc7-4a56-a09a-757ce6f4832a
3 Content-Type: application/json
4 Content-Length: 319
5
6 {
7     "ownerId":"251839141158",
8     "creationToken":"myFileSystem1",
9     "PerformanceMode" : "generalPurpose",
10     "fileSystemId":"fs-47a2c22e",
11     "CreationTime":"1403301078",
12     "LifeCycleState":"creating",
```

```
13    "numberOfMountTargets":0,
14    "sizeInBytes":{
15        "value":1024,
16        "timestamp":"1403301078"
17    }
18 }
```

See Also

For more information about using this API in one of the language-specific AWS SDKs, see the following:

- AWS Command Line Interface
- AWS SDK for .NET
- AWS SDK for C++
- AWS SDK for Go
- AWS SDK for Java
- AWS SDK for JavaScript
- AWS SDK for PHP V3
- AWS SDK for Python
- AWS SDK for Ruby V2

CreateMountTarget

Creates a mount target for a file system. You can then mount the file system on EC2 instances via the mount target.

You can create one mount target in each Availability Zone in your VPC. All EC2 instances in a VPC within a given Availability Zone share a single mount target for a given file system. If you have multiple subnets in an Availability Zone, you create a mount target in one of the subnets. EC2 instances do not need to be in the same subnet as the mount target in order to access their file system. For more information, see Amazon EFS: How it Works.

In the request, you also specify a file system ID for which you are creating the mount target and the file system's lifecycle state must be `available`. For more information, see DescribeFileSystems.

In the request, you also provide a subnet ID, which determines the following:

- VPC in which Amazon EFS creates the mount target
- Availability Zone in which Amazon EFS creates the mount target
- IP address range from which Amazon EFS selects the IP address of the mount target (if you don't specify an IP address in the request)

After creating the mount target, Amazon EFS returns a response that includes, a `MountTargetId` and an `IpAddress`. You use this IP address when mounting the file system in an EC2 instance. You can also use the mount target's DNS name when mounting the file system. The EC2 instance on which you mount the file system via the mount target can resolve the mount target's DNS name to its IP address. For more information, see How it Works: Implementation Overview.

Note that you can create mount targets for a file system in only one VPC, and there can be only one mount target per Availability Zone. That is, if the file system already has one or more mount targets created for it, the subnet specified in the request to add another mount target must meet the following requirements:

- Must belong to the same VPC as the subnets of the existing mount targets
- Must not be in the same Availability Zone as any of the subnets of the existing mount targets

If the request satisfies the requirements, Amazon EFS does the following:

- Creates a new mount target in the specified subnet.

- Also creates a new network interface in the subnet as follows:

  - If the request provides an `IpAddress`, Amazon EFS assigns that IP address to the network interface. Otherwise, Amazon EFS assigns a free address in the subnet (in the same way that the Amazon EC2 `CreateNetworkInterface` call does when a request does not specify a primary private IP address).
  - If the request provides `SecurityGroups`, this network interface is associated with those security groups. Otherwise, it belongs to the default security group for the subnet's VPC.
  - Assigns the description `Mount target fsmt-id for file system fs-id` where `fsmt-id` is the mount target ID, and `fs-id` is the `FileSystemId`.
  - Sets the `requesterManaged` property of the network interface to `true`, and the `requesterId` value to `EFS`.

  Each Amazon EFS mount target has one corresponding requester-managed EC2 network interface. After the network interface is created, Amazon EFS sets the `NetworkInterfaceId` field in the mount target's description to the network interface ID, and the `IpAddress` field to its address. If network interface creation fails, the entire `CreateMountTarget` operation fails.

Note
The `CreateMountTarget` call returns only after creating the network interface, but while the mount target state is still `creating`, you can check the mount target creation status by calling the DescribeMountTargets operation, which among other things returns the mount target state.

We recommend you create a mount target in each of the Availability Zones. There are cost considerations for using a file system in an Availability Zone through a mount target created in another Availability Zone. For more information, see Amazon EFS. In addition, by always using a mount target local to the instance's Availability Zone, you eliminate a partial failure scenario. If the Availability Zone in which your mount target is created goes down, then you won't be able to access your file system through that mount target.

This operation requires permissions for the following action on the file system:

- elasticfilesystem:CreateMountTarget

This operation also requires permissions for the following Amazon EC2 actions:

- ec2:DescribeSubnets
- ec2:DescribeNetworkInterfaces
- ec2:CreateNetworkInterface

Request Syntax

```
1 POST /2015-02-01/mount-targets HTTP/1.1
2 Content-type: application/json
3
4 {
5     "[FileSystemId](#efs-CreateMountTarget-request-FileSystemId)": "string",
6     "[IpAddress](#efs-CreateMountTarget-request-IpAddress)": "string",
7     "[SecurityGroups](#efs-CreateMountTarget-request-SecurityGroups)": [ "string" ],
8     "[SubnetId](#efs-CreateMountTarget-request-SubnetId)": "string"
9 }
```

URI Request Parameters

The request does not use any URI parameters.

Request Body

The request accepts the following data in JSON format.

** FileSystemId ** ID of the file system for which to create the mount target.
Type: String
Required: Yes

** IpAddress ** Valid IPv4 address within the address range of the specified subnet.
Type: String
Required: No

** SecurityGroups ** Up to five VPC security group IDs, of the form sg-xxxxxxxx. These must be for the same VPC as subnet specified.
Type: Array of strings
Array Members: Maximum number of 5 items.
Required: No

** SubnetId ** ID of the subnet to add the mount target in.
Type: String
Required: Yes

Response Syntax

```
1  HTTP/1.1 200
2  Content-type: application/json
3
4  {
5      "[FileSystemId](#efs-CreateMountTarget-response-FileSystemId)": "string",
6      "[IpAddress](#efs-CreateMountTarget-response-IpAddress)": "string",
7      "[LifeCycleState](#efs-CreateMountTarget-response-LifeCycleState)": "string",
8      "[MountTargetId](#efs-CreateMountTarget-response-MountTargetId)": "string",
9      "[NetworkInterfaceId](#efs-CreateMountTarget-response-NetworkInterfaceId)": "string",
10     "[OwnerId](#efs-CreateMountTarget-response-OwnerId)": "string",
11     "[SubnetId](#efs-CreateMountTarget-response-SubnetId)": "string"
12 }
```

Response Elements

If the action is successful, the service sends back an HTTP 200 response.

The following data is returned in JSON format by the service.

** FileSystemId ** ID of the file system for which the mount target is intended.
Type: String

** IpAddress ** Address at which the file system may be mounted via the mount target.
Type: String

** LifeCycleState ** Lifecycle state of the mount target.
Type: String
Valid Values:`creating` | `available` | `deleting` | `deleted`

** MountTargetId ** System-assigned mount target ID.
Type: String

** NetworkInterfaceId ** ID of the network interface that Amazon EFS created when it created the mount target.
Type: String

** OwnerId ** AWS account ID that owns the resource.
Type: String

** SubnetId ** ID of the mount target's subnet.
Type: String

Errors

BadRequest
Returned if the request is malformed or contains an error such as an invalid parameter value or a missing required parameter.
HTTP Status Code: 400

FileSystemNotFound
Returned if the specified `FileSystemId` does not exist in the requester's AWS account.
HTTP Status Code: 404

IncorrectFileSystemLifeCycleState
Returned if the file system's life cycle state is not "created".
HTTP Status Code: 409

InternalServerError

Returned if an error occurred on the server side.
HTTP Status Code: 500

IpAddressInUse

Returned if the request specified an `IpAddress` that is already in use in the subnet.
HTTP Status Code: 409

MountTargetConflict

Returned if the mount target would violate one of the specified restrictions based on the file system's existing mount targets.
HTTP Status Code: 409

NetworkInterfaceLimitExceeded

The calling account has reached the ENI limit for the specific AWS region. Client should try to delete some ENIs or get its account limit raised. For more information, see Amazon VPC Limits in the Amazon Virtual Private Cloud User Guide (see the Network interfaces per VPC entry in the table).
HTTP Status Code: 409

NoFreeAddressesInSubnet

Returned if `IpAddress` was not specified in the request and there are no free IP addresses in the subnet.
HTTP Status Code: 409

SecurityGroupLimitExceeded

Returned if the size of `SecurityGroups` specified in the request is greater than five.
HTTP Status Code: 400

SecurityGroupNotFound

Returned if one of the specified security groups does not exist in the subnet's VPC.
HTTP Status Code: 400

SubnetNotFound

Returned if there is no subnet with ID `SubnetId` provided in the request.
HTTP Status Code: 400

UnsupportedAvailabilityZone

HTTP Status Code: 400

Examples

Example 1: Add a mount target to a file system

The following request creates a mount target for a file system. The request specifies values for only the required `FileSystemId` and `SubnetId` parameters. The request does not provide the optional `IpAddress` and `SecurityGroups` parameters. For `IpAddress`, the operation uses one of the available IP addresses in the specified subnet. And, the operation uses the default security group associated with the VPC for the `SecurityGroups`.

Sample Request

```
1 POST /2015-02-01/mount-targets HTTP/1.1
2 Host: elasticfilesystem.us-west-2.amazonaws.com
3 x-amz-date: 20140620T221118Z
4 Authorization: <...>
5 Content-Type: application/json
6 Content-Length: 160
7
8 {"SubnetId": "subnet-748c5d03", "FileSystemId": "fs-e2a6438b"}
```

Sample Response

```
1 HTTP/1.1 200 OK
2 x-amzn-RequestId: c3616af3-33fa-40ad-ae0d-d3895a2c3a1f
3 Content-Type: application/json
4 Content-Length: 252
5
6 {
7     "MountTargetId": "fsmt-55a4413c",
8     "NetworkInterfaceId": "eni-d95852af",
9     "FileSystemId": "fs-e2a6438b",
10    "LifeCycleState": "available",
11    "SubnetId": "subnet-748c5d03",
12    "OwnerId": "231243201240",
13    "IpAddress": "172.31.22.183"
14 }
```

Example 2: Add a mount target to a file system

The following request specifies all the request parameters to create a mount target.

Sample Request

```
1 POST /2015-02-01/mount-targets HTTP/1.1
2 Host: elasticfilesystem.us-west-2.amazonaws.com
3 x-amz-date: 20140620T221118Z
4 Authorization: <...>
5 Content-Type: application/json
6 Content-Length: 160
7
8 {
9     "FileSystemId":"fs-47a2c22e",
10    "SubnetId":"subnet-fd04ff94",
11    "IpAddress":"10.0.2.42",
12    "SecurityGroups":[
13       "sg-1a2b3c4d"
14    ]
15 }
```

Sample Response

```
1 HTTP/1.1 200 OK
2 x-amzn-RequestId: c3616af3-33fa-40ad-ae0d-d3895a2c3a1f
3 Content-Type: application/json
4 Content-Length: 252
5
6 {
7     "OwnerId":"251839141158",
8     "MountTargetId":"fsmt-9a13661e",
9     "FileSystemId":"fs-47a2c22e",
10    "SubnetId":"subnet-fd04ff94",
11    "LifeCycleState":"available",
12    "IpAddress":"10.0.2.42",
```

```
13    "NetworkInterfaceId":"eni-1bcb7772"
14 }
```

See Also

For more information about using this API in one of the language-specific AWS SDKs, see the following:

- AWS Command Line Interface
- AWS SDK for .NET
- AWS SDK for C++
- AWS SDK for Go
- AWS SDK for Java
- AWS SDK for JavaScript
- AWS SDK for PHP V3
- AWS SDK for Python
- AWS SDK for Ruby V2

CreateTags

Creates or overwrites tags associated with a file system. Each tag is a key-value pair. If a tag key specified in the request already exists on the file system, this operation overwrites its value with the value provided in the request. If you add the `Name` tag to your file system, Amazon EFS returns it in the response to the DescribeFileSystems operation.

This operation requires permission for the `elasticfilesystem:CreateTags` action.

Request Syntax

```
1  POST /2015-02-01/create-tags/FileSystemId HTTP/1.1
2  Content-type: application/json
3
4  {
5      "[Tags](#efs-CreateTags-request-Tags)": [
6          {
7              "[Key](API_Tag.md#efs-Type-Tag-Key)": "string",
8              "[Value](API_Tag.md#efs-Type-Tag-Value)": "string"
9          }
10     ]
11 }
```

URI Request Parameters

The request requires the following URI parameters.

** FileSystemId ** ID of the file system whose tags you want to modify (String). This operation modifies the tags only, not the file system.

Request Body

The request accepts the following data in JSON format.

** Tags ** Array of `Tag` objects to add. Each `Tag` object is a key-value pair.
Type: Array of Tag objects
Required: Yes

Response Syntax

```
1  HTTP/1.1 204
```

Response Elements

If the action is successful, the service sends back an HTTP 204 response with an empty HTTP body.

Errors

BadRequest
Returned if the request is malformed or contains an error such as an invalid parameter value or a missing required

parameter.
HTTP Status Code: 400

FileSystemNotFound
Returned if the specified `FileSystemId` does not exist in the requester's AWS account.
HTTP Status Code: 404

InternalServerError
Returned if an error occurred on the server side.
HTTP Status Code: 500

Example

Create tags on a file system

The following request creates three tags (`"key1"`, `"key2"`, and `"key3"`) on the specified file system.

Sample Request

```
 1 POST /2015-02-01/create-tags/fs-e2a6438b HTTP/1.1
 2 Host: elasticfilesystem.us-west-2.amazonaws.com
 3 x-amz-date: 20140620T221118Z
 4 Authorization: <...>
 5 Content-Type: application/json
 6 Content-Length: 160
 7
 8 {
 9     "Tags": [
10         {
11             "Value": "value1",
12             "Key": "key1"
13         },
14         {
15             "Value": "value2",
16             "Key": "key2"
17         },
18         {
19             "Value": "value3",
20             "Key": "key3"
21         }
22     ]
23 }
```

Sample Response

```
 1 HTTP/1.1 204 no content
 2 x-amzn-RequestId: c3616af3-33fa-40ad-ae0d-d3895a2c3a1f
```

See Also

For more information about using this API in one of the language-specific AWS SDKs, see the following:

- AWS Command Line Interface

- AWS SDK for .NET
- AWS SDK for C++
- AWS SDK for Go
- AWS SDK for Java
- AWS SDK for JavaScript
- AWS SDK for PHP V3
- AWS SDK for Python
- AWS SDK for Ruby V2

DeleteFileSystem

Deletes a file system, permanently severing access to its contents. Upon return, the file system no longer exists and you can't access any contents of the deleted file system.

You can't delete a file system that is in use. That is, if the file system has any mount targets, you must first delete them. For more information, see DescribeMountTargets and DeleteMountTarget.

Note
The `DeleteFileSystem` call returns while the file system state is still `deleting`. You can check the file system deletion status by calling the DescribeFileSystems operation, which returns a list of file systems in your account. If you pass file system ID or creation token for the deleted file system, the DescribeFileSystems returns a `404 FileSystemNotFound` error.

This operation requires permissions for the `elasticfilesystem:DeleteFileSystem` action.

Request Syntax

```
1 DELETE /2015-02-01/file-systems/FileSystemId HTTP/1.1
```

URI Request Parameters

The request requires the following URI parameters.

** FileSystemId ** ID of the file system you want to delete.

Request Body

The request does not have a request body.

Response Syntax

```
1 HTTP/1.1 204
```

Response Elements

If the action is successful, the service sends back an HTTP 204 response with an empty HTTP body.

Errors

BadRequest
Returned if the request is malformed or contains an error such as an invalid parameter value or a missing required parameter.
HTTP Status Code: 400

FileSystemInUse
Returned if a file system has mount targets.
HTTP Status Code: 409

FileSystemNotFound
Returned if the specified `FileSystemId` does not exist in the requester's AWS account.
HTTP Status Code: 404

InternalServerError

Returned if an error occurred on the server side.

HTTP Status Code: 500

Example

Delete a file system

The following example sends a DELETE request to the `file-systems` endpoint (`elasticfilesystem.us-west-2.amazonaws.com/2015-02-01/file-systems/fs-47a2c22e`) to delete a file system whose ID is `fs-47a2c22e`.

Sample Request

```
1 DELETE /2015-02-01/file-systems/fs-47a2c22e HTTP/1.1
2 Host: elasticfilesystem.us-west-2.amazonaws.com
3 x-amz-date: 20140622T233021Z
4 Authorization: <...>
```

Sample Response

```
1 HTTP/1.1 204 No Content
2 x-amzn-RequestId: a2d125b3-7ebd-4d6a-ab3d-5548630bff33
3 Content-Length: 0
```

See Also

For more information about using this API in one of the language-specific AWS SDKs, see the following:

- AWS Command Line Interface
- AWS SDK for .NET
- AWS SDK for C++
- AWS SDK for Go
- AWS SDK for Java
- AWS SDK for JavaScript
- AWS SDK for PHP V3
- AWS SDK for Python
- AWS SDK for Ruby V2

DeleteMountTarget

Deletes the specified mount target.

This operation forcibly breaks any mounts of the file system via the mount target that is being deleted, which might disrupt instances or applications using those mounts. To avoid applications getting cut off abruptly, you might consider unmounting any mounts of the mount target, if feasible. The operation also deletes the associated network interface. Uncommitted writes may be lost, but breaking a mount target using this operation does not corrupt the file system itself. The file system you created remains. You can mount an EC2 instance in your VPC via another mount target.

This operation requires permissions for the following action on the file system:

- `elasticfilesystem:DeleteMountTarget`

Note
The `DeleteMountTarget` call returns while the mount target state is still `deleting`. You can check the mount target deletion by calling the DescribeMountTargets operation, which returns a list of mount target descriptions for the given file system.

The operation also requires permissions for the following Amazon EC2 action on the mount target's network interface:

- `ec2:DeleteNetworkInterface`

Request Syntax

```
1 DELETE /2015-02-01/mount-targets/MountTargetId HTTP/1.1
```

URI Request Parameters

The request requires the following URI parameters.

** MountTargetId ** ID of the mount target to delete (String).

Request Body

The request does not have a request body.

Response Syntax

```
1 HTTP/1.1 204
```

Response Elements

If the action is successful, the service sends back an HTTP 204 response with an empty HTTP body.

Errors

BadRequest
Returned if the request is malformed or contains an error such as an invalid parameter value or a missing required parameter.
HTTP Status Code: 400

DependencyTimeout

The service timed out trying to fulfill the request, and the client should try the call again.
HTTP Status Code: 504

InternalServerError

Returned if an error occurred on the server side.
HTTP Status Code: 500

MountTargetNotFound

Returned if there is no mount target with the specified ID found in the caller's account.
HTTP Status Code: 404

Example

Remove a file system's mount target

The following example sends a DELETE request to delete a specific mount target.

Sample Request

```
1 DELETE /2015-02-01/mount-targets/fsmt-9a13661e HTTP/1.1
2 Host: elasticfilesystem.us-west-2.amazonaws.com
3 x-amz-date: 20140622T232908Z
4 Authorization: <...>
```

Sample Response

```
1 HTTP/1.1 204 No Content
2 x-amzn-RequestId: 76787670-2797-48ee-a34f-fce2ce122fef
```

See Also

For more information about using this API in one of the language-specific AWS SDKs, see the following:

- AWS Command Line Interface
- AWS SDK for .NET
- AWS SDK for C++
- AWS SDK for Go
- AWS SDK for Java
- AWS SDK for JavaScript
- AWS SDK for PHP V3
- AWS SDK for Python
- AWS SDK for Ruby V2

DeleteTags

Deletes the specified tags from a file system. If the `DeleteTags` request includes a tag key that does not exist, Amazon EFS ignores it and doesn't cause an error. For more information about tags and related restrictions, see Tag Restrictions in the *AWS Billing and Cost Management User Guide*.

This operation requires permissions for the `elasticfilesystem:DeleteTags` action.

Request Syntax

```
1 POST /2015-02-01/delete-tags/FileSystemId HTTP/1.1
2 Content-type: application/json
3
4 {
5    "[TagKeys](#efs-DeleteTags-request-TagKeys)": [ "string" ]
6 }
```

URI Request Parameters

The request requires the following URI parameters.

** FileSystemId ** ID of the file system whose tags you want to delete (String).

Request Body

The request accepts the following data in JSON format.

** TagKeys ** List of tag keys to delete.
Type: Array of strings
Length Constraints: Minimum length of 1. Maximum length of 128.
Required: Yes

Response Syntax

```
1 HTTP/1.1 204
```

Response Elements

If the action is successful, the service sends back an HTTP 204 response with an empty HTTP body.

Errors

BadRequest
Returned if the request is malformed or contains an error such as an invalid parameter value or a missing required parameter.
HTTP Status Code: 400

FileSystemNotFound
Returned if the specified `FileSystemId` does not exist in the requester's AWS account.
HTTP Status Code: 404

InternalServerError

Returned if an error occurred on the server side.
HTTP Status Code: 500

Example

Delete tags from a file system

The following request deletes the tag key2 from the tag set associated with the file system.

Sample Request

```
1 POST /2015-02-01/delete-tags/fs-e2a6438b HTTP/1.1
2 Host: elasticfilesystem.us-west-2.amazonaws.com
3 x-amz-date: 20140620T215123Z
4 Authorization: <...>
5 Content-Type: application/json
6 Content-Length: 223
7
8 {
9     "TagKeys":[
10         "key2"
11     ]
12 }
```

Sample Response

```
1 HTTP/1.1 204 No Content
2 x-amzn-RequestId: ec08ae47-3409-49f3-9e90-64a5f981bb2b
```

See Also

For more information about using this API in one of the language-specific AWS SDKs, see the following:

- AWS Command Line Interface
- AWS SDK for .NET
- AWS SDK for C++
- AWS SDK for Go
- AWS SDK for Java
- AWS SDK for JavaScript
- AWS SDK for PHP V3
- AWS SDK for Python
- AWS SDK for Ruby V2

DescribeFileSystems

Returns the description of a specific Amazon EFS file system if either the file system `CreationToken` or the `FileSystemId` is provided. Otherwise, it returns descriptions of all file systems owned by the caller's AWS account in the AWS Region of the endpoint that you're calling.

When retrieving all file system descriptions, you can optionally specify the `MaxItems` parameter to limit the number of descriptions in a response. If more file system descriptions remain, Amazon EFS returns a `NextMarker`, an opaque token, in the response. In this case, you should send a subsequent request with the `Marker` request parameter set to the value of `NextMarker`.

To retrieve a list of your file system descriptions, this operation is used in an iterative process, where `DescribeFileSystems` is called first without the `Marker` and then the operation continues to call it with the `Marker` parameter set to the value of the `NextMarker` from the previous response until the response has no `NextMarker`.

The implementation may return fewer than `MaxItems` file system descriptions while still including a `NextMarker` value.

The order of file systems returned in the response of one `DescribeFileSystems` call and the order of file systems returned across the responses of a multi-call iteration is unspecified.

This operation requires permissions for the `elasticfilesystem:DescribeFileSystems` action.

Request Syntax

```
1 GET /2015-02-01/file-systems?CreationToken=CreationToken&FileSystemId=FileSystemId&Marker=Marker
    &MaxItems=MaxItems HTTP/1.1
```

URI Request Parameters

The request requires the following URI parameters.

** CreationToken ** (Optional) Restricts the list to the file system with this creation token (String). You specify a creation token when you create an Amazon EFS file system.
Length Constraints: Minimum length of 1. Maximum length of 64.

** FileSystemId ** (Optional) ID of the file system whose description you want to retrieve (String).

** Marker ** (Optional) Opaque pagination token returned from a previous `DescribeFileSystems` operation (String). If present, specifies to continue the list from where the returning call had left off.

** MaxItems ** (Optional) Specifies the maximum number of file systems to return in the response (integer). This parameter value must be greater than 0. The number of items that Amazon EFS returns is the minimum of the `MaxItems` parameter specified in the request and the service's internal maximum number of items per page. Valid Range: Minimum value of 1.

Request Body

The request does not have a request body.

Response Syntax

```
1  HTTP/1.1 200
2  Content-type: application/json
3
4  {
5      "[FileSystems] (#efs-DescribeFileSystems-response-FileSystems)": [
6          {
7              "[CreationTime] (API_FileSystemDescription.md#efs-Type-FileSystemDescription-
                   CreationTime)": number,
8              "[CreationToken] (API_FileSystemDescription.md#efs-Type-FileSystemDescription-
                   CreationToken)": "string",
9              "[Encrypted] (API_FileSystemDescription.md#efs-Type-FileSystemDescription-Encrypted)":
                   boolean,
10             "[FileSystemId] (API_FileSystemDescription.md#efs-Type-FileSystemDescription-
                   FileSystemId)": "string",
11             "[KmsKeyId] (API_FileSystemDescription.md#efs-Type-FileSystemDescription-KmsKeyId)": "
                   string",
12             "[LifeCycleState] (API_FileSystemDescription.md#efs-Type-FileSystemDescription-
                   LifeCycleState)": "string",
13             "[Name] (API_FileSystemDescription.md#efs-Type-FileSystemDescription-Name)": "string",
14             "[NumberOfMountTargets] (API_FileSystemDescription.md#efs-Type-FileSystemDescription-
                   NumberOfMountTargets)": number,
15             "[OwnerId] (API_FileSystemDescription.md#efs-Type-FileSystemDescription-OwnerId)": "
                   string",
16             "[PerformanceMode] (API_FileSystemDescription.md#efs-Type-FileSystemDescription-
                   PerformanceMode)": "string",
17             "[SizeInBytes] (API_FileSystemDescription.md#efs-Type-FileSystemDescription-SizeInBytes)
                   ": {
18                 "[Timestamp] (API_FileSystemSize.md#efs-Type-FileSystemSize-Timestamp)": number,
19                 "[Value] (API_FileSystemSize.md#efs-Type-FileSystemSize-Value)": number
20             }
21         }
22     ],
23     "[Marker] (#efs-DescribeFileSystems-response-Marker)": "string",
24     "[NextMarker] (#efs-DescribeFileSystems-response-NextMarker)": "string"
25 }
```

Response Elements

If the action is successful, the service sends back an HTTP 200 response.

The following data is returned in JSON format by the service.

** FileSystems ** Array of file system descriptions.
Type: Array of FileSystemDescription objects

** Marker ** Present if provided by caller in the request (String).
Type: String

** NextMarker ** Present if there are more file systems than returned in the response (String). You can use the NextMarker in the subsequent request to fetch the descriptions.
Type: String

Errors

BadRequest
Returned if the request is malformed or contains an error such as an invalid parameter value or a missing required

213

parameter.
HTTP Status Code: 400

FileSystemNotFound
Returned if the specified `FileSystemId` does not exist in the requester's AWS account.
HTTP Status Code: 404

InternalServerError
Returned if an error occurred on the server side.
HTTP Status Code: 500

Example

Retrieve list of ten file systems

The following example sends a GET request to the `file-systems` endpoint (`elasticfilesystem.us-west-2. amazonaws.com/2015-02-01/file-systems`). The request specifies a `MaxItems` query parameter to limit the number of file system descriptions to 10.

Sample Request

```
1 GET /2015-02-01/file-systems?MaxItems=10 HTTP/1.1
2 Host: elasticfilesystem.us-west-2.amazonaws.com
3 x-amz-date: 20140622T191208Z
4 Authorization: <...>
```

Sample Response

```
1  HTTP/1.1 200 OK
2  x-amzn-RequestId: ab5f2427-3ab3-4002-868e-30a77a88f739
3  Content-Type: application/json
4  Content-Length: 499
5  {
6     "FileSystems":[
7        {
8           "OwnerId":"251839141158",
9           "CreationToken":"MyFileSystem1",
10          "FileSystemId":"fs-47a2c22e",
11          "PerformanceMode" : "generalPurpose",
12          "CreationTime":"1403301078",
13          "LifeCycleState":"created",
14          "Name":"my first file system",
15          "NumberOfMountTargets":1,
16          "SizeInBytes":{
17             "Value":29313417216,
18             "Timestamp":"1403301078"
19          }
20       }
21    ]
22 }
```

See Also

For more information about using this API in one of the language-specific AWS SDKs, see the following:

- AWS Command Line Interface
- AWS SDK for .NET
- AWS SDK for C++
- AWS SDK for Go
- AWS SDK for Java
- AWS SDK for JavaScript
- AWS SDK for PHP V3
- AWS SDK for Python
- AWS SDK for Ruby V2

DescribeMountTargets

Returns the descriptions of all the current mount targets, or a specific mount target, for a file system. When requesting all of the current mount targets, the order of mount targets returned in the response is unspecified.

This operation requires permissions for the `elasticfilesystem:DescribeMountTargets` action, on either the file system ID that you specify in `FileSystemId`, or on the file system of the mount target that you specify in `MountTargetId`.

Request Syntax

```
1 GET /2015-02-01/mount-targets?FileSystemId=FileSystemId&Marker=Marker&MaxItems=MaxItems&
      MountTargetId=MountTargetId HTTP/1.1
```

URI Request Parameters

The request requires the following URI parameters.

** FileSystemId ** (Optional) ID of the file system whose mount targets you want to list (String). It must be included in your request if `MountTargetId` is not included.

** Marker ** (Optional) Opaque pagination token returned from a previous `DescribeMountTargets` operation (String). If present, it specifies to continue the list from where the previous returning call left off.

** MaxItems ** (Optional) Maximum number of mount targets to return in the response. It must be an integer with a value greater than zero.
Valid Range: Minimum value of 1.

** MountTargetId ** (Optional) ID of the mount target that you want to have described (String). It must be included in your request if `FileSystemId` is not included.

Request Body

The request does not have a request body.

Response Syntax

```
1 HTTP/1.1 200
2 Content-type: application/json
3
4 {
5    "[Marker](#efs-DescribeMountTargets-response-Marker)": "string",
6    "[MountTargets](#efs-DescribeMountTargets-response-MountTargets)": [
7       {
8          "[FileSystemId](API_MountTargetDescription.md#efs-Type-MountTargetDescription-
             FileSystemId)": "string",
9          "[IpAddress](API_MountTargetDescription.md#efs-Type-MountTargetDescription-IpAddress)":
             "string",
10         "[LifeCycleState](API_MountTargetDescription.md#efs-Type-MountTargetDescription-
             LifeCycleState)": "string",
11         "[MountTargetId](API_MountTargetDescription.md#efs-Type-MountTargetDescription-
             MountTargetId)": "string",
12         "[NetworkInterfaceId](API_MountTargetDescription.md#efs-Type-MountTargetDescription-
             NetworkInterfaceId)": "string",
```

```
13          "[OwnerId](API_MountTargetDescription.md#efs-Type-MountTargetDescription-OwnerId)": "
                string",
14          "[SubnetId](API_MountTargetDescription.md#efs-Type-MountTargetDescription-SubnetId)": "
                string"
15      }
16    ],
17    "[NextMarker](#efs-DescribeMountTargets-response-NextMarker)": "string"
18 }
```

Response Elements

If the action is successful, the service sends back an HTTP 200 response.

The following data is returned in JSON format by the service.

** Marker ** If the request included the `Marker`, the response returns that value in this field.
Type: String

** MountTargets ** Returns the file system's mount targets as an array of `MountTargetDescription` objects.
Type: Array of MountTargetDescription objects

** NextMarker ** If a value is present, there are more mount targets to return. In a subsequent request, you can provide `Marker` in your request with this value to retrieve the next set of mount targets.
Type: String

Errors

BadRequest
Returned if the request is malformed or contains an error such as an invalid parameter value or a missing required parameter.
HTTP Status Code: 400

FileSystemNotFound
Returned if the specified `FileSystemId` does not exist in the requester's AWS account.
HTTP Status Code: 404

InternalServerError
Returned if an error occurred on the server side.
HTTP Status Code: 500

MountTargetNotFound
Returned if there is no mount target with the specified ID found in the caller's account.
HTTP Status Code: 404

Example

Retrieve descriptions mount targets created for a file system

The following request retrieves descriptions of mount targets created for the specified file system.

Sample Request

```
1 GET /2015-02-01/mount-targets?FileSystemId=fs-47a2c22e HTTP/1.1
2 Host: elasticfilesystem.us-west-2.amazonaws.com
3 x-amz-date: 20140622T191252Z
4 Authorization: <...>
```

Sample Response

```
1  HTTP/1.1 200 OK
2  x-amzn-RequestId: ab5f2427-3ab3-4002-868e-30a77a88f739
3  Content-Type: application/json
4  Content-Length: 357
5
6  {
7     "MountTargets":[
8        {
9           "OwnerId":"251839141158",
10          "MountTargetId":"fsmt-9a13661e",
11          "FileSystemId":"fs-47a2c22e",
12          "SubnetId":"subnet-fd04ff94",
13          "LifeCycleState":"added",
14          "IpAddress":"10.0.2.42",
15          "NetworkInterfaceId":"eni-1bcb7772"
16       }
17    ]
18 }
```

See Also

For more information about using this API in one of the language-specific AWS SDKs, see the following:

- AWS Command Line Interface
- AWS SDK for .NET
- AWS SDK for C++
- AWS SDK for Go
- AWS SDK for Java
- AWS SDK for JavaScript
- AWS SDK for PHP V3
- AWS SDK for Python
- AWS SDK for Ruby V2

DescribeMountTargetSecurityGroups

Returns the security groups currently in effect for a mount target. This operation requires that the network interface of the mount target has been created and the lifecycle state of the mount target is not deleted.

This operation requires permissions for the following actions:

- elasticfilesystem:DescribeMountTargetSecurityGroups action on the mount target's file system.
- ec2:DescribeNetworkInterfaceAttribute action on the mount target's network interface.

Request Syntax

```
1 GET /2015-02-01/mount-targets/MountTargetId/security-groups HTTP/1.1
```

URI Request Parameters

The request requires the following URI parameters.

** MountTargetId ** ID of the mount target whose security groups you want to retrieve.

Request Body

The request does not have a request body.

Response Syntax

```
1 HTTP/1.1 200
2 Content-type: application/json
3
4 {
5    "[SecurityGroups](#efs-DescribeMountTargetSecurityGroups-response-SecurityGroups)": [ "string
       " ]
6 }
```

Response Elements

If the action is successful, the service sends back an HTTP 200 response.

The following data is returned in JSON format by the service.

** SecurityGroups ** Array of security groups.
Type: Array of strings
Array Members: Maximum number of 5 items.

Errors

BadRequest
Returned if the request is malformed or contains an error such as an invalid parameter value or a missing required parameter.
HTTP Status Code: 400

IncorrectMountTargetState
Returned if the mount target is not in the correct state for the operation.
HTTP Status Code: 409

InternalServerError
Returned if an error occurred on the server side.
HTTP Status Code: 500

MountTargetNotFound
Returned if there is no mount target with the specified ID found in the caller's account.
HTTP Status Code: 404

Example

Retrieve security groups in effect for a file system

The following example retrieves the security groups that are in effect for the network interface associated with a mount target.

Sample Request

```
1 GET /2015-02-01/mount-targets/fsmt-9a13661e/security-groups HTTP/1.1
2 Host: elasticfilesystem.us-west-2.amazonaws.com
3 x-amz-date: 20140620T223513Z
4 Authorization: <...>
```

Sample Response

```
1 HTTP/1.1 200 OK
2 x-amzn-RequestId: 088fb0b4-0c1d-4af7-9de1-933207fbdb46
3 Content-Length: 57
4
5 {
6 "SecurityGroups" : [
7 "sg-188d9f74"
8 ]
9 }
```

See Also

For more information about using this API in one of the language-specific AWS SDKs, see the following:

- AWS Command Line Interface
- AWS SDK for .NET
- AWS SDK for C++
- AWS SDK for Go
- AWS SDK for Java
- AWS SDK for JavaScript
- AWS SDK for PHP V3
- AWS SDK for Python
- AWS SDK for Ruby V2

DescribeTags

Returns the tags associated with a file system. The order of tags returned in the response of one `DescribeTags` call and the order of tags returned across the responses of a multi-call iteration (when using pagination) is unspecified.

This operation requires permissions for the `elasticfilesystem:DescribeTags` action.

Request Syntax

```
1 GET /2015-02-01/tags/FileSystemId/?Marker=Marker&MaxItems=MaxItems HTTP/1.1
```

URI Request Parameters

The request requires the following URI parameters.

** FileSystemId ** ID of the file system whose tag set you want to retrieve.

** Marker ** (Optional) Opaque pagination token returned from a previous `DescribeTags` operation (String). If present, it specifies to continue the list from where the previous call left off.

** MaxItems ** (Optional) Maximum number of file system tags to return in the response. It must be an integer with a value greater than zero.
Valid Range: Minimum value of 1.

Request Body

The request does not have a request body.

Response Syntax

```
1  HTTP/1.1 200
2  Content-type: application/json
3
4  {
5      "[Marker](#efs-DescribeTags-response-Marker)": "string",
6      "[NextMarker](#efs-DescribeTags-response-NextMarker)": "string",
7      "[Tags](#efs-DescribeTags-response-Tags)": [
8          {
9              "[Key](API_Tag.md#efs-Type-Tag-Key)": "string",
10             "[Value](API_Tag.md#efs-Type-Tag-Value)": "string"
11         }
12     ]
13 }
```

Response Elements

If the action is successful, the service sends back an HTTP 200 response.

The following data is returned in JSON format by the service.

** Marker ** If the request included a `Marker`, the response returns that value in this field.
Type: String

** NextMarker ** If a value is present, there are more tags to return. In a subsequent request, you can provide the value of `NextMarker` as the value of the `Marker` parameter in your next request to retrieve the next set of tags.
Type: String

** Tags ** Returns tags associated with the file system as an array of `Tag` objects.
Type: Array of Tag objects

Errors

BadRequest
Returned if the request is malformed or contains an error such as an invalid parameter value or a missing required parameter.
HTTP Status Code: 400

FileSystemNotFound
Returned if the specified `FileSystemId` does not exist in the requester's AWS account.
HTTP Status Code: 404

InternalServerError
Returned if an error occurred on the server side.
HTTP Status Code: 500

Example

Retrieve tags associated with a file system

The following request retrieves tags (key-value pairs) associated with the specified file system.

Sample Request

```
1 GET /2015-02-01/tags/fs-e2a6438b/ HTTP/1.1
2 Host: elasticfilesystem.us-west-2.amazonaws.com
3 x-amz-date: 20140620T215404Z
4 Authorization: <...>
```

Sample Response

```
1 HTTP/1.1 200 OK
2 x-amzn-RequestId: f264e454-7859-4f15-8169-1c0d5b0b04f5
3 Content-Type: application/json
4 Content-Length: 288
5
6 {
7     "Tags":[
8         {
9             "Key":"Name",
10            "Value":"my first file system"
11        },
12        {
13            "Key":"Fleet",
14            "Value":"Development"
15        },
```

```
16          {
17              "Key":"Developer",
18              "Value":"Alice"
19          }
20      ]
21  }
```

See Also

For more information about using this API in one of the language-specific AWS SDKs, see the following:

- AWS Command Line Interface
- AWS SDK for .NET
- AWS SDK for C++
- AWS SDK for Go
- AWS SDK for Java
- AWS SDK for JavaScript
- AWS SDK for PHP V3
- AWS SDK for Python
- AWS SDK for Ruby V2

ModifyMountTargetSecurityGroups

Modifies the set of security groups in effect for a mount target.

When you create a mount target, Amazon EFS also creates a new network interface. For more information, see CreateMountTarget. This operation replaces the security groups in effect for the network interface associated with a mount target, with the `SecurityGroups` provided in the request. This operation requires that the network interface of the mount target has been created and the lifecycle state of the mount target is not `deleted`.

The operation requires permissions for the following actions:

- `elasticfilesystem:ModifyMountTargetSecurityGroups` action on the mount target's file system.
- `ec2:ModifyNetworkInterfaceAttribute` action on the mount target's network interface.

Request Syntax

```
1 PUT /2015-02-01/mount-targets/MountTargetId/security-groups HTTP/1.1
2 Content-type: application/json
3
4 {
5    "[SecurityGroups](#efs-ModifyMountTargetSecurityGroups-request-SecurityGroups)": [ "string" ]
6 }
```

URI Request Parameters

The request requires the following URI parameters.

** MountTargetId ** ID of the mount target whose security groups you want to modify.

Request Body

The request accepts the following data in JSON format.

** SecurityGroups ** Array of up to five VPC security group IDs.
Type: Array of strings
Array Members: Maximum number of 5 items.
Required: No

Response Syntax

```
1 HTTP/1.1 204
```

Response Elements

If the action is successful, the service sends back an HTTP 204 response with an empty HTTP body.

Errors

BadRequest
Returned if the request is malformed or contains an error such as an invalid parameter value or a missing required parameter.
HTTP Status Code: 400

IncorrectMountTargetState
Returned if the mount target is not in the correct state for the operation.
HTTP Status Code: 409

InternalServerError
Returned if an error occurred on the server side.
HTTP Status Code: 500

MountTargetNotFound
Returned if there is no mount target with the specified ID found in the caller's account.
HTTP Status Code: 404

SecurityGroupLimitExceeded
Returned if the size of `SecurityGroups` specified in the request is greater than five.
HTTP Status Code: 400

SecurityGroupNotFound
Returned if one of the specified security groups does not exist in the subnet's VPC.
HTTP Status Code: 400

Example

Replace a mount target's security groups

The following example replaces security groups in effect for the network interface associated with a mount target.

Sample Request

```
1 PUT /2015-02-01/mount-targets/fsmt-9a13661e/security-groups HTTP/1.1
2 Host: elasticfilesystem.us-west-2.amazonaws.com
3 x-amz-date: 20140620T223446Z
4 Authorization: <...>
5 Content-Type: application/json
6 Content-Length: 57
7
8 {
9 "SecurityGroups" : [
10 "sg-188d9f74"
11 ]
12 }
```

Sample Response

```
1 HTTP/1.1 204 No Content
2 x-amzn-RequestId: 088fb0b4-0c1d-4af7-9de1-933207fbdb46
```

See Also

For more information about using this API in one of the language-specific AWS SDKs, see the following:

- AWS Command Line Interface
- AWS SDK for .NET
- AWS SDK for C++
- AWS SDK for Go

- AWS SDK for Java
- AWS SDK for JavaScript
- AWS SDK for PHP V3
- AWS SDK for Python
- AWS SDK for Ruby V2

Data Types

The following data types are supported:

- FileSystemDescription
- FileSystemSize
- MountTargetDescription
- Tag

FileSystemDescription

Description of the file system.

Contents

CreationTime Time that the file system was created, in seconds (since 1970-01-01T00:00:00Z).
Type: Timestamp
Required: Yes

CreationToken Opaque string specified in the request.
Type: String
Length Constraints: Minimum length of 1. Maximum length of 64.
Required: Yes

Encrypted A Boolean value that, if true, indicates that the file system is encrypted.
Type: Boolean
Required: No

FileSystemId ID of the file system, assigned by Amazon EFS.
Type: String
Required: Yes

KmsKeyId The ID of an AWS Key Management Service (AWS KMS) customer master key (CMK) that was used to protect the encrypted file system.
Type: String
Length Constraints: Minimum length of 1. Maximum length of 2048.
Required: No

LifeCycleState Lifecycle phase of the file system.
Type: String
Valid Values:`creating | available | deleting | deleted`
Required: Yes

Name You can add tags to a file system, including a `Name` tag. For more information, see CreateTags. If the file system has a `Name` tag, Amazon EFS returns the value in this field.
Type: String
Length Constraints: Maximum length of 256.
Required: No

NumberOfMountTargets Current number of mount targets that the file system has. For more information, see CreateMountTarget.
Type: Integer
Valid Range: Minimum value of 0.
Required: Yes

OwnerId AWS account that created the file system. If the file system was created by an IAM user, the parent account to which the user belongs is the owner.
Type: String
Required: Yes

PerformanceMode The `PerformanceMode` of the file system.
Type: String
Valid Values:`generalPurpose | maxIO`
Required: Yes

SizeInBytes Latest known metered size (in bytes) of data stored in the file system, in bytes, in its `Value` field, and the time at which that size was determined in its `Timestamp` field. The `Timestamp` value is the integer number of seconds since 1970-01-01T00:00:00Z. Note that the value does not represent the size of a consistent snapshot of the file system, but it is eventually consistent when there are no writes to the file system. That is, the value will represent actual size only if the file system is not modified for a period longer than a couple of hours. Otherwise, the value is not the exact size the file system was at any instant in time.

Type: FileSystemSize object

Required: Yes

See Also

For more information about using this API in one of the language-specific AWS SDKs, see the following:

- AWS SDK for C++
- AWS SDK for Go
- AWS SDK for Java
- AWS SDK for Ruby V2

FileSystemSize

Latest known metered size (in bytes) of data stored in the file system, in its `Value` field, and the time at which that size was determined in its `Timestamp` field. Note that the value does not represent the size of a consistent snapshot of the file system, but it is eventually consistent when there are no writes to the file system. That is, the value will represent the actual size only if the file system is not modified for a period longer than a couple of hours. Otherwise, the value is not necessarily the exact size the file system was at any instant in time.

Contents

Timestamp Time at which the size of data, returned in the `Value` field, was determined. The value is the integer number of seconds since 1970-01-01T00:00:00Z.
Type: Timestamp
Required: No

Value Latest known metered size (in bytes) of data stored in the file system.
Type: Long
Valid Range: Minimum value of 0.
Required: Yes

See Also

For more information about using this API in one of the language-specific AWS SDKs, see the following:

- AWS SDK for C++
- AWS SDK for Go
- AWS SDK for Java
- AWS SDK for Ruby V2

MountTargetDescription

Provides a description of a mount target.

Contents

FileSystemId ID of the file system for which the mount target is intended.
Type: String
Required: Yes

IpAddress Address at which the file system may be mounted via the mount target.
Type: String
Required: No

LifeCycleState Lifecycle state of the mount target.
Type: String
Valid Values:`creating | available | deleting | deleted`
Required: Yes

MountTargetId System-assigned mount target ID.
Type: String
Required: Yes

NetworkInterfaceId ID of the network interface that Amazon EFS created when it created the mount target.
Type: String
Required: No

OwnerId AWS account ID that owns the resource.
Type: String
Required: No

SubnetId ID of the mount target's subnet.
Type: String
Required: Yes

See Also

For more information about using this API in one of the language-specific AWS SDKs, see the following:

- AWS SDK for C++
- AWS SDK for Go
- AWS SDK for Java
- AWS SDK for Ruby V2

Tag

A tag is a key-value pair. Allowed characters: letters, whitespace, and numbers, representable in UTF-8, and the following characters:+ - = . _ : /

Contents

Key Tag key (String). The key can't start with `aws:`.
Type: String
Length Constraints: Minimum length of 1. Maximum length of 128.
Required: Yes

Value Value of the tag key.
Type: String
Length Constraints: Maximum length of 256.
Required: Yes

See Also

For more information about using this API in one of the language-specific AWS SDKs, see the following:

- AWS SDK for C++
- AWS SDK for Go
- AWS SDK for Java
- AWS SDK for Ruby V2

Additional Information for Amazon EFS

Following, you can find some additional information about Amazon EFS, including features that are still supported but not necessarily recommended.

Topics

- Backing Up Amazon EFS File Systems Using AWS Data Pipeline
- Mounting File Systems Without the EFS Mount Helper

Backing Up Amazon EFS File Systems Using AWS Data Pipeline

If you need to be able to recover from unintended changes or deletions in your Amazon EFS file systems, we recommend that you use the EFS-to-EFS Backup Solution. This solution is suitable for all Amazon EFS file systems in all AWS Regions. It includes an AWS CloudFormation template that launches, configures, and runs the AWS services required to deploy this solution. This solution follows AWS best practices for security and availability.

You can also back up EFS file systems by using AWS Data Pipeline. In this backup solution, you create a data pipeline by using the AWS Data Pipeline service. This pipeline copies data from your Amazon EFS file system (called the *production file system*) to another Amazon EFS file system (called the *backup file system*).

This solution consists of AWS Data Pipeline templates that implement the following:

- Automated EFS backups based on a schedule that you define (for example, hourly, daily, weekly, or monthly).
- Automated rotation of the backups, where the oldest backup is replaced with the newest backup based on the number of backups that you want to retain.
- Quicker backups using rsync, which only back up the changes made between one backup to the next.
- Efficient storage of backups using hard links. A *hard link* is a directory entry that associates a name with a file in a file system. By setting up a hard link, you can perform a full restoration of data from any backup while only storing what changed from backup to backup.

After you set up the backup solution, this walkthrough shows you how to access your backups to restore your data. This backup solution depends on running scripts that are hosted on GitHub, and is therefore subject to GitHub availability. If you'd prefer to eliminate this reliance and host the scripts in an Amazon S3 bucket instead, see Hosting the rsync Scripts in an Amazon S3 Bucket.

Important

This solution requires using AWS Data Pipeline in the same AWS Region as your file system. Because AWS Data Pipeline is not supported in US East (Ohio), this solution doesn't work in that AWS Region. We recommend that if you want to back up your file system using this solution, you use your file system in one of the other supported AWS Regions.

Topics

- Performance for Amazon EFS Backups Using AWS Data Pipeline
- Considerations for Amazon EFS Backup by Using AWS Data Pipeline
- Assumptions for Amazon EFS Backup with AWS Data Pipeline
- How to Back Up an Amazon EFS File System with AWS Data Pipeline
- Additional Backup Resources

Performance for Amazon EFS Backups Using AWS Data Pipeline

When performing data backups and restorations, your file system performance is subject to Amazon EFS Performance, including baseline and burst throughput capacity. The throughput used by your backup solution counts toward your total file system throughput. The following table provides some recommendations for the Amazon EFS file system and Amazon EC2 instance sizes that work for this solution, assuming that your backup window is 15 minutes long.

EFS Size (30 MB Average File Size)	Daily Change Volume	Remaining Burst Hours	Minimum Number of Backup Agents
256 GB	Less than 25 GB	6.75	1 - m3.medium
512 GB	Less than 50 GB	7.75	1 - m3.large
1.0 TB	Less than 75 GB	11.75	2 - m3.large*
1.5 TB	Less than 125 GB	11.75	2 - m3.xlarge*

EFS Size (30 MB Average File Size)	Daily Change Volume	Remaining Hours	Burst	Minimum Number of Backup Agents
2.0 TB	Less than 175 GB	11.75		3 - m3.large*
3.0 TB	Less than 250 GB	11.75		4 - m3.xlarge*

* These estimates are based on the assumption that data stored in an EFS file system that is 1 TB or larger is organized so that the backup can be spread across multiple backup nodes. The multiple-node example scripts divide the backup load across nodes based on the contents of the first-level directory of your EFS file system.

For example, if there are two backup nodes, one node backs up all of the even files and directories located in the first-level directory. The odd node does the same for the odd files and directories. In another example, with six directories in the Amazon EFS file system and four backup nodes, the first node backs up the first and the fifth directories. The second node backs up the second and the sixth directories, and the third and fourth nodes back up the third and the fourth directories respectively.

Considerations for Amazon EFS Backup by Using AWS Data Pipeline

Consider the following when you're deciding whether to implement an Amazon EFS backup solution using AWS Data Pipeline:

- This approach to EFS backup involves a number of AWS resources. For this solution, you need to create the following:
  - One production file system and one backup file system that contains a full copy of the production file system. The system also contains any incremental changes to your data over the backup rotation period.
  - Amazon EC2 instances, whose lifecycles are managed by AWS Data Pipeline, that perform restorations and scheduled backups.
  - One regularly scheduled AWS Data Pipeline for backing up data.
  - An AWS Data Pipeline for restoring backups.

When this solution is implemented, it results in billing to your account for these services. For more information, see the pricing pages for Amazon EFS, Amazon EC2, and AWS Data Pipeline.

- This solution isn't an offline backup solution. To ensure a fully consistent and complete backup, pause any file writes to the file system or unmount the file system while the backup occurs. We recommend that you perform all backups during scheduled downtime or off hours.

Assumptions for Amazon EFS Backup with AWS Data Pipeline

This walkthrough makes several assumptions and declares example values as follows:

- Before you get started, this walkthrough assumes that you already completed Getting Started.
- After you've completed the Getting Started exercise, you have two security groups, a VPC subnet, and a file system mount target for the file system that you want to back up. For the rest of this walkthrough, you use the following example values:
  - The ID of the file system that you back up in this walkthrough is `fs-12345678`.
  - The security group for the file system that is associated with the mount target is called `efs-mt-sg` (`sg-1111111a`).
  - The security group that grants Amazon EC2 instances the ability to connect to the production EFS mount point is called `efs-ec2-sg` (`sg-1111111b`).
  - The VPC subnet has the ID value of `subnet-abcd1234`.
  - The source file system mount target IP address for the file system that you want to back up is `10.0.1.32:/`.

- The example assumes that the production file system is a content management system serving media files with an average size of 30 MB.

The preceding assumptions and examples are reflected in the following initial setup diagram.

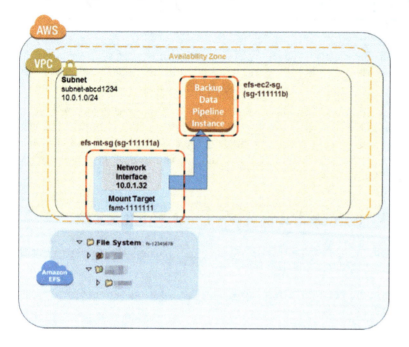

How to Back Up an Amazon EFS File System with AWS Data Pipeline

Follow the steps in this section to back up or restore your Amazon EFS file system with AWS Data Pipeline.

Topics

- Step 1: Create Your Backup Amazon EFS File System
- Step 2: Download the AWS Data Pipeline Template for Backups
- Step 3: Create a Data Pipeline for Backup
- Step 4: Access Your Amazon EFS Backups

Step 1: Create Your Backup Amazon EFS File System

In this walkthrough, you create separate security groups, file systems, and mount points to separate your backups from your data source. In this first step, you create those resources:

1. First, create two new security groups. The example security group for the backup mount target is `efs-backup-mt-sg (sg-9999999a)`. The example security group for the EC2 instance to access the mount target is `efs-backup-ec2-sg (sg-9999999b)`. Remember to create these security groups in the same VPC as the EFS volume that you want to back up. In this example, the VPC associated with the `subnet-abcd1234` subnet. For more information about creating security groups, see Creating Security Groups.

2. Next, create a backup Amazon EFS file system. In this example, the file system ID is `fs-abcdefaa`. For more information about creating file systems, see Creating an Amazon Elastic File System.

3. Finally, create a mount point for the EFS backup file system and assume that it has the value of `10.0.1.75:/`. For more information about creating mount targets, see Creating Mount Targets.

After you've completed this first step, your setup should look similar to the following example diagram.

236

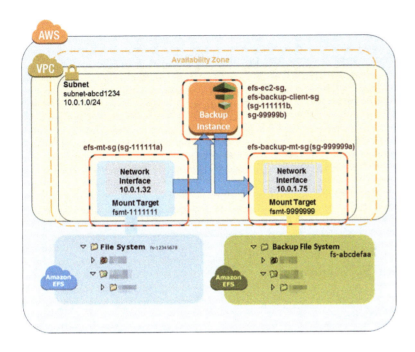

Step 2: Download the AWS Data Pipeline Template for Backups

AWS Data Pipeline helps you reliably process and move data between different AWS compute and storage services at specified intervals. By using the AWS Data Pipeline console, you can create preconfigured pipeline definitions, known as templates. You can use these templates to get started with AWS Data Pipeline quickly. For this walkthrough, a template is provided to make the process of setting up your backup pipeline easier.

When implemented, this template creates a data pipeline that launches a single Amazon EC2 instance on the schedule that you specify to back up data from the production file system to the backup file system. This template has a number of placeholder values. You provide the matching values for those placeholders in the **Parameters** section of the AWS Data Pipeline console. Download the AWS Data Pipeline template for backups at 1-Node-EFSBackupDataPipeline.json from GitHub.

Note
This template also references and runs a script to perform the backup commands. You can download the script before creating the pipeline to review what it does. To review the script, download efs-backup.sh from GitHub. This backup solution depends on running scripts that are hosted on GitHub and is subject to GitHub availability. If you'd prefer to eliminate this reliance and host the scripts in an Amazon S3 bucket instead, see Hosting the rsync Scripts in an Amazon S3 Bucket.

Step 3: Create a Data Pipeline for Backup

Use the following procedure to create your data pipeline.

To create a data pipeline for Amazon EFS backups

1. Open the AWS Data Pipeline console at https://console.aws.amazon.com/datapipeline/. **Important** Make sure that you're working in the same AWS Region as your Amazon EFS file systems.

2. Choose **Create new pipeline**.

3. Add values for **Name** and optionally for **Description**.

4. For **Source**, choose **Import a definition**, and then choose **Load local file**.

5. In the file explorer, navigate to the template that you saved in Step 2: Download the AWS Data Pipeline Template for Backups, and then choose **Open**.

6. In **Parameters**, provide the details for both your backup and production EFS file systems.

Parameters	
Production EFS mount target IP address.	10.0.1.32:/
Security group that can connect to the Production EFS mount point.	sg-1111111b
Interval for backups.	daily
Security group that can connect to the Backup EFS mount point.	sg-9999999b
Number of backups to retain.	7
Backup EFS mount target IP address.	10.0.1.75:/
VPC subnet for your backup EC2 instance (ideally the same subnet used for the production EFS mount point).	subnet-1234abcd
Instance type for creating backups.	m3.medium
Name for the directory that will contain your backups.	backup-fs-12345678
Shell command to run.	wget https://raw.githubusercontent.com/awslabs/data-pipeline-

7. Configure the options in **Schedule** to define your Amazon EFS backup schedule. The backup in the example runs once every day, and the backups are kept for a week. When a backup is seven days old, it is replaced with next oldest backup.

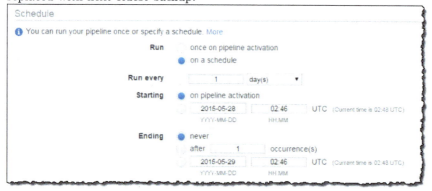

Schedule

🛈 You can run your pipeline once or specify a schedule. More

Run   once on pipeline activation
           ● on a schedule
Run every [1] day(s) ▾
Starting   ● on pipeline activation
           [2015-05-28] [02:46] UTC (Current time is 02:48 UTC)
             YYYY-MM-DD   HH:MM
Ending   ● never
           after [1] occurrence(s)
           [2015-05-29] [02:46] UTC (Current time is 02:48 UTC)
             YYYY-MM-DD   HH:MM

Note

We recommend that you specify a run time that occurs during your off-peak hours.

8. (Optional) Specify an Amazon S3 location for storing pipeline logs, configure a custom IAM role, or add tags to describe your pipeline.

9. When your pipeline is configured, choose **Activate**.

You've now configured and activated your Amazon EFS backup data pipeline. For more information about AWS Data Pipeline, see the AWS Data Pipeline Developer Guide. At this stage, you can perform the backup now as a test, or you can wait until the backup is performed at the scheduled time.

Step 4: Access Your Amazon EFS Backups

Your Amazon EFS backup has now been created, activated, and is running on the schedule you defined. This step outlines how you can access your EFS backups. Your backups are stored in the EFS backup file system that you created in the following format.

```
1 backup-efs-mount-target:/efs-backup-id/[backup interval].[0-backup retention]-->
```

Using the values from the example scenario, the backup of the file system is located in `10.1.0.75:/fs-12345678/`
`daily.[0-6]`, where `daily.0` is the most recent backup and `daily.6` is the oldest of the seven rotating backups.

Accessing your backups gives you the ability to restore data to your production file system. You can choose to restore an entire file system, or you can choose to restore individual files.

Step 4.1: Restore an Entire Amazon EFS Backup

Restoring a backup copy of an Amazon EFS file system requires another AWS Data Pipeline, similar to the one you configured in Step 3: Create a Data Pipeline for Backup. However, this restoration pipeline works in the reverse of the backup pipeline. Typically, these restorations aren't scheduled to begin automatically.

As with backups, restores can be done in parallel to meet your recovery time objective. Keep in mind that when you create a data pipeline, you need to schedule when you want it run. If you choose to run on activation, you start the restoration process immediately. We recommend that you only create a restoration pipeline when you need to do a restoration, or when you already have a specific window of time in mind.

Burst capacity is consumed by both the backup EFS and restoration EFS. For more information about performance, see Amazon EFS Performance. The following procedure shows you how to create and implement your restoration pipeline.

To create a data pipeline for EFS data restoration

1. Download the data pipeline template for restoring data from your backup EFS file system. This template launches a single Amazon EC2 instance based on the specified size. It launches only when you specify it to launch. Download the AWS Data Pipeline template for backups at 1-Node-EFSRestoreDataPipeline.json from GitHub. **Note**
   This template also references and runs a script to perform the restoration commands. You can download the script before creating the pipeline to review what it does. To review the script, download efs-restore.sh from GitHub.

2. Open the AWS Data Pipeline console at https://console.aws.amazon.com/datapipeline/. **Important**
   Make sure that you're working in the same AWS Region as your Amazon EFS file systems and Amazon EC2.

3. Choose **Create new pipeline**.

4. Add values for **Name** and optionally for **Description**.

5. For **Source**, choose **Import a definition**, and then choose **Load local file**.

6. In the file explorer, navigate to the template that you saved in Step 1: Create Your Backup Amazon EFS File System, and then choose **Open**.

7. In **Parameters**, provide the details for both your backup and production EFS file systems.

```
Parameters

Production EFS mount target IP address.        10.0.1.32:/

Security group that can connect to the         sg-1111111b
Production EFS mount point.

Instance type for performing the               m3.large
restore.

Security group that can connect to the         sg-9999999b
Backup EFS mount point.

Name for the directory that already            backup-fs-12345678
contains your backups.

Backup number to restore (0 = the most         0
recent backup).

Backup EFS mount target IP address.            10.0.1.75:/

Interval that you chose for the backup         daily
your going to restore.

VPC subnet for your restoration EC2            subnet-1234abcd
instance (ideally the same subnet used
for the backup EFS mount point).
```

8. Because you typically perform restorations only when you need them, you can schedule the restoration to run **once on pipeline activation**. Or schedule a one-time restoration at a future time of your choosing, like during an off-peak window of time.

9. (Optional) Specify an Amazon S3 location for storing pipeline logs, configure a custom IAM role, or add tags to describe your pipeline.

10. When your pipeline is configured, choose **Activate**.

You've now configured and activated your Amazon EFS restoration data pipeline. Now when you need to restore a backup to your production EFS file system, you just activate it from the AWS Data Pipeline console. For more information, see the http://docs.aws.amazon.com/datapipeline/latest/DeveloperGuide/.

Step 4.2: Restore Individual Files from Your Amazon EFS Backups

You can restore files from your Amazon EFS file system backups by launching an Amazon EC2 instance to temporarily mount both the production and backup EFS file systems. The EC2 instance must be a member of both of the EFS client security groups (in this example, **efs-ec2-sg** and **efs-backup-clients-sg**). Both EFS mount targets can be mounted by this restoration instance. For example, a recovery EC2 instance can create the following mount points. Here, the `-o ro` option is used to mount the Backup EFS as read-only to prevent accidentally modifying the backup when attempting to restore from a backup.

```
1 mount -t nfs source-efs-mount-target:/ /mnt/data
```

```
1 mount -t nfs -o ro backup-efs-mount-target:/fs-12345678/daily.0 /mnt/backup>
```

After you've mounted the targets, you can copy files from **/mnt/backup** to the appropriate location in **/mnt/data** in the terminal using the `cp -p` command. For example, an entire home directory (with its file system permissions) can be recursively copied with the following command.

```
1 sudo cp -rp /mnt/backup/users/my_home /mnt/data/users/my_home
```

You can restore a single file by running the following command.

```
1 sudo cp -p /mnt/backup/user/my_home/.profile /mnt/data/users/my_home/.profile
```

Warning

When you are manually restoring individual data files, be careful that you don't accidentally modify the backup itself. Otherwise, you might corrupt it.

Additional Backup Resources

The backup solution presented in this walkthrough uses templates for AWS Data Pipeline. The templates used in Step 2: Download the AWS Data Pipeline Template for Backups and Step 4.1: Restore an Entire Amazon EFS Backup both use a single Amazon EC2 instance to perform their work. However, there's no real limit to the number of parallel instances that you can run for backing up or restoring your data in Amazon EFS file systems. In this topic, you can find links to other AWS Data Pipeline templates configured for multiple EC2 instances that you can download and use for your backup solution. You can also find instructions for how to modify the templates to include additional instances.

Topics

- Using Additional Templates
- Adding Additional Backup Instances
- Adding Additional Restoration Instances
- Hosting the rsync Scripts in an Amazon S3 Bucket

Using Additional Templates

You can download the following additional templates from GitHub:

- 2-Node-EFSBackupPipeline.json – This template starts two parallel Amazon EC2 instances to back up your production Amazon EFS file system.
- 2-Node-EFSRestorePipeline.json – This template starts two parallel Amazon EC2 instances to restore a backup of your production Amazon EFS file system.

Adding Additional Backup Instances

You can add additional nodes to the backup templates used in this walkthrough. To add a node, modify the following sections of the `2-Node-EFSBackupDataPipeline.json` template.

Important
If you're using additional nodes, you can't use spaces in file names and directories stored in the top-level directory. If you do, those files and directories aren't backed up or restored. All files and subdirectories that are at least one level below the top level are backed up and restored as expected.

- Create an additional EC2Resource for each additional node you want to create (in this example, a fourth EC2 instance).

```
1 {
2 "id": "EC2Resource4",
3 "terminateAfter": "70 Minutes",
4 "instanceType": "#{myInstanceType}",
5 "name": "EC2Resource4",
6 "type": "Ec2Resource",
7 "securityGroupIds" : [ "#{mySrcSecGroupID}","#{myBackupSecGroupID}" ],
8 "subnetId": "#{mySubnetID}",
9 "associatePublicIpAddress": "true"
10 },
```

- Create an additional data pipeline activity for each additional node (in this case, activity `BackupPart4`), make sure to configure the following sections:

  - Update the `runsOn` reference to point to the EC2Resource created previously (`EC2Resource4` in the following example).

241

- Increment the last two `scriptArgument` values to equal the backup part that each node is responsible for and the total number of nodes. For "2" and "3" in the example following, the backup part is "3" for the fourth node because in this example our modulus logic needs to count starting with 0.

```
1  {
2  "id": "BackupPart4",
3  "name": "BackupPart4",
4  "runsOn": {
5  "ref": "EC2Resource4"
6  },
7  "command": "wget https://raw.githubusercontent.com/awslabs/data-pipeline-samples/master/
       samples/EFSBackup/efs-backup-rsync.sh\nchmod a+x efs-backup-rsync.sh\n./efs-backup-
       rsync.sh $1 $2 $3 $4 $5 $6 $7",
8  "scriptArgument": ["#{myEfsSource}","#{myEfsBackup}", "#{myInterval}", "#{myRetainedBackups
       }","#{myEfsID}", "3", "4"],
9  "type": "ShellCommandActivity",
10 "dependsOn": {
11 "ref": "InitBackup"
12 },
13 "stage": "true"
14 },
```

- Increment the last value in all existing `scriptArgument` values to the number of nodes (in this example, "4").

```
1  {
2  "id": "BackupPart1",
3  ...
4  "scriptArgument": ["#{myEfsSource}","#{myEfsBackup}", "#{myInterval}", "#{myRetainedBackups
       }","#{myEfsID}", "1", "4"],
5  ...
6  },
7  {
8  "id": "BackupPart2",
9  ...
10 "scriptArgument": ["#{myEfsSource}","#{myEfsBackup}", "#{myInterval}", "#{myRetainedBackups
       }","#{myEfsID}", "2", "4"],
11 ...
12 },
13 {
14 "id": "BackupPart3",
15 ...
16 "scriptArgument": ["#{myEfsSource}","#{myEfsBackup}", "#{myInterval}", "#{myRetainedBackups
       }","#{myEfsID}", "0", "4"],
17 ...
18 },
```

- Update `FinalizeBackup` activity and add the new backup activity to the `dependsOn` list (`BackupPart4` in this case).

```
1  {
2  "id": "FinalizeBackup", "name": "FinalizeBackup", "runsOn": { "ref":
3  "EC2Resource1" }, "command": "wget
4  https://raw.githubusercontent.com/awslabs/data-pipeline-samples/master/samples/EFSBackup/
       efs-backup-end.sh\nchmod a+x
5  efs-backup-end.sh\n./efs-backup-end.sh $1 $2", "scriptArgument": ["#{myInterval}",
```

```
6 "#{myEfsID}"], "type": "ShellCommandActivity", "dependsOn": [ { "ref": "BackupPart1" },
7 { "ref": "BackupPart2" }, { "ref": "BackupPart3" }, { "ref": "BackupPart4" } ], "stage":
8 "true"
```

Adding Additional Restoration Instances

You can add nodes to the restoration templates used in this walkthrough. To add a node, modify the following sections of the 2-Node-EFSRestorePipeline.json template.

- Create an additional EC2Resource for each additional node you want to create (in this case, a third EC2 instance called EC2Resource3).

```
1 {
2 "id": "EC2Resource3",
3 "terminateAfter": "70 Minutes",
4 "instanceType": "#{myInstanceType}",
5 "name": "EC2Resource3",
6 "type": "Ec2Resource",
7 "securityGroupIds" : [ "#{mySrcSecGroupID}","#{myBackupSecGroupID}" ],
8 "subnetId": "#{mySubnetID}",
9 "associatePublicIpAddress": "true"
10 },
```

- Create an additional data pipeline activity for each additional node (in this case, Activity RestorePart3). Make sure to configure the following sections:
    - Update the runsOn reference to point to the EC2Resource created previously (in this example, EC2Resource3).
    - Increment the last two scriptArgument values to equal the backup part that each node is responsible for and the total number of nodes. For "2" and "3" in the example following, the backup part is "3" for the fourth node because in this example our modulus logic needs to count starting with 0.

```
1 {
2 "id": "RestorePart3",
3 "name": "RestorePart3",
4 "runsOn": {
5 "ref": "EC2Resource3"
6 },
7 "command": "wget https://raw.githubusercontent.com/awslabs/data-pipeline-samples/master/
      samples/EFSBackup/efs-restore-rsync.sh\nchmod a+x efs-restore-rsync.sh\n./efs-backup-
      rsync.sh $1 $2 $3 $4 $5 $6 $7",
8 "scriptArgument": ["#{myEfsSource}","#{myEfsBackup}", "#{myInterval}", "#{myBackup}","#{
      myEfsID}", "2", "3"],
9 "type": "ShellCommandActivity",
10 "dependsOn": {
11 "ref": "InitBackup"
12 },
13 "stage": "true"
14 },
```

- Increment the last value in all existing scriptArgument values to the number of nodes (in this example, "3").

```
1 {
2 "id": "RestorePart1",
3 ...
```

```
4   "scriptArgument": ["#{myEfsSource}","#{myEfsBackup}", "#{myInterval}", "#{myBackup}","#{
        myEfsID}", "1", "3"],
5   ...
6  },
7  {
8   "id": "RestorePart2",
9   ...
10  "scriptArgument": ["#{myEfsSource}","#{myEfsBackup}", "#{myInterval}", "#{myBackup}","#{
        myEfsID}", "0", "3"],
11  ...
12 },
```

Hosting the rsync Scripts in an Amazon S3 Bucket

This backup solution is dependent on running rsync scripts that are hosted in a GitHub repository on the internet. Therefore, this backup solution is subject to the GitHub repository being available. This requirement means that if the GitHub repository removes these scripts, or if the GitHub website goes offline, the backup solution as implemented preceding doesn't function.

If you'd prefer to eliminate this GitHub dependency, you can choose to host the scripts in an Amazon S3 bucket that you own instead. Following, you can find the steps necessary to host the scripts yourself.

To host the rsync scripts in your own Amazon S3 bucket

1. **Sign Up for AWS** – If you already have an AWS account, go ahead and skip to the next step. Otherwise, see Sign up for AWS.

2. **Create an AWS Identity and Access Management User** – If you already have an IAM user, go ahead and skip to the next step. Otherwise, see Create an IAM User.

3. **Create an Amazon S3 bucket** – If you already have a bucket that you want to host the rsync scripts in, go ahead and skip to the next step. Otherwise, see Create a Bucket in the *Amazon Simple Storage Service Getting Started Guide.*

4. **Download the rsync scripts and templates** – Download all of the rsync scripts and templates in the EFSBackup folder from GitHub. Make a note of the location on your computer where you downloaded these files.

5. **Upload the rsync scripts to your S3 bucket** – For instructions on how to upload objects into your S3 bucket, see Add an Object to a Bucket in the *Amazon Simple Storage Service Getting Started Guide.*

6. Change the permissions on the uploaded rsync scripts to allow **Everyone** to **Open/Download** them. For instructions on how to change the permissions on an object in your S3 bucket, see Editing Object Permissions in the *Amazon Simple Storage Service Console User Guide.*

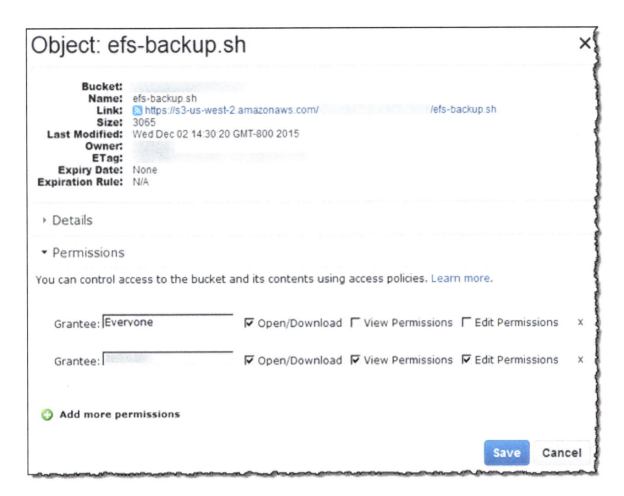

7. **Update your templates** – Modify the `wget` statement in the `shellCmd` parameter to point to the Amazon S3 bucket where you put the startup script. Save the updated template, and use that template when you're following the procedure in Step 3: Create a Data Pipeline for Backup. **Note**
We recommend that you limit access to your Amazon S3 bucket to include the IAM account that activates the AWS Data Pipeline for this backup solution. For more information, see Editing Bucket Permissions in the *Amazon Simple Storage Service Console User Guide*.

You are now hosting the rsync scripts for this backup solution, and your backups are no longer dependent on GitHub availability.

Mounting File Systems Without the EFS Mount Helper

Note

In this section, you can learn how to mount your Amazon EFS file system without the amazon-efs-utils package. To use encryption of data in transit with your file system, you must mount your file system with Transport Layer Security (TLS). To do so, we recommend using the amazon-efs-utils package. For more information, see Using the amazon-efs-utils Tools

Following, you can learn how to install the Network File System (NFS) client and how to mount your Amazon EFS file system on an Amazon EC2 instance. You also can find an explanation of the `mount` command and the available options for specifying your file system's Domain Name System (DNS) name in the `mount` command. In addition, you can find how to use the file `fstab` to automatically remount your file system after any system restarts.

Note

Before you can mount a file system, you must create, configure, and launch your related AWS resources. For detailed instructions, see Getting Started with Amazon Elastic File System.

Topics

- NFS Support
- Installing the NFS Client
- Mounting on Amazon EC2 with a DNS Name
- Mounting with an IP Address
- Mounting Automatically

NFS Support

Amazon EFS supports the Network File System versions 4.0 and 4.1 (NFSv4) and NFSv4.0 protocols when mounting your file systems on Amazon EC2 instances. Although NFSv4.0 is supported, we recommend that you use NFSv4.1. Mounting your Amazon EFS file system on your Amazon EC2 instance also requires an NFS client that supports your chosen NFSv4 protocol.

For optimal performance and to avoid a variety of known NFS client bugs, we recommend working with a recent Linux kernel. If you are using an enterprise Linux distribution, we recommend the following:

- Amazon Linux 2015.09 or newer
- RHEL 7.3 or newer
- RHEL 6.9 with kernel 2.6.32-704 or newer
- All versions of Ubuntu 16.04
- Ubuntu 14.04 with kernel 3.13.0-83 or newer
- SLES 12 Sp2 or later

If you are using another distribution or a custom kernel, we recommend kernel version 4.3 or newer.

Note

Using Amazon EFS with Amazon EC2 instances based on Microsoft Windows is not supported.

Troubleshooting AMI and Kernel Versions

To troubleshoot issues related to certain AMI or kernel versions when using Amazon EFS from an EC2 instance, see Troubleshooting AMI and Kernel Issues.

Installing the NFS Client

To mount your Amazon EFS file system on your Amazon EC2 instance, first you need to install an NFS client. To connect to your EC2 instance and install an NFS client, you need the public DNS name of the EC2 instance and a user name to log in. That user name for your instance is typically `ec2-user`.

To connect your EC2 instance and install the NFS client

1. Connect to your EC2 instance. Note the following about connecting to the instance:

   - To connect to your instance from a computer running Mac OS or Linux, specify the .pem file to your Secure Shell (SSH) client with the `-i` option and the path to your private key.
   - To connect to your instance from a computer running Windows, you can use either MindTerm or PuTTY. If you plan to use PuTTY, you need to install it and use the following procedure to convert the .pem file to a .ppk file.

   For more information, see the following topics in the *Amazon EC2 User Guide for Linux Instances*:

   - Connecting to Your Linux Instance from Windows Using PuTTY
   - Connecting to Your Linux Instance Using SSH

   The key file cannot be publicly viewable for SSH. You can use the `chmod 400` *filename*`.pem` command to set these permissions. For more information, see Create a Key Pair.

2. (Optional) Get updates and reboot.

```
1 $ sudo yum -y update
2 $ sudo reboot
```

3. After the reboot, reconnect to your EC2 instance.

4. Install the NFS client.

   If you're using an Amazon Linux AMI or Red Hat Linux AMI, install the NFS client with the following command.

```
1 $ sudo yum -y install nfs-utils
```

   If you're using an Ubuntu Amazon EC2 AMI, install the NFS client with the following command.

```
1 $ sudo apt-get -y install nfs-common
```

If you use a custom kernel (that is, if you build a custom AMI), you need to include at a minimum the NFSv4.1 client kernel module and the right NFS4 userspace mount helper.

Note
If you choose **Amazon Linux AMI 2016.03.0** or **Amazon Linux AMI 2016.09.0** when launching your Amazon EC2 instance, you don't need to install `nfs-utils` because it's already included in the AMI by default.

Next: Mount Your File System
Use one of the following procedures to mount your file system.

- Mounting on Amazon EC2 with a DNS Name
- Mounting with an IP Address
- Mounting Your Amazon EFS File System Automatically

Mounting on Amazon EC2 with a DNS Name

You can mount an Amazon EFS file system on an Amazon EC2 instance using DNS names. You can do this with a DNS name for the file system, or a DNS name for a mount target.

- **File system DNS name** – Using the file system's DNS name is your simplest mounting option. The file system DNS name automatically resolves to the mount target's IP address in the Availability Zone of the connecting Amazon EC2 instance. You can get this DNS name from the console, or if you have the file system ID, you can construct it using the following convention.

```
1 file-system-id.efs.aws-region.amazonaws.com
```

  Using the file system DNS name, you can mount a file system on your Amazon EC2 instance with the following command.

```
1 sudo mount -t nfs -o nfsvers=4.1,rsize=1048576,wsize=1048576,hard,timeo=600,retrans=2,
    noresvport file-system-id.efs.aws-region.amazonaws.com:/ efs-mount-point
```

- **Mount target DNS name** – In December 2016, we introduced file system DNS names. We continue to provide a DNS name for each Availability Zone mount target for backward compatibility. The generic form of a mount target DNS name is as follows.

```
1 availability-zone.file-system-id.efs.aws-region.amazonaws.com
```

  In some cases, you might delete a mount target and then create a new one in the same Availability Zone. In such a case, the DNS name for that new mount target in that Availability Zone is the same as the DNS name for the old mount target.

For a list of AWS Regions that support Amazon EFS, see Amazon Elastic File System in the *AWS General Reference*.

To be able to use a DNS name in the `mount` command, the following must be true:

- The connecting EC2 instance must be inside a VPC and must be configured to use the DNS server provided by Amazon. For information about Amazon DNS server, see DHCP Options Sets in the *Amazon VPC User Guide*.
- The VPC of the connecting EC2 instance must have DNS hostnames enabled. For more information, see Viewing DNS Hostnames for Your EC2 Instance in the *Amazon VPC User Guide*.

Note
We recommend that you wait 90 seconds after creating a mount target before you mount your file system. This wait lets the DNS records propagate fully in the AWS Region where the file system is.

Mounting with an IP Address

As an alternative to mounting your Amazon EFS file system with the DNS name, Amazon EC2 instances can mount a file system using a mount target's IP address. Mounting by IP address works in environments where DNS is disabled, such as VPCs with DNS hostnames disabled, and EC2-Classic instances mounting using ClassicLink. For more information on ClassicLink, see ClassicLink in the *Amazon EC2 User Guide for Linux Instances.*

You can also configure mounting a file system using the mount target IP address as a fallback option for applications configured to mount the file system using its DNS name by default. When connecting to a mount target IP address, EC2 instances should mount using the mount target IP address in the same Availability Zone as the connecting instance.

You can get the mount target IP address for your EFS file system through the console using the following procedure.

To obtain the mount target IP address for your EFS file system

1. Open the Amazon Elastic File System console at https://console.aws.amazon.com/efs/.

2. Choose the **Name** value of your EFS file system for **File systems**.

3. In the **Mount targets** table, identify the **Availability Zone** that you want to use to mount your EFS file system to your EC2 instance.

4. Make a note of the **IP address** associated with your chosen **Availability Zone**.

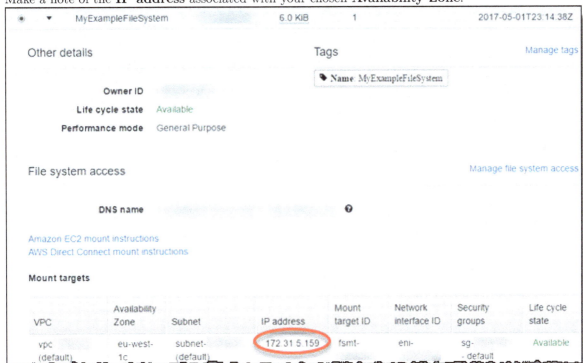

You can specify the IP address of a mount target in the `mount` command, as shown following.

```
1 $ sudo mount -t nfs -o nfsvers=4.1,rsize=1048576,wsize=1048576,hard,timeo=600,retrans=2,
    noresvport mount-target-IP:/   ~/efs-mount-point
```

Mounting Automatically

You can use the file `fstab` to automatically mount your Amazon EFS file system whenever the Amazon EC2 instance that it's mounted on reboots. You can set up automatic mounting in two ways. You can update the `/etc/fstab` file in your EC2 instance after you connect to the instance for the first time, or you can configure automatic mounting of your EFS file system when you create your EC2 instance.

Updating an Existing EC2 Instance to Mount Automatically

To automatically remount your Amazon EFS file system directory when the Amazon EC2 instance reboots, you can use the file `fstab`. The file `fstab` contains information about file systems, and the command `mount -a`, which runs during instance startup, mounts the file systems listed in the `fstab` file.

Note

Before you can update the /etc/fstab file of your EC2 instance, make sure that you've already created your Amazon EFS file system and that you're connected to your Amazon EC2 instance. For more information, see Step 2: Create Your Amazon EFS File System in the Amazon EFS Getting Started exercise.

To update the /etc/fstab file in your EC2 instance

1. Connect to your EC2 instance, and open the `/etc/fstab` file in an editor.

2. Add the following line to the `/etc/fstab` file.

```
1 mount-target-DNS:/ efs-mount-point nfs4 nfsvers=4.1,rsize=1048576,wsize=1048576,hard,timeo
    =600,retrans=2,_netdev,noresvport 0 0
```

   If you want to copy the contents of your `/etc/fstab` file between EC2 instances in different Availability Zones (AZ), we recommend that you use the file system DNS name. Don't copy the `/etc/fstab` file between AZs if you're using the mount target DNS name. If you do, then each file system has a unique DNS name for each Availability Zone with a mount target. For more information about DNS names, see Mounting on Amazon EC2 with a DNS Name.

3. Save the changes to the file.

Your EC2 instance is now configured to mount the EFS file system whenever it restarts.

Note

If your Amazon EC2 instance needs to start regardless of the status of your mounted Amazon EFS file system, add the `nofail` option to your file system's entry in your `etc/fstab` file.

The line of code you added to the /etc/fstab file sets the following.

Field	Description
`mount-target-DNS:/`	The Domain Name Server (DNS) name for the file system that you want to mount. This is the same value used in **mount** commands to mount the subdirectory of your EFS file system.
`efs-mount-point`	The mount point for the EFS file system on your EC2 instance.
`nfs4`	The type of file system. For EFS, this type is always `nfs4`.
`mount options`	Mount options for the file system. This is a comma-separated list of the following options: [See the AWS documentation website for more details] For more information, see Additional Mounting Considerations.

250

Field	Description
0	A nonzero value indicates that the file system should be backed up by dump. For EFS, this value should be 0.
0	The order in which fsck checks file systems at boot. For EFS file systems, this value should be 0 to indicate that fsck should not run at startup.

Document History

The following table describes important changes to the *Amazon Elastic File System User Guide.*

- **API version**: 2015-02-01
- **Latest documentation update**: May 30, 2018

Change	Description	Date Changed
Additional AWS Region support added	Amazon EFS is now available to all users in the Asia Pacific (Seoul) AWS Region.	In this release
Added CloudWatch metric math support	Metric math enables you to query multiple CloudWatch metrics and use math expressions to create new time series based on these metrics. For more information, see Using Metric Math with Amazon EFS.	April 4, 2018
Added the amazon-efs-utils set of open-source tools, and added encryption in transit	The amazon-efs-utils tools are a set of open-source executable files that simplifies aspects of using Amazon EFS, like mounting. There's no additional cost to use amazon-efs-utils, and you can download these tools from GitHub. For more information, see Using the amazon-efs-utils Tools. Also in this release, Amazon EFS now supports encryption in transit through Transport Layer Security (TLS) tunneling. For more information, see Encrypting Data and Metadata in EFS.	April 4, 2018
Updated file system limits per AWS Region	Amazon EFS has increased the limit on the number of file systems for all accounts in all AWS Regions. For more information, see Resource Limits.	March 15, 2018
Additional AWS Region support added	Amazon EFS is now available to all users in the US West (N. California) AWS Region.	March 14, 2018

Change	Description	Date Changed
Amazon EFS File Sync (EFS File Sync)	Amazon EFS now supports copying files from your on-premises data center or from the cloud to Amazon EFS by using EFS File Sync. EFS File Sync copies file systems accessed using Network File System (NFS) version 3 or NFS version 4 to Amazon EFS file systems. To get started, see Amazon EFS File Sync.	November 22, 2017
Data encryption at rest	Amazon EFS now supports data encryption at rest. For more information, see Encrypting Data and Metadata in EFS.	August 14, 2017
Additional region support added	Amazon EFS is now available to all users in the EU (Frankfurt) region.	July 20, 2017
File system names using Domain Name System (DNS)	Amazon EFS now supports DNS names for file systems. A file system's DNS name automatically resolves to a mount target's IP address in the Availability Zone for the connecting Amazon EC2 instance. For more information, see Mounting on Amazon EC2 with a DNS Name.	December 20, 2016
Increased tag support for file systems	Amazon EFS now supports 50 tags per file system. For more information on tags in Amazon EFS, see Managing File System Tags.	August 29, 2016
General availability	Amazon EFS is now generally available to all users in the US East (N. Virginia), US West (Oregon), and EU (Ireland) regions.	June 28, 2016
File system limit increase	The number of Amazon EFS file systems that can be created per account per region increased from 5 to 10.	August 21, 2015
Updated Getting Started exercise	The Getting Started exercise has been updated to simplify the getting started process.	August 17, 2015
New guide	This is the first release of the *Amazon Elastic File System User Guide*.	May 26, 2015